Camp Haan
The History of Riverside's World War II Anti-Aircraft Training Center

KEITH A. BEAULIEU

KEITH A. BEAULIEU

**Camp Haan
The History of Riverside's World War II Anti-Aircraft
Training Center**

Copyright © 2023 by Keith A. Beaulieu
All Rights Reserved.

No part of this document may be reproduced or transmitted in any form or by any means, electronic, mechanical, photocopying, recording, or otherwise, without prior written permission.

Requests for permission to make copies of any part of the work should be submitted to the publisher.

Cover Photograph courtesy of Yeager Family Library, March Field Air Museum

Published by Keith A. Beaulieu
Cape51@yahoo.com

Printed in the United States of America
First Printing: August 2023

ISBN 978-1-7360792-0-1 (paperback)
ISBN 978-1-7360792-1-8 (hardback)

First edition, 2023

10 9 8 7 6 5 4 3 2 1

KEITH A. BEAULIEU

Major General William George Haan
For whom Camp Haan was named.

October 4, 1863 – October 26, 1924
Interred at Arlington National Cemetery
Section 4, Site 3045

CAMP HAAN
THE HISTORY OF RIVERSIDE'S WORLD WAR II ANTI-AIRCRAFT TRAINING CENTER

DEDICATION

Dedicated to the civilian and military personnel who served and traveled through Camp Haan.
It has been my privilege to tell the story.

Aerial of Camp Haan looking South down the regimental area. Regimental Area 5 in the center of the picture (June 1941).

Source: Yeager Family Library, March Field Air Museum

CAMP HAAN
THE HISTORY OF RIVERSIDE'S WORLD WAR II ANTI-AIRCRAFT TRAINING CENTER

CONTENTS

	Acknowledgments	i
1	Pre-World War II	1
2	Birth of a Camp	6
3	U.S. Army Construction Division	11
4	Construction	27
5	Infrastructure	60
6	World War II Years	112
7	Post-World War II	187
8	Camp Haan Today	205

Appendix 1	Land Acquisition
Appendix 2	Buildings
Appendix 3	Sample Weekly Chapel Activities
Appendix 4	Camp Haan Building Disposition
Appendix 5	Known Units

ACKNOWLEDGMENTS

Writing this book was not done by me alone; I received research help from multiple sources to gather source material. I thank Ruth McCormick, Sterling Jenson, William K. Woerz III, Steve Lech, Glenn Wenzel, WSGM Daniel M. Sebby, Mary Graves, Mark Gallagher, Mark Berhow, Jim Rhett, Ben Major, Todd Schnnuth, Alison Thurman, Sara Goodwins, and Lille Foster.

A special thanks to James Huntoon and the rest of the National Archives Riverside staff.

While researching this book, I acquired several artifacts from Camp Haan. The pictures of the artifacts and bits of history I acquired. After this project, all artifacts will be donated so others researching history can enjoy them.

An extra special thanks are owed to my wife, Charlene, and my daughter, Mackenzie, for putting up with my latest nerdy endeavor.

INTRODUCTION

I did not grow up in Riverside, far from it. I grew up on the west coast of Florida. We moved here in 2013 after I retired from the Air Force. As a lifelong lover of history, specifically military history, I found March Field and the surrounding areas fascinating. As I was enjoying learning about the area, there was a brief mention of a couple of Army camps in and around Riverside, Camp Anza, and Camp Haan. I quickly found information on Camp Anza due to Frank Teurlay's work, but there needed to be more I could find on Camp Haan. This just piqued my interest even more.

As I did a cursory search on Camp Haan, I found nothing about the camp beyond a few paragraphs and one picture of the camp from the air in 1941. I realized that if I wanted to know more, I would have to dig it up myself through the museums, archives, and historical societies.

Before World War II, the U.S. Army established a camp west of March Field. The camp was named Camp Haan after Major General William Haan. Camp Haan served the Army's needs from 1941 to 1946 as the largest antiaircraft training center on the west coast. Thousands of military personnel were trained at the camp and nearby Camp Irwin and the Mohave range on the way to the western front.

CAMP HAAN
THE HISTORY OF RIVERSIDE'S WORLD WAR II ANTI-AIRCRAFT TRAINING CENTER

Camp Haan served as a POW camp for German and Italian POWs. The POWs worked in the camp laundry and bakery and provided local citrus growers as day laborers. 1945 the camp was designated as the Southwestern branch of the U.S. Disciplinary Barracks.

Camp Haan was designated as an Army Disciplinary Barracks in 1945, one of eight in the country to house military general prisoners.

At the war's end, Camp Haan transitioned to a debarkation and surplus center before being declared a surplus camp in 1947 and assigned to the War Assets Administration. Just after that and through 1948, the buildings and utilities on the camp were sold off to veterans, government organizations, schools, municipalities, religious organizations, and private citizens.

The lack of information about Camp Haan launched me on this journey. In doing so, I now have a deeper understanding of building cantonments, the conditions, and generally, how life was during World War II. Unfortunately, I have not found any among the living to interview to get first-hand accounts. I am sadly a few years too late; however, there are a few brief mentions and accounts documented from various sources that I will quote and paraphrase over the course of this book to provide that personal perspective of their time at the camp.

I wrote this book because of a love for history, and I believe history is generational. Camp Haan's history has been largely forgotten except in the archives; I hope this project brings to light Camp Haan's contribution to the community and the country. It has been almost eight decades since the closure of Camp Haan, and the world has long forgotten the camp. I endeavor to think that this presentation of the camp, as it was then, through the descriptions and data I have collated that families and descendants of the men and women will now be able to grasp a piece of the world that cannot be brought back.

Keith

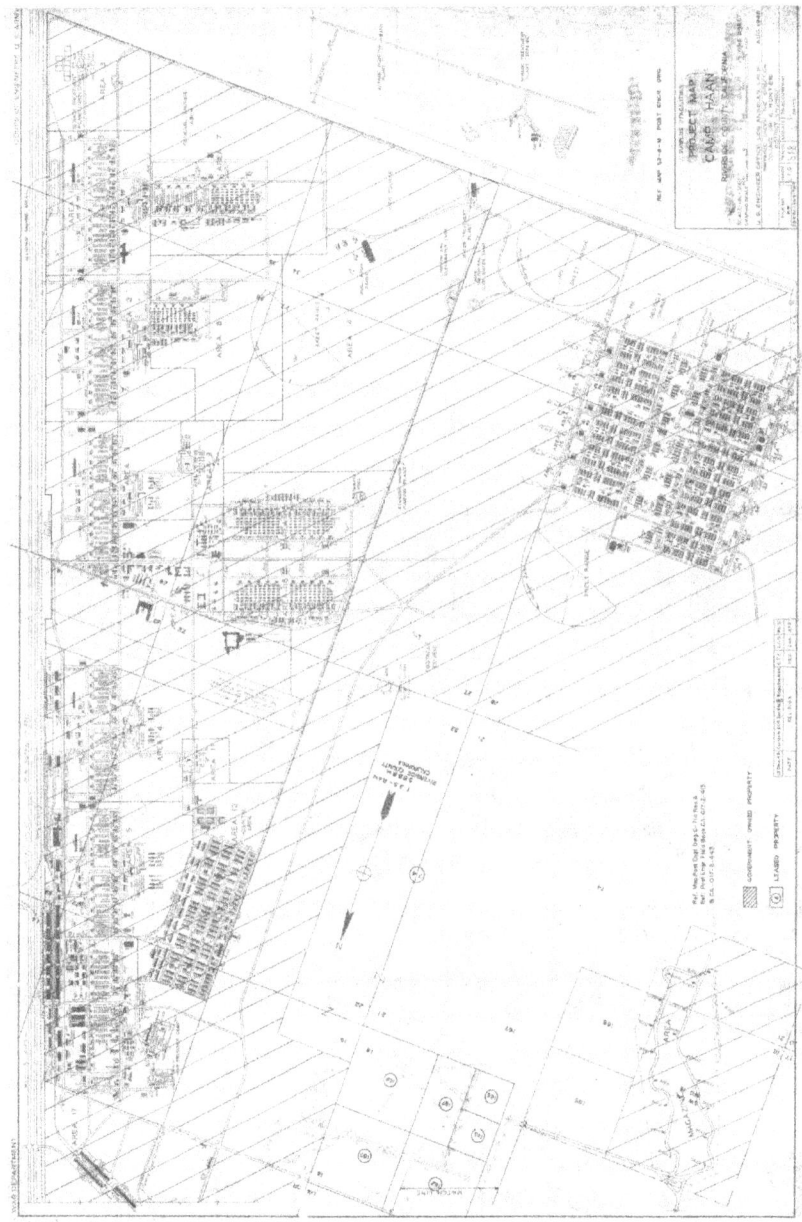

Full map of Camp Haan including the Topside areas. August 1946

CAMP HAAN
THE HISTORY OF RIVERSIDE'S WORLD WAR II ANTI-AIRCRAFT TRAINING CENTER

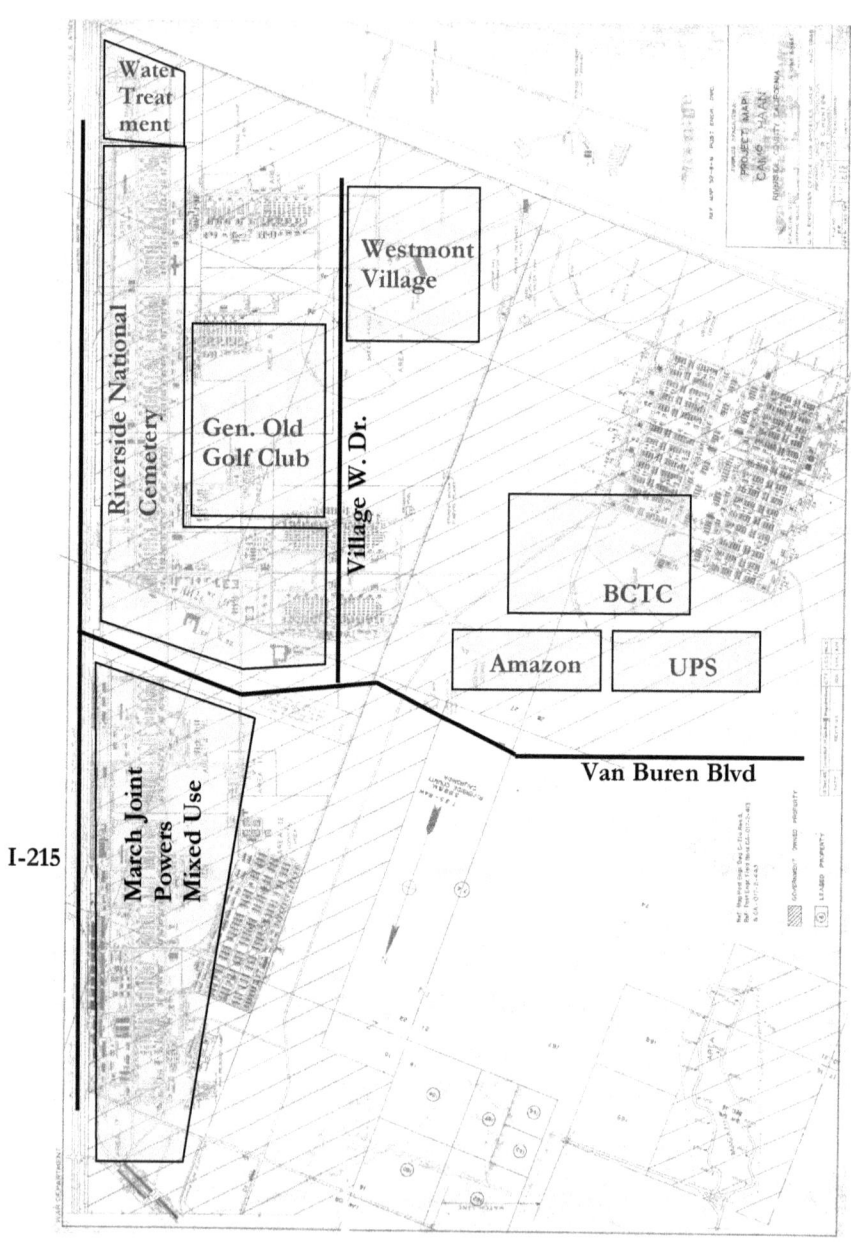

Full Camp Haan map with present day approximations

KEITH A. BEAULIEU

CHAPTER 1
PRE-WORLD WAR II

The years leading up to the declaration of war were a tumultuous time for America. The United States lost 100,000 men fighting in World War I, the stock market crashed, leading to the Great Depression, and millions were out of work and desperate. On the other side of the world, nationalism swept through Germany, reeling against the punitive measures outlined in the Treaty of Versailles. China and Japan were locked in a brutal war, and the Spanish Civil War had broken out; some would say that these were precursors to the upcoming World War.

Although the United States was drawn into World War I toward its end, the bloody conflict left Americans weary of war, and isolationism became the new standard. There was a significant pushback against any kind of involvement in foreign affairs. Critics argued that U.S. involvement in World War I had been driven by the banks and manufacturers with business interests. These criticisms fed into America's growing isolationism. Between 1935 and 1939, Congress passed five different Neutrality Acts that forbid U.S. involvement in foreign conflicts[1] and the exporting of arms, ammunition, and implements of war to foreign nations.[2]

After World War I, the War Department was largely de-funded. In 1937 the War Department, desperate for new equipment, proposed an expenditure to produce modern weapons and vehicles. Congress rejected the proposal. There were reports of army trainees training with broomsticks because they could not get a hold of firearms. In one instance, the National Guard went through training maneuvers with mortars in the back of a truck labeled as tanks. Training budgets amounted to less than 5% of the annual War Department appropriations. The scarcity of equipment and supply, it made it nearly impossible to have divisional-level training.³ Munitions appropriations were scant. For some perspective, before 1939, the Medical Department and the Quartermaster Corps were limited to $20,000 each year (approximately $361,000 in today's dollars when corrected for inflation). Despite requesting additional funding in 1937 for $123,000 to maintain clothing, equipment, and military vehicles, Congress only appropriated $2,000. The United States was not war-ready.

In the fall of 1939, Germany invaded Poland. Shortly after, Great Britain and France declared war on Nazi Germany, effectively beginning World War II. For many Americans, this was the first in many realities that forced the United States to prepare.

Mobilization⁴ in the United States began in the 1920s after the Army used up its World War I surplus. Mobilization plans submitted between 1931 and 1939 emphasized the need for the procurement of materials and supplies necessary to maintain a functioning military and have reserve commodities for national emergencies. This industrial mobilization dealt with broad aspects of planning and training.

By the time 1940 rolled around, things were not going well. Great Britain and France were entangled in a war against Nazi Germany for almost a year; France signed an armistice in June of 1940, leaving Great Britain as the single country fighting Nazi Germany. Even though Nazi Germany, Japan, and Italy pursued conquest and expansion, The United States was still in lockstep with isolationist world politics. Although America officially remained neutral; however, many Americans supported Great Britain. It was only a matter of time before the United States would be dragged into the war. Pushed into action by Hitler's victories in Europe, Congress finally appropriated a bill and necessary powers for the United States to mobilize. This invoked no patriotic response or duty to respond as it did in World War I. The country displayed a "business-as-usual" mentality, still trying to pick up the pieces from the great depression.

CAMP HAAN
THE HISTORY OF RIVERSIDE'S WORLD WAR II ANTI-AIRCRAFT TRAINING CENTER

In his 1940 State of the Union Address, Roosevelt announced, "We are committed to an all-inclusive national defense. We are committed to full support of all those resolute peoples everywhere who are resisting aggression and are thereby keeping war away from our hemisphere. We are committed to the proposition that principles of morality and considerations for our security will never permit us to acquiesce in a peace dictated by aggressors and sponsored by appeasers."[5] Congress affirmed this sentiment by the passing Lend-Lease Act; the United States could now supply Great Britain with military equipment.

Realizing that entrance into the war was inevitable, Roosevelt, with the support of Congress appropriated over a billion dollars to begin construction of plants and manufacturing facilities that would support the war. This funding also directed the construction of temporary military facilities and training facilities to house an expanded wartime army[6]. The Army Quartermaster General began to prepare plans to construct or expand military forts ahead of the anticipated Selective Service Act of 1940. On September 16, 1940, after the fall of France that June and a swastika displayed on the Eiffel Tower, Congress passed the Selective Service Act; it brought about the first peacetime conscription in United States history. The downstream effect of the Selective Service Act of 1940 would take the Army's manning from 270,000 in 1939 to over 1.2 million by the middle of 1940.[7] America began to mobilize.

Through the Protective Mobilization Plan, Roosevelt called for not only the expansion of American forces but also infrastructure and munitions.[8] The U.S. mobilization pace picked up in the wake of German military successes in the spring of 1940.

When Germany invaded the Soviet Union on June 22, 1941, President Roosevelt asked that the War Department, chiefly Secretary of War Henry Stimson and Secretary of the Navy Frank Knox, put together production requirements to "defeat our potential enemies."[9] The War Department returned with a report that identified the troop basis and resources required to equip and maintain to defeat Germany, Italy, and Japan. They called it the Victory Program. This program offered the Roosevelt administration the first real insight into it would take in resources. The numbers were stunning; America was nowhere near the projected numbers. In the Victory Program estimates, the total of the estimated army before the United States was openly at war, was remarkably close to the total achieved four years later. In hindsight, the Victory Program's total manpower projections were 8,795,658, and the actual peak strength (air and ground) reported on 31 May 1945 was 8,291,336. Although the manning projections were remarkably close, the item-by-item projections on the number of divisions were estimated at 236% of what was used. This overestimate was beneficial though, as it was used principally to communicate the amount of equipment needed to be manufactured. The number of men proposed in the Victory Program for antiaircraft artillery units was 464,695, far more than the actual May 1945 total of 246,943.[10]

Although full-scale mobilization remained impossible because America was not yet in the war, the U.S. government started the financial transition from conservation of resources to abundance. Mobilization between 1940 and December 7, 1941, was not considered total mobilization but rather mobilization to prepare to modernize the military in defending the United States. Appropriations came faster than the Army could absorb them, over $8 billion in 1940 and $26 billion in 1941, towering above half-billion dollars allotted for expansion early in 1939. By the fall of 1941, production was full speed ahead for the M-1 rifle, the .50 caliber machine gun, the Browning automatic rifle, and the Thompson Machine gun. Production of the standard utility vehicles (1/4-ton jeep, 3/4-ton weapons carrier, 2 1/2-ton cargo trucks, etc...) also ramped up as well as the M-4 medium tank, the mainstay of the armored division until the development of the M-26. The Quartermaster Corps began constructing 17 supply depots, 42 ordinance plants, and several chemical warfare plants in the United States, 57% of which were complete by December 1941.

As the Army grew and equipment was acquired, it required a great deal of organization and management. Part of this organization was the physical infrastructure to house troops and equipment. Except for airfield construction and off-continent bases, all camp

CAMP HAAN
THE HISTORY OF RIVERSIDE'S WORLD WAR II ANTI-AIRCRAFT TRAINING CENTER

construction was assigned to the Quartermaster General. As an integral part of the mobilization plan, building construction had to keep up with the surging army size. In addition to camps and forts areas, large, sparsely populated areas were also needed for training and fighting maneuvers.

By the time Japan attacked Pearl Harbor, Congress had spent more on Army procurement for mobilization than it had for both the Army and the Navy during all of World War I[11].

CHAPTER 2
BIRTH OF A CAMP

Before World War II, the War Department only had 20 personnel on staff experienced in real estate.[12] This posed a problem for mobilization efforts. Since mobilization required large amounts of land to be purchased in a relatively quick fashion, the War Department started to employ private firms to help augment. This was only a stop-gap measure, as the private contract and acquisition fees were exceedingly high. The Quartermaster Corps sought out and recruited real estate experts from the Lands Division of the Department of Justice to help process the purchases.

Where available, the Army purchased the lands from the federal government; or made effort to lease the land for 5-10 years. Whenever purchasing or leasing lands failed to drive results, the Chief of Engineers was permitted to use eminent domain to obtain the property. Even so, this was not a small proposition; in 1940, the War Department owned approximately 2 million acres of land that had been accumulating slowly since 1917. For this mobilization effort, the War Department needed 8 million more acres. Ultimately, 6 million acres came from federally-owned land and were transferred to the War Department. At its peak, the real estate program expended $340 million dollars ($6.2 billion today) and had 3,500 installations on 38 million acres of land.[13] This represented an area relative in size to the state of Iowa.

CAMP HAAN
THE HISTORY OF RIVERSIDE'S WORLD WAR II ANTI-AIRCRAFT TRAINING CENTER

Construction of camps and forts, storage depots, industrial facilities, and munitions facilities fell under the scope of the Quartermaster Corps. The 3,500 installations provided housing, training, transportation, and supplies for 5.3 million troops. Peak construction activity was in July 1942, with $729 million in construction contracts.[14]

Cantonments were erected all over the United States during World War I and World War II. A cantonment is a temporary garrison built by the Army to provide training facilities for troops. Cantonments were also designated as munitions and testing sites[15]. Later during World War II, cantonments were used as detention camps for prisoners of war, disciplinary barracks, processing stations, and logistical hubs. Cantonments were not inherently defensive structures; many of the cantonments had only chain-link fences and soldiers assigned as a patrolling watch as a determent. Additionally, many of the cantonments were built in large open, flat, and remote spaces away from the general population.

The architectural features of the cantonments were groups of barracks, parade fields, headquarters buildings, and supporting structures. These building arrangements were duplicated often and duplicated as a standard set of plans.

Many of the cantonments of World War II were based on the design principles of the World War I cantonments; however, the precedent was established during the second half of the 1800s during the expansion west. The temporary nature of the cantonments allowed for the continual movement of the expanding west. These cantonments were used to house troops and act as supply depots.

CAMP HAAN
THE HISTORY OF RIVERSIDE'S WORLD WAR II ANTI-AIRCRAFT TRAINING CENTER

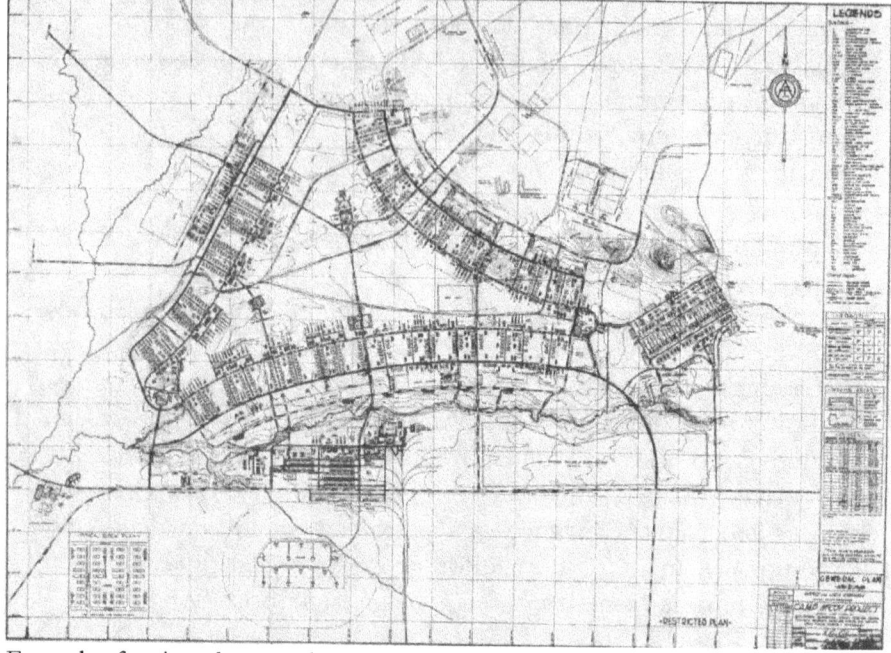

Example of a triangular camp layout.
Source: Wasch, D.; Bush, P.; Landreth, K; Glass, J. (nd) World War II and the U.S. Army Mobilization Program: A History of 700 and 800 Series Cantonment Construction. Legacy Resource Management Program, Department of Defense.

During the Spanish-American War[16] in the late 1800s, cantonments proved particularly useful as supply depots and aided in the necessity of marshaling supplies to foreign campaigns. They were also used to train troops; this meant that housing and training space was needed.

World War I Cantonments

At the start of World War I, the Army again wanted to use cantonments; however, they had a problem. The first was that they needed to be able to support thousands of troops. Secondly, the cantonments had to have adequate sources of food and water, and sewerage. Sewerage was an important lesson from the Spanish-American War, where up to 10 percent of all Army troops contracted typhoid fever. Future planning of cantonments had to address the issues. The Army turned to Colonel Frank McClellan

Gunby, assisted by Major George Gibbs, Jr., noted experts on Army camp planning[17].

Colonel Frank M. Gunby[18] was the Officer in Charge of the Engineering Branch of the Construction Division of the Army. He was a crucial team member in preparing plans for cantonments during WWI. He took that experience in cantonment building and applied that to WWII cantonments and expedited the building of cantonments in 1940.[19]

Major George Gibbs Jr., with a degree in landscape architecture, worked for the Construction Division, specializing in camp planning. During the Depression, he worked for the U.S. Forest Service and supervised the construction of Civilian Conservation Corps (CCC) projects in California. He was handpicked to work in France for the Quartermaster General's Graves Registration Service (GRS), ultimately designing the site plan for the Meuse-Argonne American Cemetery.[20]

A flurry of new cantonments were to be built. The War College approved two cantonment layouts: linear and u-shaped. Camp Lewis[21] was to be the largest.

Camp Lewis, established in 1917, became a cantonment of 44,685 soldiers. One of the chief criteria for the camp layout was based on the structure of an infantry division. The approved plan grouped buildings based on the regiment plus administrative buildings, supply, and a post exchange[22]. The decision was made to cluster the buildings around brigades of two regiments each in rectangular blocks with streets as wide as 50 feet to serve as a natural firebreak, could be used for troop formations, and as parade areas. These groupings were recreated for several regimental groupings on the property, considering the War College-approved layouts, terrain, and drainage, creating a u-shaped plan.

As early as the 1930s, the Army advocated for the extensive use of prefabricated wooden temporary structures that troops, conservation corps[23] manpower, or unskilled labor could erect and easily take down to re-mobilize.

World War II Cantonments

In contrast to World War I linear and u-shaped layouts, cantonment layouts of World War II were typically triangular or rectangular, at least in design. This way, each side of the layout was a brigade. One advantage of structuring the camps in triangular and rectangular shapes was having training areas adjacent to each brigade without troop movement into other brigade areas.

Although there were standards of design and blueprints for construction, local constructing quartermasters would have some discretion in adapting the standards to the local conditions, environment, and availability of materials.[24] Principle orders of World War II cantonments was that of the typical layout was based on the cantonment's function and Army requirements. "Every unit, large and small, would remain intact. Companies would be grouped into battalions and battalions into regiments. Regimental areas would adjoin a central parade ground. Hospitals would be in isolated spots, away from the noise and dirt. Storage Depots and motor parks would be near railway sidings or along main roads.[25]" Prisoner of war camps would be in a separate area, and the women and African American (colored)[26] troops would have their area with facilities.

The camps were arranged in gridded streets and straight rows of buildings in a quadrangular arrangement. This turned out to be more ideal than practical; seldom could the pattern be adhered to strictly, and changes were often necessary to adjust to the terrain[27].

Camps designed in 1940 were largely designed from plans produced by engineers of the J. B. McCrary Corporation. Their designs of Camp Stewart, Georgia influenced the design of later anti-aircraft training centers, and the design of the armored division camp at Fort Benning became the prototype for similar projects.[28] One of the first Camps built under the mobilization plan was Camp Edwards on September 12, 1940, and initially out of the gate, the constructing Quartermasters encountered problems with supply, contracting, and labor.

CHAPTER 3
U.S. ARMY CONSTRUCTION DIVISION

Before Camp Haan existed, the Army had been working on the challenge of housing mass troops in the event of a full-scale emergency or war declaration. One such unsung hero whose work changed the face of cantonment construction in the immediate years prior to the United States' entrance into WWII, was Colonel Charles D. Hartman.[29]

Colonel Charles D. Hartman
Chief of Construction

Colonel Hartman was a West Point graduate, infantry officer, and spent the first part of his career in the infantry. Later he was transferred to the Graves Registration Service (GRS),

Quartermaster General, and served as the Director of Sales for the War Department. Considering all his personal accomplishments, Col. Hartman was most notably known for his work with the Quartermasters Corps.

Colonel Hartman started his career as a construction officer November 1917 and served the Quartermasters Corps through World War I. He then returned to lead the Construction Division in 1934, it was there he discovered that the drawing from World War I, the 600 series, and the 700 series were in rough shape, "consisting of a few tracings for barracks, mess hall, and storehouses.[30]" The details of the plans were missing, and lumber sizes listed in the plan were no longer commercially produced. Colonel Hartman set on a personal mission to repair the damage the best he could.

Hampered by a lack of funding during this time, Col. Hartman scraped together funds from various other projects in the Construction Division and whatever fund he could allocate from the Works Progress Administration (WPA) and called for a complete revision of the drawings. By 1938, Col. Hartman had the necessary architects and draftsmen to begin to make progress on the project. General A. Owen Seaman, who served as Quartermaster General of the Construction Division under General Henry H. Arnold admitted," I didn't think we would ever need these cantonments."[31] To further the sentiment, up to that point, the Army's mobilization plan didn't require the construction of cantonment structures. For this reason, many in the Quartermaster General denounced mobilization structures, the overall funding for updating the plans, and provided push back to Col. Hartman.

Many in Washington and on the ground favored a decentralized control of the construction. Col. Hartman was fiercely in favor of centralizing stating that, "The day was long past when non-professionals could do construction. Nowadays a corps of specialists was required. Commanders could not themselves direct Construction Quartermasters (CQMs) with any degree of competence, nor could they justify the expense of maintaining separate technical staff.³² Hartman further warned Washington that if control were to go decentralized, construction quality would be no better than the construction seen in 1917. Many described Hartman's leadership style as very guarded and wanted to maintain control of the entire decision process; he did not delegate well.

> *"In light of the lessons of the past and the recognized civilian practice, the need for a strong centralized organization is important, first, because a central organization can be more efficiently and economically managed and controlled, second, responsibility can be more readily and directly placed."*³³

Because of recent amendment changes under the Detached Service Law³⁴ in 1912, stating that no Army officer could stay in Washington (in a detached service) greater than 5 years, in August 1939, Col. Hartman was sent to California for a period of six months, presumably back to the infantry. Because of his previous experiences, Col. Hartman was then recalled back to Washington and became the head of the Construction Division on March 1, 1940 with a promotion to Bridgadier General. Upon his return he found that the previous two Quartermasters General did not advance planning aside from exhaustive studies, in fact one of them abolished the planning branch, making it all but impossible to be ready for a full-scale emergency.

As the Army soon would find out, they would need those drawings and plans.

Convinced that mobilization was about to occur, Gen. Hartman thought that he was prepared, he had the drawing redone a year or so earlier, so he thought he could just "dust off" the plans; this was when Hartman made a shocking and alarming discovery, someone had altered the plans so much so that they were useless. To add onto that, not all the plans were there; some of the plans seemed to have disappeared. In Hartman's eyes he was staring at imminent mobilization and he didn't have plans to build out the cantonments.

Pulling from experiences in WWI construction, Hartman reorganized the Construction Division like what it was during WWI, but to enact any massive construction plan, Hartman needed manpower. In 1940, there were 824 regular Army Quartermasters, only 100 of which had any construction experience. Hartman had few options, commanders were not willing to give up officers in the regular Army, and Hartman could not tap reservists or National Guard members until the Selective Service Act was passed. He then looked to civil service; the depression left the construction industry barren, so Hartman sought out the older generation because they had the necessary skills. This, however, was dampened when the Surgeon General declared that anyone with false teeth, flat feet, high blood pressure, or overweight be rejected from service. Hartman appealed but was denied. Finally, Gen. Hartman saw some traction when he appealed to the corps area commanders to detail officers to his division. Although Hartman did not necessarily get construction men, he obtained a number of highly qualified officers. Still with this influx of manning, the demand exceeded the supply and in July 1940 the Construction Division was still short 200 officers with another 700 vacancies coming down soon. Hartman now had to pivot and rely on civil service for manpower, but the rules were equally strict for employment and location was going to be an issue since decidedly the cantonments were to be built in rural or barren areas in most cases.

Employment for the Construction Division also had its own challenges, "The Civil Service rosters contained many misfits who had lost their positions due to the depression [he later wrote]. A substantial number of these did not live in the Washington area. We found they did not have the money to travel to Washington for an interview and a heavy percentage were not qualified for our undertaking.[35]"

In order to make this happen, Hartman and his small staff had to do a little marketing and advertising; Hartman looked to the professional societies to get the word out for qualified individuals. In the end he persevered and the Construction Division began to swell gradually by August 1940.

CAMP HAAN
THE HISTORY OF RIVERSIDE'S WORLD WAR II ANTI-AIRCRAFT TRAINING CENTER

Building Site Selection

Now that Gen. Hartman had the necessary administrative staff to manage the construction projects, he turned to build requirements from the War Department. If Gen. Hartman were to meet the mobilization requirements, he knew he had to get these camps built fast and as cheaply as possible, his mandate stated that the costs would not be exorbitant. In thinking about this to put together an operational plan Hartman knew the location of the building sites had to lend themselves to rapid and economical construction, factoring in climate, terrain, soil, subsurface conditions, availability of transportation and labor, and materials. Because site selection depended on the availability of the land, Hartman was not privy to site locations in many cases. "I never knew until the directive came to me where [a] camp would be," Hartman explained in a 1941 Senate Committee hearing. He stressed the need for a thorough investigation of the proposed sites because he already had pointed out that six of the proposed locations were going to cause challenges; Camp Blanding in Florida was probably too swampy, Fort Eustis in Virginia probably had too much marshes and streams running throught it, Fort Huachuca in Arizona was too hilly for motorized units, Camps San Luis Obisbo in California and Hulen in Texas were too small for division trainings, and Fort Clark was more than 10 miles away from the railroad. This ultimately was problematic for Hartman, because he had essentially no control over the site and the conditions, yet he was responsible for the speed and cost of the construction.

First and foremost, site selection criteria were prioritized for military considerations. They needed personnel, anti-aircraft, and planes near the coast; troops needed to train in various climates and conditions. Flying fields had to be in an area with favorable weather permitting year-round training and mutations and plants had to be located to afford maximum protection and production.

700 Series[36]

Initially part of the mobilization plan, the Army had planned on housing the troops in tents, but quickly decided to provide "temporary" shelter. Consequently, Gen. Hartman and the 700 series plans took center stage and suddenly became important. The

Construction Division was supposed to be building 700 series buildings in 1939 as part of Roosevelt's limited mobilization. Drawn up hastily in Spring of 1939, mobilization structure plans began to take shape. Most of these plans were drawn up from the 1917 structures or by memory from veteran employees of the Construction Division.

Gen. Hartman scrambled and created a construction advisory committee to help fix the problem with the plans. With help from this committee that comprised of the president of the American Society of Civil Engineers, the past President of the American Institute of Architects, the President of the American Engineering Council, and the Chairman of the Construction League of America, a revised version of the 700 series plans were out in record time. When completed, the "700 series" represented the entirety of temporary wartime building plans. It contained blueprints for over 300 hundred structures of various types and included blueprints for roads and utilities and typical camps. While the structures in the 700 series looked like the 600 series of World War I, there were discernable differences in quality of life. For example, the 700 series barrack had latrines inside the barracks versus separate latrine buildings. The 700 series structures also called for concrete foundations or concrete foundation piers as opposed to wooden posts. Other modifications were aimed at reducing the ongoing maintenance costs. Canopies or "aqua medias", and overhanging eave units served to keep rain off the structure of the buildings were among the changes.

As the schedule for construction began that summer, the War Department issued its first basic directive on its construction policy on June 15, 1940. According to the directive, military construction in the United States fell under the direction of the Quartermaster Corps for all camp construction and all overseas camp and airfield construction was the responsibility of the Corps of Engineers. This directive laid down the fundamental explanation under which the Army's huge construction program was to be executed.

Gen. Hartman circulated a memo on July 19, 1940 that specified that the revised 700 series plans were the standard and instructed all other plans obsolete. Gen. Hartman would go on to become known as the person instrumental in creating and approving the 63-man barracks, which is still the basis of barrack construction used today.

The 700 series plans called for several "rules" concerning camp layout. To prevent the spread of fire through the camp, one-story buildings needed to be at least 40 feet apart; two-story buildings 50 feet apart. Firebreaks of 250 feet wide the length of the camp. Hospitals would be isolated spots, away from the noise and dirt; storage depots and motor parks would be placed near or alongside railways.

Gen. Hartman also laid out mandates on how the buildings would be constructed. Cantonments were built based on the company and include two 63-man barracks with inside lavatories, one mess hall, one recreation hall, and one supply building. It also mandated that as the cantonments expanded, the ratio of barracks to mess halls would remain constant.

A relatively late challenge in the design of the 700 series plans was the fact that even into the fall of 1940, while construction had already begun at camps, Army G-3[37] was still reorganizing and changing the number of personnel per unit. "The size of the infantry company, the basic unit around which most camps were designed, was not fixed until construction was well underway.[38]" There were reports of frustrated contractors and quartermasters that construction had to be stopped and ripped out to accommodate changes to the series to comply, even though the changes had no significantly impact to structure. Finally, after going back and forth on numerous changes, the Construction Division set forth a policy that the changes should be incorporated unless the cantonment's construction was at an advanced stage or not practical from that point in the construction. This gave the construction quartermaster in the field the ability to make the decision if and when a change needed to be made based on what he was seeing on the ground.

CAMP HAAN
THE HISTORY OF RIVERSIDE'S WORLD WAR II ANTI-AIRCRAFT TRAINING CENTER

As the first camps were starting to be built in the fall of 1940, it was generally understood that shelter was a decisive factor; in response, the newly pined Gen. Hartman publicized his latest estimate that housing for one to two million men could be ready in three or four months. But he also warned of things that could cause delays such as strikes, bad weather, and shortages of materials.[39] Hartman knew that the winter months were approaching and historically construction slowed significantly in the winter months, if not for the actual labor, but the availability of materials due to reduced staffing at the plants and manufacturing facilities making the products that were being installed in the cantonments.

Gen. Hartman was all about constructing a sound structure, according to the plans, on schedule, and under budget. Frills were not something that General Hartman considered nor did he think it belonged in his planning. Initially, the buildings in the camps were not to be painted, Army Chief of Staff General Moore agreed with Hartman and saw it as expensive and a not needed expense; Hartman thought they should only paint the exterior of buildings in effort to reduce ongoing maintenance costs. Only when President Roosevelt visited Camp Meade in Maryland and said he wanted to see the buildings painted, did policy change in November 1940.[40] However, like several of the other variations in construction methods, this policy seemed to be applied sporadically. Some camps had their exterior buildings painted, while others were just clad with the bitumen paper anchored down by wood stripping, and some buildings were constructed of adobe.

The 700 series structures were considered temporary and designed to only last from 5-20 years. As World War II mobilization continued, construction continued to evolve from the 700 series to the 800 series, the Modified Theater-of-Operations (T.O) series, and T.O 700 series. The T.O variants of the 700 and 800 series buildings were wartime "minimalist" versions of the parent series, most of these T.O. structures survived beyond World War II.

A key part of mobilization construction was speed. To accomplish the builds in the timeframe needed the construction needed to be as simple as possible. Complex framing details were avoided and most of the interior finishes were generally omitted; electrical and plumbing were also kept as simple as possible. This simplicity enabled the contractors to be able to hire unskilled labor for much of the builds. This helped to keep the wages down and keep the construction on track once the war started and when there was a shortage in skilled labor.

Despite Hartman's push to mobilize and build, many criticized him and his office for cost overruns, for taking on too much himself, not delegating, and not taking suggestions from the field. There were questions about the ability of the Construction Division to adequately maintain control as early as July 1940.[41] This prompted the Army Chief of Staff General Moore and Quartermaster General, General Gregory to consider a leadership change. In the meantime, General Gregory directed all "papers to and from the Construction Division," be routed through his office in effort to keep a close eye on General Hartman's activities, specifically personnel requests. This would mark a drastic 180 on his previous stance of letting Hartman hire his own personnel. Previously, in discussions with the Civil Service Commission, "Gregory asked the commission to step aside and let Hartman do his own hiring."

The Army was being pressured toward decentralizing the Construction Division in the fall of 1940, adamantly opposed by Hartman. It all came to a head in December of that year when General Gregory ordered Hartman to set up regional offices within the Construction Division; Hartman refused. General Gregory promptly relieved General Hartman of command of the Construction Division.

"General Gregory came into my office early in the afternoon of December 11th and I knew by the scared look on his face that he had bad news for me. He informed me that I was relieved from the construction Division at once. I did not give him the courtesy of a reply. I immediately closed my desk and departed."[42]

General Hartman

This event was recorded in Secretary of War Henry Stimson's diary:

CAMP HAAN
THE HISTORY OF RIVERSIDE'S WORLD WAR II ANTI-AIRCRAFT TRAINING CENTER

"Another crisis has come up in the Department. General Hartman, who has had charge of construction in the Quartermaster Corps, is being relieved and Lt. Col. Somervell is being placed in his place. It is a pathetic situation because Hartman has been a loyal and devoted man. He has conducted the difficult and delicate work of choosing these contractors in these bids on numerous projects without a taint of scandal of any sort thus far. But he apparently lacks the gift of organization and he has been running behind in the work."[43]

General Hartman's greatest handicap may have been the lack of qualified personnel to get the job done and the unwillingness to adapt to changing construction environments that were evolving rapidly. Almost immediately after being relieved of command, General Hartman checked himself into the hospital to receive care. He was admitted to Walter Reed on December 11, 1940 for what was officially described as he was admitted for observation and treatment following a long period of overwork. Gen. Hartman remained on sick leave until April 1941, where he then served as commander of the Quartermaster Replacement Center at Fort Lee. He suffered a near fatal heart attack in March of 1942. General Hartman retired on disability from the U.S. Army on April 30, 1943 after 39 years of service. He would pass away in 1962.

In a December 13, 1940 War Department press release, Colonel Brehon Somervell was appointed to replace Hartman.

Colonel Brehon Somervell

Col. Somervell favored a decentralized system. When he took over, he immediately reorganized[44] the Construction Division by reducing the number of branches and breaking out the country into nine territorial construction zones each with a zone Quartermaster.⁴⁵ Somervell quickly replaced some of Gen. Hartman's men with is own, although a majority of them stayed in the division. He also hired prominent engineers, architects, and sonstruction men in each of the nine territories; men such as C. Herrick Hammond and Edward T. Foley. Somervell made substantial progress in the first few months reorganizing the division and planting some of the country's best in key positions. November 1940 saw the transfer of airfield construction to to the Engineering Corps; this took an additional load off of Somervell's division; however, this was a minor respite. Somervell knew that in the following months, eight National Guard divisions and eitghty miscellaneous units were to be sent to their camps in January and February on top of the requirement that five hospitals were scheduled to be open by March 1.⁴⁶

In Washington, Col. Somervell was tasked to complete a cost overrun study and he concluded that 25-35 percent of the increase was due to cost of labor and material, 50-60 percent to additional requirements, and 15-25 percent to changes in plans or underestimations of costs.⁴⁷ An independent study was completed by Saville & Blackburn, an engineering firm, and confirmed the debt that the construction division was accruing, in fact it was more. Somervell was in a position where he had to request additional funding to support the construction of the cantonments.

The 700 series came under intense scrutiny by Somervell and his division and changes were, yet again made to the 700 series plans. Most notably, northern camps benefited from the changes and construction was being "beefed up." Roofing members were increased in size, the number and size of bracings were increased, and roof bracing members were strengthened to account for increased snow load. These changes led to the beginning of a new series. In April 1941, the ok was given to start experimenting on alternative types of construction such as; masonry, tile, cinder blocks, plaster , and stucco. They even experimented with a metal pre-fabricated barrack concept.

CAMP HAAN
THE HISTORY OF RIVERSIDE'S WORLD WAR II ANTI-AIRCRAFT TRAINING CENTER

Throughout the course of cantonment construction for mobilization, it has been estimated that over 100,000 Series 700 buildings have been built. At the peak of construction, housing for over 1 million military personnel was constructed in just 10 months.

800 Series

In February and March 1941, work began on making changes to the Quartermaster plans for the 700 series, because the new designs were markedly different from the 700 series, Somervell decided to classify the new plans and drawings as 800 series. When the 800 series was released, the Construction Division stated that the series was both necessary and important for a number of reasons: (1)

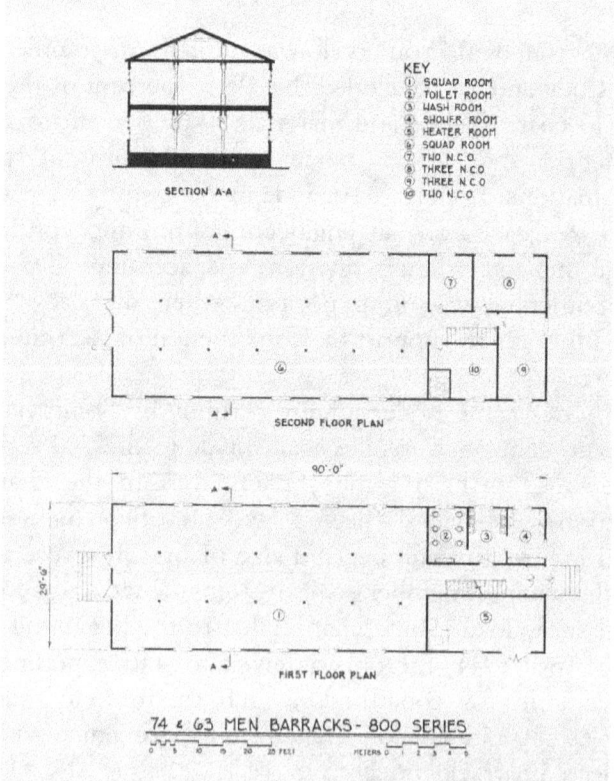

Source: Wasch, D.; Bush, P.; Landreth, K; Glass, J. (nd) World War II and the U.S. Army Mobilization Program: A History of 700 and 800 Series Cantonment Construction. Legacy Resource Management Program, Department of Defense.

building were more functional, (2) building were more livable (increased quality of life), (3) structurally safer, (4) overall cost was higher but fewer buildings were needed, and (5) fewer the buildings meant that the ongoing or utility costs would be overall less.[48] Another notable change in policy is that the 800 series allowed specifications to permit alternative types of construction, such as masonry, plaster, and stucco.

The 800 series barracks plan and shape were essentially unchanged but improved upon the 700 series. Studs were placed 2 feet on center versus the 3 feet on center that the 700 series called for. Additionally, bracing was added to the structures for camps in earthquake prone areas (same for camps in hurricane prone areas), larger squad rooms, and taller ceiling heights.

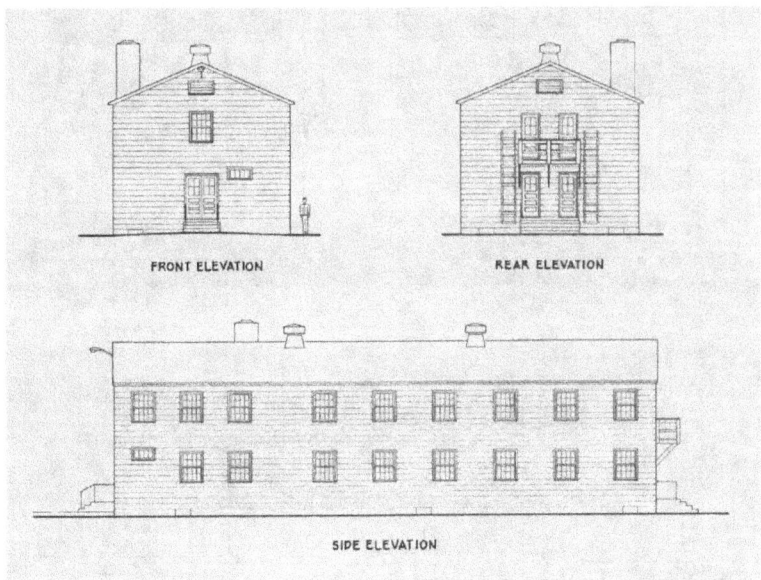

Source: Wasch, D.; Bush, P.; Landreth, K; Glass, J. (nd) World War II and the U.S. Army Mobilization Program: A History of 700 and 800 Series Cantonment Construction. Legacy Resource Management Program, Department of Defense.

CAMP HAAN
THE HISTORY OF RIVERSIDE'S WORLD WAR II ANTI-AIRCRAFT TRAINING CENTER

The 63-man barracks gave way to 74-man barracks in the 800 series because it was better fitted for the size of the companies and reduce the number of barracks needed at the camps.

Other notable changes from the 700 to 800 series included the warehouses were larger to accommodate more storage space, mess halls were re-arranged to flow more efficiently, and all the building in the series were arguably better ventilated and insulated. The 800 series also called for the removal of tents in favor of hutments.

Because the barracks' footprint changed, this also changed the way the camps were being laid out. The cantonment planning progressed from October 1940 to May 1942. In doing so, the

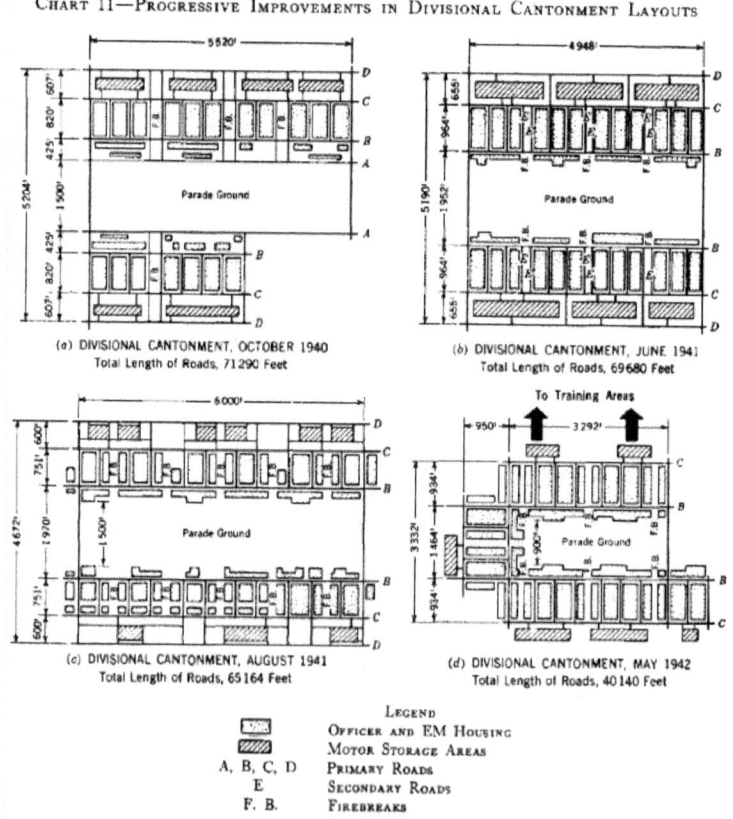

CHART 11—PROGRESSIVE IMPROVEMENTS IN DIVISIONAL CANTONMENT LAYOUTS

(a) DIVISIONAL CANTONMENT, OCTOBER 1940
Total Length of Roads, 71 290 Feet

(b) DIVISIONAL CANTONMENT, JUNE 1941
Total Length of Roads, 69 680 Feet

(c) DIVISIONAL CANTONMENT, AUGUST 1941
Total Length of Roads, 65 164 Feet

(d) DIVISIONAL CANTONMENT, MAY 1942
Total Length of Roads, 40 140 Feet

LEGEND
- Officer and EM Housing
- Motor Storage Areas
- A, B, C, D Primary Roads
- E Secondary Roads
- F. B. Firebreaks

Source: Leon Zach, "Site Planning of Cantonment and Community Housing," *Civil Engineering*, August 1945, pp. 364–65.

Source: Fine, L; Remington, Jesse (1989) The Corps of Engineers: Construction in the United States. Center of Military History: Washington DC.

cantonments under the 800 series plans required less linear feet of road.⁴⁹

Through the successive progressions in layouts, the Construction Division was able to reduce the roadage by 44%.

The 800 series buildings; however, were not well received in the field. Many commanders preferred the 700 series and called the 800 series building "too permanent."

Toward the end of 1941, both the 700 series and 800 series plans were authorized. Construction quartermasters were told to replace the 700 series plans with those of the 800 series except in special circumstances. These special circumstances included: extension of a 700 series building, constructing new buildings in a 700 series type camp, or when the 800 series were not feasible. Almost all the temporary cantonments were built with a mix of 700 & 800 series buildings. Because of the multitude of changes that occurred in both the 700 and 800 series during the actual construction of the cantonments, camps would have two identical structures built sided-by-side that have different aesthetics. For example, one 63-man barrack may have the aqua medias, while the other one would not.

In October 1942, the War Department canceled the 800 series plans opting for a more temporary building that cost less; subsequently, most of the buildings in the contoments, after December 1941 were 700 series of T.O. type.⁵⁰

Ultimately, the program cost roughly double the original cost estimates made by the General Staff in summer of 1940.⁵¹ With far greater support Col. Somervell accomplished what Gen. Hartman could not. Part of his success was that he was more flexible to the changing policies and more persuasive to polices and procedures he thought would advance his goals. Somervell would continue on in the Construction Division, become the commanding general Army Services of Supply, and be integral part of the leadership to building the massive War Department building, known now as the Pentagon.

CAMP HAAN
THE HISTORY OF RIVERSIDE'S WORLD WAR II ANTI-AIRCRAFT TRAINING CENTER

World War II cantonment construction would be the first mobilization construction project since World War I; it was also the first mobilization construction program relying heavily on industry and civilian contractors and engineers. Despite the series 700 & 800 building being called "temporary," the Quartermasters estimated the lifespan of the buildings of 5 to 20 years[52]. In reality, these structures would survive decades and serve the civilian community long after the war. In a 1993 U.S. Army Corps of Engineers report estimated that over 26,000 World War II structures still existed, and many were still being used[53]. This is a testament to the quality of construction and materials that were used in combination with the utility and the civilian need for the buildings after the war.

CHAPTER 4
CONSTRUCTION

Concurrent with the buildup in troops, the Army and the War Department were purchasing and leasing large tracts of land to build temporary cantonments for housing and training troops. Camp Haan, like many camps in World War I and World War II, was designed to be a cantonment.

Since the War Department imposed budget constraints stressed that construction costs would not be exorbitant, building sites were looked at that could be rapidly set up and economical to do so. All things were considered, climate, soil type, terrain, availability of transportation, sub surface composition, and availability of labor and utilities. Because having a military installation built near a city or a town would bring in revenue to the community, the site selection process also had political and social implications.

Selecting the site would be the first challenge in a series of challenges that had to be overcome. Camp Haan was to become the largest west coast anti-aircraft training center in the nation. For this to happen, certain U.S. Army criteria had to be met:

1. The site had reasonable access to water

2. The site had to be able to have natural drainage or be gradable to facilitate drainage

3. The site had to have accessible rail and highway facilities

4. The site had to have or access to an artillery firing range

5. The site had to have adjoining field space for field maneuvers

6. Cost and availability of property were a factor

7. The site had to have access to food supplies (farms, markets, towns)

Even though these criteria were meant to be doctrine, in many cases, the site selection process was delegated down to junior officers with little to no experience in site surveying and planning. In some cases, that Gen. Hartman alluded to, sites were being picked that no one even set eyes on. Luckily, the site for what would be Camp Haan was close to March Field, so the commanders did know the area.

Site #1

The primary site was selected by Lt. Col. Robert H. Van Volkenburgh and Major Bunting, was in Perris, California, just south of March Field in the San Jacinto drainage basin. An architect-Engineer contract was signed on September 25, 1940, and site surveys began. The Army knew the location for the camp would be challenging and with no access to water, wells would have to be drilled and developed. Before any other work was done on the site, wells were drilled and the water was tested. The Army quickly found out that the water was of bad quality and the site was abandoned by the Army on September 30, 1940.[54]

Site #2

Lt. Col. Robert H. Van Volkenburgh and Major Bunting scrambled to find an additional location, and it was under their nose, or aptly just to the west of March Field. On October 12, 1940, settled on an area of land about 10 miles southeast of Riverside, California also known as the Alessandro tract. As early as August 1940, the War Department, while hedging their bets on finding suitable land for a cantonment, were in negotiations with landowners and the

Riverside Chamber of Commerce[55] for the new Army post[56]. Originally, the plan was to purchase 950 acres to house and train up to 10,000 military personnel.[57] The area selected was primarily used for farming. The area was chosen for multiple reasons. First, the camp would be near what would become the Mohave artillery range (Camp Irwin). Secondly, the proximity to the Los Angeles Port of Embarkation[58] that shipped personnel, equipment, and supply to China and the India-Burma theaters was ideal. Third, the location of the proposed camp was near a rail line. Fourth, the weather afforded year-round training. Finally, it was ideal to set up

March Airfield in May 1938. The large swath of farmland to the west is the future site of Camp Haan. Source: UC Santa Barbara Library

an antiaircraft artillery training center in reasonable approximation to the west coast where they would have to set up defensive positions against Japan. Another advantage to having an anti-artillery camp across the highway from March Field was that it allowed practicing ranging and spotting of aircraft flying in and out of March field.

CAMP HAAN
THE HISTORY OF RIVERSIDE'S WORLD WAR II ANTI-AIRCRAFT TRAINING CENTER

Back in Washington, the funding for the construction of the camp was delayed by Congress and this delayed the purchases of land and ultimately the start of construction. By the time Congress passed the third supplemental defense bill, appropriating building funds, fall was approaching. This concerned General Hartman because he knew that construction would stop or be slowed with the approaching winter. Before ground was even broke at the cantonment, Secretary of War, Henry Stimson was quoted that he intended to place as many as 12,500 men at the encampment across from March Field. This represented a further modification to the original estimates by Stimson of 5,000.[59] That number would fluctuate upwards during the building of the camp until 30,000 men were being considered.

Finally, shortly after Labor Day 1940, the bottleneck finally broke. Construction authorization and directives began to flow into General Hartman's desk; 26 camps, 1 general hospital, 2 airfields, 1 munitions plant, and numerous smaller projects. By October there were 300 additional directives on Hartman's desk that were greenlit for construction.

Because of the immediate need for housing, much of the planning and design of the camp had to occur concurrently, so the U.S. Army selected the architect-engineer contract. This brought the architects, engineers, and construction contractors together on the job all at the same time at the same site. Because accurate cost estimates varied based on geographic region, the government opted for a cost plus a fixed fee to the contractor for management services.

Building a camp for 30,000 military personnel and contracted civilians is a large undertaking, too large for most construction companies of the days, so several companies were put on contract; each managing their piece, and all activities were to be overseen on-site by the Constructing Quartermaster.

CAMP HAAN
THE HISTORY OF RIVERSIDE'S WORLD WAR II ANTI-AIRCRAFT TRAINING CENTER

Acquisition

The initial land for the camp was acquired through a combination of fee, leases, permits, and easements and consisted of 1,809.39 acres. The largest acreage known as the Alessandro Tract was sold the War Department from Caroline M. Trautwein. That plot of land was closer to March Field, where present-day Riverside National Cemetery sits. The initial build and main camp of Camp Haan lie on sloping land paralleling the state highway (old 395, now 215), four miles in length. Although acquisition would begin in August 1940, it was not until August of 1942 when all the legal documents and transfer of titles were finalized. By then, the War Department had already decided to expand the camp and was purchasing and leasing additional land. Much of the first expansion of Camp Haan was designed to fill out some of the quality-of-life issues that were not a priority in the original buildout. These items included chapels, paved sidewalks, and additional buildings in the hospital area. It also included new regimental areas that would include 215 more hutments, six mess halls, a post exchange, a gas station, administrative-type buildings, a motor repair shop, and two

> **ADVERTISEMENT**
> OFFICE OF THE CONSTRUCTING QUARTERMASTER, CAMP HAAN, RIVERSIDE COUNTY, CALIFORNIA—Sealed bids will be received in triplicate at this office until 11:00 A.M., June 17, 1941, and then publicly opened, for the construction and completion of 68 buildings and appurtenant work at Camp Haan. Plans and specifications are available at the Office of the Constructing Quartermaster at Camp Haan upon payment of deposit of $10.00. Certified or cashier's check (10%) must accompany bid. Any bid extending the completion date beyond August 9, 1941, will not be accepted. Inv. No. QM-6694-41-2.

Source: San Bernardino County Sun, Wednesday, June 11, 1941

warehouses. This expansion also included the requisite utilities that comes with the expansion[60]. By April 3, 1941, the War

Departmentt announced an imminent project start.[61] Shortly after the work began.

In June of 1941, advertisements went out to the civilian community for the planned expansion while the War Department was expanding land acquisition activities.

Although most of the expansion was focused on the camp, there was also some civilian infrastructure improved in the surrounding areas. The war department announced in July 1941 that $4,000,000 was being allotted to the state of California for roadwork vital to the defense program. The money was specifically earmarked for four (4) projects:

1. Widen Box Spring highway. This was the main route out of Riverside to March Field and Camp Haan

2. Widen Dracea Street Intersection

3. Widen two lanes of Dracea Street to four lanes from March Field to Camp Haan

4. Widen Iowa Avenue at the San Bernardino-Riverside County line to accommodate large Army trucks going north to Camp Irwin.[62]

By August 1941, Van Buren Blvd from Camp Anza to Camp Haan was constructed. The road continued through Camp Haan to U.S. 395 (present-day I-215). The portion traversing through the camp was open to the public during the day.[63] This afforded civilians a closer look at Army life since the roadway transected the camp.

By November 1942, the north and west areas of the original camp expansion have been completed; the hospital wings were finished, and the War Department continued its planned expansion of Camp Haan, that same month, by exercising the War Powers Act. Notably, 32 properties were purchased through the declaration of taking, through the War Powers Act (WPA)[64] and seven properties were donated by the landowners.

CAMP HAAN
THE HISTORY OF RIVERSIDE'S WORLD WAR II ANTI-AIRCRAFT TRAINING CENTER

As the War Department continued to take steps toward expansion and the war heating up over in Europe, security was beefed up between June and Dec 1941, as a 10-ft chain linked fence topped with barbed wire was installed around the camp. Floodlights were also installed at ratio of 59 lights per linear mile. This was to protect ammunition and other critical storage areas but was also use as a deterrent for curious civilians, make it harder for the troops to just walk off, and add a layer of protection to the camp that was not there in the initial build. Early on, the only protection that Camp Haan was afforded was scant military police patrols augmented by March Field and the fact that the camp was out in the eastern part of Riverside in a very sparsely populated area.[65]

The additional areas of Camp Haan were built as an expansion in 1943 to further expand the anti-air training. The first area was

> Reproduced from the holdings of the *National Archives at Riverside*
>
> WAR DEPARTMENT
> Washington, D. C.
>
> Certificate No. 23   11 August 1943
>
> In accordance with the provisions of Section I of the Military Appropriation Act of 1944, Public No. 108 - 78th Congress, approved 1 July 1943, the following named projects for the acquisition of land are hereby approved by me:
>
> | Name of Project | Approximate Acreage | Amount |
> |---|---|---|
> | Camp Haan, Calif. (For Sewage Treatment Plant and Effluent Line) | 187.673 | $10,235.00 |
>
> HENRY L. STIMSON
> Secretary of War

Certificate No. 23 authorizing the expansion of Camp Haan.
Source: National Archives at Riverside

187.673 acres for a sewage treatment plant and effluent line.[66] The second and most expansive area would be referred to as the "Topside" area of Camp Haan because this area was built on the southwest side of Camp Haan on an elevated plateau west of Regimental Area 1. This consisted of 5,414.35 acres. The Topside area would add 13 more battalion areas (approximately 13,000 more men) to the camp's infrastructure. The Topside area was such a major expansion that the existing electrical into the camp could not support the expansion, so the Topside part of the camp was fed from an entirely separate electrical substation.[67] Gutter and curbing projects commenced camp wide and sidewalks were installed around the headquarters area. The entire camp underwent

CAMP HAAN
THE HISTORY OF RIVERSIDE'S WORLD WAR II ANTI-AIRCRAFT TRAINING CENTER

beatification through the planting of thousands of coulter pines, fan palms, Monterey pines, incense cedar, and rose bushes. In total, 10,000 trees and hundreds of bushes and shrubs were planted.[68]

Construction Begins

Going back to the original construction of the camp, the War Department and local Army Construction Quartermasters signed contracts with builder contractors. They hired J.B Lippincott and O.G Bowen as the architectural engineers for the project and Stanley R. Gould as the architect consultant.

Joseph Barlow Lippincott was a very well-known civil engineer on the west coast. He also served as the supervising engineer of for the Federal Reclamation Service, where he helped investigate sources of water for Los Angeles – which directly led to the Owens River Dam and later was named the Assistant Chief Engineer for the construction of the Los Angeles Aqueduct[69]. In 1913, Lippincott left public service and entered private practice, headquartering at 2835 Gilroy Street, Los Angeles, CA. In 1914, he served as the first President of the Southern California Association of Members of the American Society of Civil Engineers.

For firms like Lippincott and Bowen to qualify for the contract, the War Department did some due diligence through the Construction Division to ensure the firm would offer strong organization backed by capital, experience, and key personnel to complete the project in the least possible time.

Joseph Barlow Lippincott (1864-1942)
Source: http://cookfamilygenealogy.org/

Lippincott and Bowen, in coordination with the approved plans from the War College, artillery officers, and Quartermaster

General, began to design the camp layout. Quartermasters assigned to camp during construction were the on-site managers. Quartermasters were key part of the team to come up with the design for the layout in line with Army regulations as much as possible with terrain considerations.

During the preliminary stages, Major Joseph Bergheim, served as the Acting Constructing Quartermaster at Camp Haan until Major Harry Larson arrived on station on October 15, 1940.[70] Because of the series 700 plan changes, Maj. Larson ordered a stoppage of work on the site on October 23, 1940. Work stoppages were quite common during this period in the mobilization program; changes to personnel unit sizes and anticipated personnel total numbers necessitated many changes. In October 1940, the War Department, more specifically the Construction Division, published 35 new tables of organizations and equipment, in November 379 more , and December 30 more.[71] While Lippincott and Bowen were incorporating all the changes the Construction Division were laying out in the plans and blueprints, in the meantime, construction was directed to be started on the water main that would connect the camp to Riverside.

On October 31, 1940, supplement no. 1 was given to Lippincott and Bowen and necessitated that a new site plan layout needed to be completed. Moreover, all the mess hall plans had to be redrawn because of new size regulations directed by the Army. To make matters worse, on November 7, 1940, Major Larson told Lippincott and Bowen that the site plan needed to be revised yet again due to updated runway restrictions from nearby March Field affecting the maximum height of structures in the camp. This frustrated Lippincott and Bowen because a lot of work and man hours were needed to change and re-draw the site plans yet again.

Construction moved from the planning phase to the actual construction and began on the anti-aircraft training center camp west of March Field mid-November of 1940; however, Lippincott and Bowen were less than pleased with Major Larson as the Constructing Quartermaster (C.Q.M). An excerpt from

Lippincott's and Bowen's completion report confirms the frustration,

> "Major Harry Larson was relieved from duty at this post and Captain Kenneth H. Newton was appointed Constructing Quartermaster. Up to this time much difficulty was experienced by the Architect-Engineer and the contractor getting decisions, approvals, and cooperation from the C.Q.M and a considerable delay in the work may be credited to this fact."[72]

Final approval for the site plan, except for the headquarters and quartermaster area, was secured on November 12, 1940. On November 16, 1940, Major Larson was relieved and Captain Kenneth H. Newton[73] was appointed Construction Quartermaster for the remainder of the build.[74] The reasons for Major Larson being relieved were not conveyed in Lippincott and Bowens completion report, but it was evident that the parties did not get along. They had nothing but praise for Captain Newton, citing that, "After Captain Newton took charge, no delays were encountered, due to his actions and a fine spirit of cooperation."[75]

U. S. To Buy Land For Army Base

WASHINGTON, Oct. 22. — (UP)—The War department will purchase 950 acres of land near March Field, Calif., for an anti-aircraft firing center at a tent camp, housing approximately 10,000 men, it was learned today.

Officials said the department's representatives are not yet in the field to buy the land, but 950 acres will be necessary.

When the land is purchased and the camp established, five units, each with 75 officers and 1800 enlisted men, will be stationed there. They are the 251st coast artillery, 215th coast artillery, 216th coast artillery, 217th coast artillery and 65th coast artillery, all anti-aircraft organizations. In addition, the headquarters and headquarters battery of the 101st coast artillery brigade, with 10 officers and 72 enlisted men, will be stationed there.

Source: Santa Ana Register, Tuesday, October 22, 1940, P. 8

CAMP HAAN
THE HISTORY OF RIVERSIDE'S WORLD WAR II ANTI-AIRCRAFT TRAINING CENTER

Once camp construction began, the hired contractors began to feverously hire skilled and unskilled workers. In some cases, workers from the Civilian Conservation Corps were used. Men from all over the country seeking work to better their positions in the post-depression economies flocked to the locations where the camps were being built. Men responsible for the actual construction of Camp Haan were known to have come from a far away as the Midwest for work. Between July 1940 and December 1940, the number of men employed for all military construction projects, Army wide, increased from 5,380 to 396,255. Thousands of men were hired by various contractors during the Camp Haan build.

Building delays

All evidence and the initial land surveys leading up to selecting the site steered everyone to believe that the Alessandro Tract would be relatively quick to construct the camp, since the land was relatively flat, barren, and mostly used for dry agriculture. This turned out to be a mistaken assumption.

Construction work at Camp Haan has been slowed down considerably during recent rains by muddy roads. Camp was nicknamed Lake Haan.
Times photo

Source: Los Angeles Times, Monday, March 10, 1941

CAMP HAAN
THE HISTORY OF RIVERSIDE'S WORLD WAR II ANTI-AIRCRAFT TRAINING CENTER

The Army found that the Alessandro Tract of land was riddled with boulders, large and small, grain stubble, and the ground proved to be extremely hard. When the contractors went to break ground and dig trenches for the initial sewer and water lines, they found that ground was so hard that they had to take jackhammers to it.[76] This was further complicated by the area's local wildlife resistance being kicked out of their habitat; there were numerous instances where workers were bitten by rattlesnakes and coyotes were prevalent on the job site.

Further complicating the construction, the winter of 1940 was unseasonably wet and cold for the Riverside area. Los Angeles recorded its, "heaviest and most continuous rainfall in forty-three years.[77]" All the cleared land that Camp Haan was being built on turned to a sea of mud with the rain and because of the rolling terrain and the runoff, it created little lakes of retained water. The season broke all weather records for total precipitation and the number of days of rain:

Number of days of rain: 43
Total Precipitation: 21.51 inches[78]

Lippincott and Bowen reported to the Army, as an example of the conditions, that Pinkerton and Jameson, a contractor, estimated a thirty-day delay and a monetary loss in road construction alone over $35,000 due to weather.[79] The contractor would get the roadway leveled and properly graded and their efforts would be disrupted by rain requiring that they start over several times.

CAMP HAAN
THE HISTORY OF RIVERSIDE'S WORLD WAR II ANTI-AIRCRAFT TRAINING
CENTER

Camp Haan under construction.
Source: Yeager Family Library, March Field Air Museum

CAMP HAAN
THE HISTORY OF RIVERSIDE'S WORLD WAR II ANTI-AIRCRAFT TRAINING CENTER

Camp Haan under construction.
Source: Yeager Family Library, March Field Air Museum

CAMP HAAN
THE HISTORY OF RIVERSIDE'S WORLD WAR II ANTI-AIRCRAFT TRAINING CENTER

Camp Haan under construction.
Source: Yeager Family Library, March Field Air Museum

CAMP HAAN
THE HISTORY OF RIVERSIDE'S WORLD WAR II ANTI-AIRCRAFT TRAINING
CENTER

Camp Haan under construction.
Source: Yeager Family Library, March Field Air Museum

Camp Haan under construction. Notice the B-24 overhead
Source: Yeager Family Library, March Field Air Museum

CAMP HAAN
THE HISTORY OF RIVERSIDE'S WORLD WAR II ANTI-AIRCRAFT TRAINING CENTER

Camp Haan under construction.
Source: Yeager Family Library, March Field Air Museum

Camp Haan under construction. Notice the chapel in the background.
Source: Yeager Family Library, March Field Air Museum

CAMP HAAN
THE HISTORY OF RIVERSIDE'S WORLD WAR II ANTI-AIRCRAFT TRAINING CENTER

Camp Haan under construction.
Source: Yeager Family Library, March Field Air Museum

Camp Haan under construction.
Source: Yeager Family Library, March Field Air Museum

CAMP HAAN
THE HISTORY OF RIVERSIDE'S WORLD WAR II ANTI-AIRCRAFT TRAINING CENTER

Camp Haan under construction.
Source: Yeager Family Library, March Field Air Museum

Camp Haan under construction. "A" Tent construction in the regimental area.
Source: Yeager Family Library, March Field Air Museum

CAMP HAAN
THE HISTORY OF RIVERSIDE'S WORLD WAR II ANTI-AIRCRAFT TRAINING CENTER

Originally, the Construction Division gave the contractors the final completion date and allowed them to prioritize their operations, but as building delays started to creep up and Washington began questioning the delays and policies that the Construction Division was broadcasting. The War Department guided the Construction Division to set forth a new policy in November of 1940 that directed, "contractors would coordinate their plans with the scheduled dates of troop arrivals. Barracks and mess halls would have top priority, and so would hospital wings for the first arrivals.[80]" The thought process behind this was to make the camps minimally operational so that troops could move in and begin training and then contractors could finish up the remainder construction projects while the camp was occupied.

Weather wasn't the only delay; there were also delays due to resource availability. Lumber was the most serious bottleneck; however, several other hard to procure items caused delays as well; kitchen and hospital equipment, lavatory fixtures, and stoves proved hard to come by. Manufacturers were unable to keep up with the demand in late 1940. Shortages in the skilled labor to build the camp also ranked high as a delaying factor, in fact all the camps had skilled labor shortages.

In December 1940, Commanding officers and support staff began arriving at the camp to prepare for the first wave of U.S. troops to arrive by train. Also, by this time, the railyard was teeming with activities as trains were arriving with construction material as were key provisions, supplies, and equipment for camp operational activities. It was not uncommon during this time to see a fury of activity in the adjacent rail yards by the Quartermasters at all hours of the day and night unloading trucks, tentage, cots, and other supplies from the trains in preparation for the U.S. Troops.[81]

Completion of Camp Haan Anti-Aircraft Training Center was estimated, by the Construction Division, to be January 1, 1941; however, once January came, its completion date was pushed to February 15, 1941.[82] The Army adhered to the War Production Board's minimum standards of wartime production by making a

CAMP HAAN
THE HISTORY OF RIVERSIDE'S WORLD WAR II ANTI-AIRCRAFT TRAINING CENTER

"no frills" camp, so there would not be landscaping budgeted in the build.

The army declared the camp "minimally in service" on January 10, 1941. On the same day, the Army published General Order No. 1,

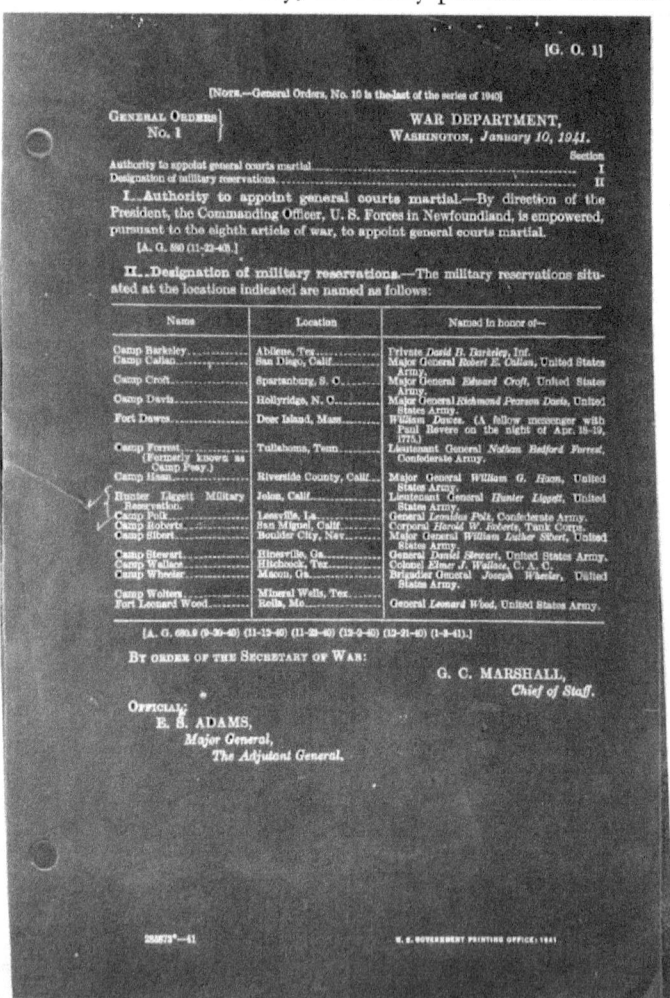

General Order No. 1 officially naming Camp Haan.
Source: National Archives and Record Administration Riverside

CAMP HAAN
THE HISTORY OF RIVERSIDE'S WORLD WAR II ANTI-AIRCRAFT TRAINING CENTER

formally giving the camp a name; the anti-aircraft training center in Riverside, California would officially be called Camp Haan after Major General William George Haan, a senior general in the United States Army during World War I.

Construction was still underway when the first train of soldiers arrived at the depots. Only a few of the regimental areas were complete and even the station hospital was still under construction. An advance contingent, the 215th and the 216th of the Minnesota

Camp Haan to Be Title of Army Center

(By Associated Press)

RIVERSIDE, Jan. 10. — Camp Haan has been officially designated as the name of the new anti-aircraft training center erected adjacent to March field, it was announced today.

The name honors Maj. Gen. William George Haan, one-time assistant chief of staff of the army, who commanded the 32nd division in the Meuse-Argonne offensive in France in the World war. He died in 1924.

Troops are due to arrive at the camp beginning Jan. 15.

Source: San Bernardino County Sun Saturday, January 11, 1941.

National Guard arrived the second week on 17 January 1941, it involved 6 officers and 100 men led by Captain Edward Johnson[83]; followed by the main contingent of 4,000 men arriving January 17-20, 1941.[84] The 78th, a regular Army unit, moved over from March Field leaving their relatively comfortable accommodations in an aircraft hangar.

Recalling when he first arrived at Camp Haan, Bowen Smith said, "We had three buildings: a latrine, a mess hall, and an orderly room."

The 217th was held back in Minnesota because their regimental area was not finished being constructed; they arrived in late February 1941. With Camp construction so far behind it was common for troop movements to be delayed. If the troop movements were not delayed the soldiers would be in less-than-ideal conditions. At Camp Shelby, the troops were not delayed and arrived at unfinished projects and troops had to wade into water to get to their tents; Soldiers at Camp Blanding in Florida were experiencing similar conditions. At Camp Barkley, there were not enough latrines built. These rough, unsanitary conditions also caused epidemics in some of the camps. Camp San Luis Obispo had reported 970 military personnel with the measles and Camp Lewis, at one point, had approximately 11% of their personnel out with measles.

Theodore P. Foster, enlisted on February 27, 1941 at Kalamazoo, Michigan and was sent to Camp Haan for training; commented on the new camp in letters home to his family and friends:

Camp Haan is a new camp, and being in California, the tents are all that is necessary. There are 4 ½ miles of tents along the highway [highway 395], usually about 10 in a row. To the north, you can go about 15 miles without seeing a house or road, and on the other three sides, there are snow-capped mountains in the background, So there are plenty of wide-open spaces around us. The nearest town is Riverside, eight miles away. We live in tents with wood floors and sides...each tent has a little oil burner as its [sic] colder than the devil at night, even with three wool blankets over you[85].

CAMP HAAN
THE HISTORY OF RIVERSIDE'S WORLD WAR II ANTI-AIRCRAFT TRAINING CENTER

Then Captain William Ryan, attached to the 101st Brigade, recounted his first few months at Camp Haan:

> *The weather was rainy and cold much of those first several months – the damp cold went right through to the bones. Those who had boots were lucky because it wasn't long after the first rain that there wasn't a pair of rubber boots to be had in Riverside. The 217th didn't arrive until late February, they arrived several days after a rain and there was still a lot of water standing around. One of their captains, who was something of a stuffed shirt, was all dressed up when he stepped off the train. He stepped into a drainage ditch along side of the tracks and sank into the muddy water – what a mess he was.*[86]

Once the trains of troops started arriving, the presence of troops also hindered construction efforts. Military traffic clogged the construction roads, rail yard was offloading troops and equipment, preventing construction materials from arriving, and the troops pilfered construction materials and equipment to make their tents and day rooms more comfortable. While I have found no such evidence that pilfering existed during Camp Haan's build, it would be fair to say that the conditions provided an excellent opportunity for these actions to occur.

In May 1941. Pinkerton and Jameson, out of Corona, California, was contracted $210,000 to build additional roads, grading, gas/sewer/water lines, electric distribution, 216 tent frames, and 20 buildings at Camp Haan.[87] Although original construction directives stated the camps were to be built in two to three months, the initial construction of the camp was finished in October 1941, nearly eight months[88] later than expected. By that time, incremental improvements were already being made to the camp. On June 30, 1941 the camp was listed as having a housing capacity for 533 officers, 4,806 non-commissioned officers, and 10,954 enlisted men. The hospital had a capacity of 488 beds.[89]

Robert F. Gallagher, a young Army soldier, arrived at Camp Haan and commented that:

CAMP HAAN
THE HISTORY OF RIVERSIDE'S WORLD WAR II ANTI-AIRCRAFT TRAINING CENTER

"All the buildings were made of wood and had a temporary look about them. There wasn't a tree, bush, blade of grass, or anything else of green throughout its sprawling acres."[90]

Gallagher noted that the camp was particularly clean on his arrival; unknown to him at the time, it was the many GIs that were detailed that kept it clean.

Building and trade council advertisement.
Source: San Bernardino County Sun, Sunday, March 28, 1943.

Methods of Building the Camp

Because of the necessity for speed in construction and keeping the different contractors and work crews out of each other's way, an assembly line approach was utilized, and crews were divided into specialized teams called transit crews (e.g. – grading and paving, carpentry, framing, electrical, plumbing). Crews would transit to each building and accomplish their part of the construction process.

The first step was for the foundation transit crew to mark foundations in each area on "batter boards." Batter boards are temporary frames set beyond the corners of a planned foundation

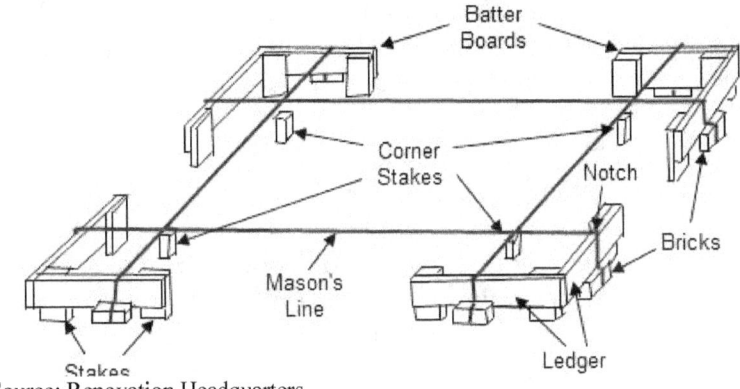

Source: Renovation Headquarters

at precise elevations. These batter boards are then used to hold layout lines to indicate the limits of the foundation.

The foundation transit crew set the pier settings. The footing setting varied depending on the soil conditions and the indicated load, but the first floor's height was 2'6" above ground[91]. While this was occurring, the plumbing transit crew would come in and lay preliminary plumbing. Meanwhile, the lumber was being delivered to the site in preparation. Once the lumber was delivered to the site, a camp sawmill was established. This was another time-saving technique used heavily during WWII cantonment construction. The construction plans called for repeated uses of standardized lengths. This enabled carpenters to turn out large quantities of lumber quickly. Rafters, sheathing, studs, headers, joints, collar beams, platform braces, and stringers could be pre-cut before being turned over to the other construction crews. One report from the Fort Meade construction stated, "a four-saw hook-up produced 150 rafters an hour and could produce as many as 300.[92]"

Once the structure was ready for framing, the construction crew subdivided it into smaller work units; one group laid the first floor, and the other unit assembled the wall frames on the ground and raised them. This was also the point where the plumbing crew would return and finish the above-ground installation. In typical construction, the siding was placed after the walls were erected, though frequently in cantonment construction, the siding was placed on the wall before being raised on the structure, and the window opening would be cut with a circular saw. Aqua medias or continuous eaves were added as either part of the second-story wall panels or were false work added afterward.

After the first floor was framed, an entirely separate crew would work the same framing process for the second floor. A separate roofing crew put together the truss segments, installed them, and covered with bituminous (asphalt) roll roofing materials. Next, a crew would come in to finish the windows and doors. Once all the framing was complete, and the building was dried in, the electrical, plumbing, and heating teams would come in and finish the installation.

Construction superintendents carefully choreographed all these separate teams and several coordinated efforts that the contractors hired.

WWII Cantonment Construction Features

Flooring

In early cantonment construction, single layer dried lumber was used to create the flooring for all series 700 buildings and tents. It was quickly realized that the drying effects of the wood due to heat caused the floors to warp and buckle. To rectify the issue, in 1941, construction crews were directed to start installing a second floor (double floor) with felt paper laid in between the layers effectively creating a subfloor and a finished floor. Floor planking consisted of 2" x 12" for 700 series. The 800 series called for 3" x 14" planking; however, due to non-availability of lumber in that size, 2" x 12" was more commonly used for 800 series and T.O. structures.

Aqua Medias
Aqua media or continuous eaves were a key feature in 700 series buildings. "The 1940s barracks have adopted a tropical item known as "aqua medias" which, in simplest terms, is a skirt over the first-floor windows which permits them to be left open during rainstorms without getting the cots wet.[93]" Officially, aqua medias had a tow-fold purpose; (1) allow for ventilation during a rainstorm without getting cots wet, and (2) reduce the weathering and rotting on the buildings and windows.

By 1941, aqua medias were falling out of favor because they were prone to leaks and water seepage. They were eventually removed from the series 800 plans, and the T.O plans.

Termite Shields
Termite shields were typically added on the structure when the foundation met the structure. The idea behind it was to prevent termites from infesting the wooden structures. But in the arid climate of southern California, Lippincott and Bowen, using their experience as builders and architects in the region, decided that they were unnecessary and recommended that the termite shields be eliminated from the plans because the shields were expensive and delayed construction. After seeking the advice of a termite specialist in the area, the C.Q.M authorized the elimination of the termite shields except for the buildings in the hospital group.[94]

Fire Egress
Fire safety was an afterthought in the early 600 and 700 series design plans. It consisted of a small balcony (approximately 40 inches by 36 inches) and a ladder nailed to the wall. Second-story egress only featured one egress option opposite from the end of the heating boilers and chimney.

In subsequent 800 series and T.O design plans, fire egress changed over to staircases. This change allowed the occupants in the barracks to evacuate faster and safer in the event of a fire.

Chimneys

Series 700 chimneys were all external to the buildings. This enabled the building to be erected before any heating installation; this sped up the construction process. The chimneys were placed four feet from the structure, and contained a red brick base, a metal stack, and guide wires from the chimney to the roof.

Example of a 700 series chimney on this structure

World War II 700 series barracks building.
Source: National Infantry Museum

World War II 700 series barracks building.
Source: National Infantry Museum

Series 800 design plans incorporated the chimney into the building structure rather than as separate structures.

Heating and Ventilation

Central to the World War II barracks was the accommodation of central heating that was added to the design for the 700 series buildings.

"The type of heating unit installed was adjustable to the available local fuel. The hot air heaters employed circulatory fans to distribute the heat overhead through metal ducts and dampers.[95]"

The heating systems could run on anthracite or bituminous coal, oil, or gas. If the system ran off coal, coal boxes were installed outside the building at the rear of the building behind the heater room

Despite an upgrade from the 600 series and WWI, the 700 series heating systems were notoriously ineffective. The buildings were either being overheated due to ineffective thermostats or ineffective due to the building being drafty.

The T.O series barracks had stove heaters rather than a central heating system. Barracks in warmer zones typically had two stove heaters, while colder zone barracks had up to six and the building was better insulated. This was in keeping with the temporary nature of the T.O. plans that made the structures with less permanent fixtures.

Painting

To the army, painting buildings was not necessary. The original cantonment plans called for the wood siding to remain unpainted despite the directed lobbying efforts of Painting and Contractors of America (PDCA):

"It is the painting that makes it habitable, gives it appearance and beauty, makes it sanitary for occupation, and prevents insects from attacking it.[96]"

President Roosevelt's directive resulted in the most significant order of paint in the industry's history, 945,062 gallons, and cost $11-$12 million. The War Department directed that all mobilization buildings be painted a standard ivory color with gray doors. This directive was directed only at the exteriors of the building, the interiors were largely left unpainted. The only interior paint authorized was within the hospital and mess halls, although pictures of interior spaces in many cantonments included painted walls and even unit murals.

Siding

Most of the siding on mobilization buildings in WWII was of wood clapboard drop siding, 2 feet by 10 feet, arranged horizontally. They also experimented with 26-gauge Steel siding. To get the buildings to match the rest of the camp, the steel was cut the same size as the wood drop siding, and the steel siding was zinc coated with a base coat and then painted over with the approved colors. As the war dragged on and additional buildings were erected in the camps, alternative building methods specific to the area were also used. For example, at Camp Haan, the use of stucco and adobe-type structures were also experimented with during expansion efforts

CAMP HAAN
THE HISTORY OF RIVERSIDE'S WORLD WAR II ANTI-AIRCRAFT TRAINING CENTER

In the end, the Army built 46 camps and cantonments that functioned like civilian municipalities with their roads, water, sewage, bakeries, storage, maintenance, electric systems, and hospitals. There were nearly 46,000 furnaces, and the camp sewage plants combined daily capacity reached 86.7 million gallons. This totaled 700 miles of gas lines, 804 miles of railway, 1,500 miles of sewer, 1,557 miles of road, 2,000 miles of water pipes, and 3,500 miles of electrical lines.

CHAPTER 5
INFRASTRUCTURE

Building infrastructure

Because camp Haan was designated as a cantonment, all the camps' buildings and subsequent expansions of the antiaircraft training center were labeled as temporary structures. Each building number started with the letter T followed by the building number. For example, the headquarters building was labeled T–1. Through research and combing through disposition records, I found many of the actual building numbers that were used while the camp was in active status, starting with T–1 through T–15021. This is not to say that there were 15,000 buildings in camp Haan, but that is as high as the numbering system has gone up through research. In fact, even though buildings were largely sequential in the different areas, there is evidence that because of wartime shortages and budgetary constraints, some of the buildings were never authorized to be built or never were built due to other constraints.

Also, through records of disposition, it appears that some of the buildings were numbered initially using one set of nomenclature and was changed at some point between 1941 and 1946 to suit other purposes or, the building numbers remain the same but the purpose of the building changed over the six years that camp on in operation.

You will see further in the reading that if I could identify the building number on the building that I am talking about, I included it in the text along with the location of that building either through the narrative or through the included maps in this book.

Infrastructure was key to making an Army cantonment. The Army had to be able to supply services for all the camp inhabitants to live and function daily. What made it particularly challenging in Camp Haan's case was that the original camp was built on a specific set of requirements. At the same time, the Army kept increasing the number of Army personnel. Once the camp's expansion was approved, the Army would have to expand the camp and the infrastructure.

Water Supply, Distribution and Sewage

Initial Build

The camp initially received water from March Field and underground reservoirs.[97] Because the surrounding communities supplied March Field with water, the local community protested. They argued that the water needed to supply both military installations would seriously deplete the available supply.[98] The War Department worked with the local municipalities and contracted in October 1941 with the Metropolitan Water District to get water from the local communities until the water supply pipeline from Camp Haan to Lake Matthews could be built. Lake Matthews dam area was completed in 1939 and saw its first water in 1940; this resource was also a major consideration in the decision to place Camp Haan where it was located. This seemed to stem the protests a bit.

In November 1941, Camp Haan notified Riverside Mayor Walter C. Davidson that construction of the supply line from Lake Matthews would take longer than expected due to supply shortages, specifically pipe valves. The government sent the letter to the mayor, exercising a clause in their contract stating that in case of unexpected contingencies, the City of Riverside would continue to supply water through the Metropolitan Water District.[99] Per the contract, Camp Haan, once completed, would receive water from the Lake Matthews. Lake Matthews is located to the Southwest of Camp Haan and received water through a 20-inch supply line to a treatment plan located on the south end of the camp. This line contained 44,165 feet of steel pipe and 9,100 feet of concrete pipe (approximately 10 miles of pipe in total) that made up the water main. The U.S. government agreed to pay a rate of eight cents per 1,000 gallons of water measured through the meter. The main camp had a 1,000,000-gallon concrete reservoir. I don't know for sure, but I would think some of this pipe still exists in the ground between Camp Haan and Lake Matthews.

A secondary 16" supply line from the City of Riverside was installed and used from 1941-1947. This originally was the primary line supplying the camp until the Lake Matthews supply line could be completed. The Iowa pumping station in the north end of the camp was owned and maintained by Riverside.

Expansion

Once the "topside" expansion occurred, a 100,000 gallons elevated (90') wooden tank was added for pressure and an additional 2,500,000-gallon steel reservoir was added for the main camp supply. Two additional pumping stations were installed when the "topside" expansion was built.

Topside Pumping Station #1
The Topside pumping station was in building T-6010 contained a total of five pumps:
- Pump 1 - Worthington centrifugal, 1450 gallon per minute pump powered by 40 horsepower General Electric motor
- Pump 2 - Worthington centrifugal, 1150 gallon per minute pump powered by 25 horsepower General Electric motor
- Pump 3- Worthington centrifugal, 1150 gallon per minute pump powered by 25 horsepower General Electric motor
- Pump 4 -Worthington centrifugal, 750 gallon per minute pump, gasoline powered for back-up/standby
- Pump 5 -Worthington centrifugal, 750 gallon per minute pump, gasoline powered for back-up/standby

This pumping station would pump water from the 1,000,000-gallon reservoir to the elevated 100,000-gallon reservoir.

Topside Pumping Station #2
Pumping station #2 was in building T-6011 and contained a total of two pumps:
- Pump 1 -Worthington centrifugal, 750 gallon per minute pump, 48 horsepower gasoline powered Waukesha motor
- Pump 2 -Worthington centrifugal, 750 gallon per minute pump, 48 horsepower gasoline powered Waukesha motor

This pumping station was installed to provide water to the topside in an emergency. It was designed to connect the 1,000,000-gallon reservoir directly to the topside area's primary water grid, bypassing the elevated wooden reservoir.

There were 450 fire hydrants on the camp and automatic sprinkler systems for all the buildings in the hospital area. The hospital buildings were the camp's only structures with sprinkler systems.

Sewage Plant
The Camps sewage system was constructed with a vitrified clay pipe. The Sewage plant (T-5901) and associated structures were built on land that was sold, permitted, or declared easements by the War Department. The plant was located at the terminus of Avenue "B" in the southeast corner of the camp in area 13. It was located essentially on the same site as the present-day water treatment plant at 22751 Nandina Ave. alongside the I-215, just southeast of the Riverside National Cemetery. Initial approval was received to begin construction on October 28, 1940.

This sewage plant was used for the central part of the camp. It was rated for up to 15,000 people. It consisted of mechanical screens followed by a two-stage sedimentation process and rapid biofilters, separate sludge digestion and chlorination of the influent and effluent. The effluent was routed to a farm south of the camp that the government reached an agreement to use 300 acres and dispose of it through irrigation. This would be the land south of present-day Nandina Avenue. In order to accomplish this, the government must install an additional three miles of high-pressure pipe with accompanying structures.[100]

After the camp's closure, the sewage plant, in its entirety, was transferred to March Field in 1947 and used to assist March Field.

Because the camp was not entirely on level ground, several lift stations were located in the main camp area. One of the sewage lift stations was located in building T-2986, at the corner of Ave B and 35th street.

Another sewage plant was built for the topside area during the topside expansion. This plant (T-9301) was in Area 14 at the far southwest of the camp just off Nandina Ave. Sludge lagoons were located southwest corner of area 14.

Incinerator

The incinerator was also built in Area 13, building T-5811, just west of the sewage plant on Avenue "D." The 10-ton incinerator and metal building were constructed on top of a 12-foot high concrete structure[101] and construction started in late June 1941 and was completed on August 25, 1941.

Camp Haan Incinerator.
Source: Camp Haan Tracer

Typical Cantonment Incinerator
Source: United States War Department. (1941). Citadels of Democracy: Camps and Plants for Men and Munitions. U.S. Government Printing Office, Washington.

Water Treatment Plant

The War Department issued a contract on Friday, November 21, 1941 to the Ocean Shore Iron Works and A. C. Le Prest Company out of San Francisco to construct the water treatment plant and accompanying reservoir at a cost of $198,455.[102]

The water treatment plant (T-6007) was constructed in the southwest corner of the camp in area 14 off Nandina Ave. In the general vicinity were also the 1-million-gallon clearwater tank (T-6008) and the 100,000-gallon elevated water tank (T-6800).

The water treatment plant, in its entirety, including the reservoirs and supply mains were transferred to March Field in 1947.

As of this printing, remnants of the water treatment plant are still located on the site and the 1-million-gallon water tank. This area is now fenced off, and construction work is ongoing to raze the remaining concrete remnants.

Electric

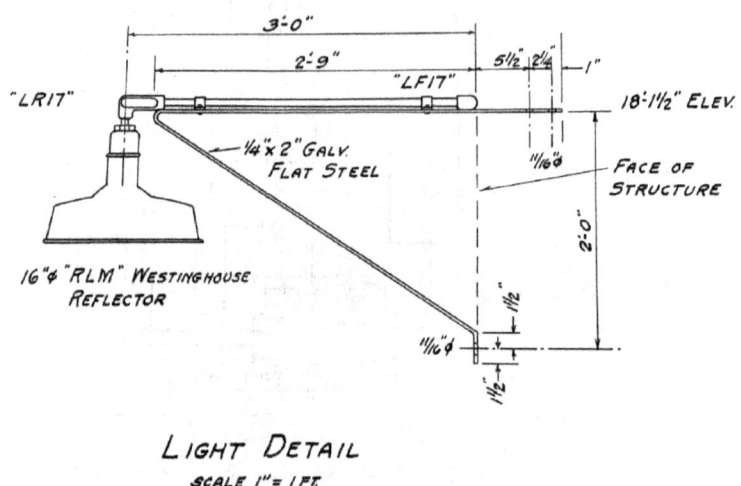

Exterior Light detail from construction plans (June 15, 1941).
Source: National Archives and Records Administration, Riverside

Electricity was supplied by the California Electric Company in Riverside, California at 33,000 volts and transformed down to the appropriate voltages through a switching station within the camp. Electric distribution around camp was mainly aerial; however, a few areas of the camp electric was placed underground, particularly in the prisoner of war camp. There were 789 wood power poles installed to distribute the electricity around camp. The camp made use of exterior lighting in the form of lamps, which was common in the 1940s; 416 lamps were mounted on the poles around camp. Most of the camp used incandescent lighting but fluorescent lighting was also used.

Fire Protection

As was previously stated, the buildings in the hospital area all had automatic sprinklers. Overall, there were five fire stations in the camp, 450 fire hydrants, forty-four fire reporting telephones and fire extinguishers in every building, and most government-owned vehicles in the camp.

By the time the camp closed and was in disposition by the WAA, the camp had four (4) designated firefighting equipment in inventory as of March 1947:

1. One (1) 1942 Chevrolet, 1.5-ton fire truck, class 500, model 900, serial #3764, U.S. Army serial number #501701.
2. One (1) 1943 Dodge, 1.5-ton fire truck, class 500, serial #PA-85, U.S. Army serial number #505266.
3. One (1) Chevrolet forestry fire truck, class 125, U.S. Army serial number #50803.
4. One (1) General Motors water tank truck, 5-ton, 1,000-gal capacity, model CCW 353, serial number #25967, U.S. Army serial #4309461.

Railroad Construction

Camp Haan paralleled the Atchison, Topeka & Santa Fe (ATSF) Railroad. Additional connections were constructed in the form of multiple spur lines to make full use of the railroad for the camp. These spur lines were made to the specifications of ATSF and tied directly into the existing railway. The site was graded, and estimated that the contractor moved 1,650,000 cubic yards of material. In all, 7,501 linear feet were laid with several turnouts. Although the railroad tracks of 1940s Camp Haan have long disappeared, there are still railroad tracks that run alongside the I-215 just as they would have back in the 1940s along the 395.

Building Types

Due to mobilization efforts in late 1940, the initial construction of Camp Haan was, as one veteran of the camp would put it, "basic primitive.[103]" All the troops were housed under canvas pyramidal tents stretched over wood frames and wood floors. The only framed buildings initially were the regimental and headquarters buildings, Officers' mess, PX, Postal station, recreation hall, mess halls, supply rooms, and latrines. There were no sidewalks at first, but they were later replaced with 2 x 6 framed sidewalks with crushed gravel. There were no trees or shrubs.

Tents Hutments/Barracks

The most important structure in World War II housing was the Army barrack that housed enlisted men. Even today, the Army barrack is a prominent structure in the Army's present-day inventory. However, tents were used quite a bit when building cantonments to make the build expedient, especially in earlier construction projects and in more southern cantonments such as southern California, Alabama, and Florida.

<u>Tents</u>
"A" tents had dimensions of 15'-10" x 15'-10" model M1934, 254

Camp Haan A Tents.
Notice the lack of landscaping and make-shift walkways places this photograph taken in 1941.Source: Personal

sq. ft. These tents were first introduced in 1934 and were canvas tent over a 2 x 4 wooden frame. Although designed to be erected and used just with the tent canvas, all the tents at Camp Haan had wood frames. The tents had screened doors measuring 2'4" by 6'6". The floors were all wood plank and could be described as "as good wind could blow them away."[104]The maximum capacity of the tent is eight (8) men (current infantry squad strength for that period) when the tent stove is not used. For reasons of greater comfort and sanitation, use of this tent was limited to six (6) men when the supply of tentage was permitted. Ventilation for the tent was via the center pole with an adjustable hood. The upper part of the tent was screened, allowing the tentage to be rolled up for ventilation or down for rain and the cold.

Each tent had 6 or 8 cots in them. These were standard military-issue canvas cots on wood frames, otherwise, there was no other furniture assigned to the tents so the soldiers would have to get creative and use their duffel bags or chests as furniture. Many tents acquired items organically, such as card tables and radios, even though Army regulations did not permit them.

"D" tents were introduced in 1941 and used to shelter two (2) officers in the field and not in combat. When necessary, this tent could be used as a small storage tent. This tent is 8 feet x 10 inches wide, 9 feet 2 inches long, and 8 feet 6 inches high. Floor is approximately 80 square feet. The tent was a square-ended tent, rectangular. All elements, such as top, side walls and reinforcements, were made of 12.29-ounce duck[105], while the sod cloth is made of 9.85-ounce duck[106]. The ridge height was 8 feet 6 inches, wall height is 3 feet 9 inches, giving a pitch of 4 feet 9 inches. Each end section has an overlapping slit forming a door, while stovepipe openings are provided at either end of the tent. Ventilation is done by rolling up the side walls and opening slits. When not in use, stovepipe openings could be used as ventilation. This wall tent is normally used for one (1) general officer, field officer, captain, or two (2) lieutenants or warrant officers.

'D" Tents

CAMP HAAN
THE HISTORY OF RIVERSIDE'S WORLD WAR II ANTI-AIRCRAFT TRAINING CENTER

Camp Haan was a "southern camp" and therefore was planned for and was built as a tent camp. The initial regimental areas were pyramidal tents with wooden frames. The author has not found evidence that Camp Haan was set up as a tent camp without the wooden wall framing.

Hutments

As the war continued, canvas became a scarce commodity and tents were converted to hutments. Money from the War Department to convert the tents into hutments was unavailable until May 1942.[107] A hutment was created by removing the canvas from the pyramidal tents and replacing it with solid wood roofing and sheathed and covered with mineral-surfaced roofing materials. The hutments generally had the same shape and dimensions as the "A" tents at 16'x16'. Hutments resembled large sheds that you commonly see in many homes across America. Hutments had the same clapboard look like the full barracks. The hutments had screen doors and screened windows that could be covered with

Typical Cantonment Hutment
Notice lack of roads and series 700 chapel in background.
Source: personal

plywood in case of rain or cold. Hutments were used in the later expansion of Camp Haan and some photographic evidence in this book show that at least some of the "A" tents were replaced by hutments around 1943.

Barracks

The decision to use the barracks versus tents was predicated on the climate and the winter of the camp's location. Generally, tents were used in the south, and wood barracks were used in the north. The Army used 700 series wood-framed barracks in states where the winter temperature got below 20 degrees in the winter. In southern states, tents were preferred, though the tents had wood floors and wood-frame construction.[108] This was not true in all cases though, sometimes, it was faster and cheaper to construct barracks versus procuring the tentage materials.

> *"One strange thing is that is a good deal cheaper to put people in temporary wooden buildings than to them in tent. You can't get the amount of tentage you need in a mobilization."*
>
> Supervising Architect
> Construction Division.

The barracks looked like those of the World War I 600 series with very few changes in structural elements with six over six double hung windows, wood drop siding, and two stories in height.

CAMP HAAN
THE HISTORY OF RIVERSIDE'S WORLD WAR II ANTI-AIRCRAFT TRAINING CENTER

The original 63-man barrack, as designed by Hartman's team, was wood frame, 29 feet 6 inches by 80 feet long, and two stories tall. The building was wood frame construction, 3 feet on center. The wooden sills rested on a concrete footing or, in later builds, concrete pads. Windows were either double-hung or casement, although double-hung were more commonly used. The six over six windows were typical, but there were provisions for eight over

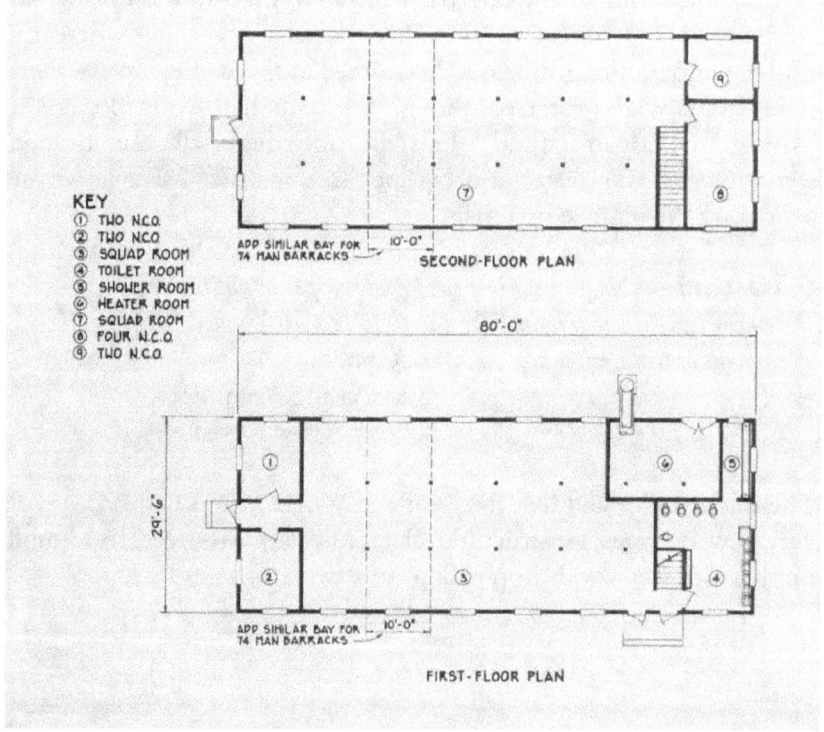

Series 700 63-man World War II Barracks floor plan.
Source: Wasch, D.; Bush, P.; Landreth, K; Glass, J. (nd) World War II and the U.S. Army Mobilization Program: A History of 700 and 800 Series Cantonment Construction. Legacy Resource Management Program, Department of Defense.

eight. Aqua medias - capped all the windows on the first and second floors. One end of the barracks was used for the heating plant and place over a concrete slab.

The barracks were heated by hot air heater with circulatory fans. The heating system was adaptable to local fuel supplies. This was a nice feature in the 700 series buildings because it allowed the camps to be flexible in finding fuel for the heaters. Chimneys were not attached to the barracks structure, instead, they were set four feet from the exterior wall and composed of brick at the bottom and steel at the top flue.

The roof was wood truss constructed, sheathed, and covered with mineral-surfaced roofing materials. The interior of the barracks was left unfinished and the draftiness of the building was well known amongst the soldiers.

There were different stages of building in the five years of Camp Haan, there was no direct evidence that actual 700 or 800 series barracks style buildings were constructed on Camp Haan in the original regimental areas; however, they were used in later expansions of the camp for the "topside" area.

Mess Halls

Mess Halls were where soldiers ate their meals and got hot coffee. Because of Camp Haan's size and the need to feed up to 30,000 hungry soldiers, there were a lot of mess halls, I have been able to verify at least 135 mess halls of varying size.

Camp
Most of the mess halls in the regimental area, used for the enlisted soldiers were 25' x 94'. Some of the mess halls were designed to have larger throughput, presumably to accommodate larger number of army soldiers during training; some of these mess halls measured 25' x 114', 20' x 132', 40' x 148' and 20' x 124'. Many of the

Typical WWII mess hall
Source: Fine, L;
Remington, Jesse (1989) the Corps of Engineers: Construction in the United States. Center of Military History: Washington DC.

building in cantonments served several functions, mess halls had some dual purposes; at times, the mess halls were used to hold training or meetings, and in some instances, used as make-shift chapels. In the early months of the camp, the troops were fed on typical Army rations provided from the Quartermasters. Each battery that operated a mess hall (there were mess halls in each of the regimental area) were given a small stipend for additional foodstuffs. In Southern California, in the heart of the Orange belt, it wasn't surprising that fresh squeezed orange jucie was a troop favorite. Vendors could be seen around camp daily distributing gallons upon gallons of orange juice around to the camp's mess halls. The local growers also set up stands right outside of the camps for a little extra business; 15 cents would get you an entire bushel[109] of oranges back in 1941.

One of the very first mess halls built with the purpose of funneling Army troops through for the AATC was the mess hall in Area 1 (T-517). This mess hall had a massive main building that measured 64' x 288' and had wings protruding from the main building that had dimensions of, 32' x 48', 48' x 80', and 20' x 42'.

Officers had their own mess halls and many of them had the same dimension of 25' x 94'; however, some of the areas had officer mess halls and recreation combined. Therefore, the building was L-shaped with dimensions were 25' x 78' and 25' x 90'.

Hospital Area
Because the hospital was a station hospital it had three separate mess halls for patients admitted to the hospital who were ambulatory. The patient mess halls (T-5674, T-5684, and T-5692) had dimensions of 37' x 150', 37' x 153', and 37' x 166' respectively. Both the officers and nurses had separate mess buildings in the hospital area. The nurse's mess (T-5608) was located at the front of the hospital area off Avenue "K". The building was T-shaped and measured 25' x 108' and 29' 44'. The designated officer mess was co-located in the officer recreation building (T-5622) and had dimensions of 30' 140'.

CAMP HAAN
THE HISTORY OF RIVERSIDE'S WORLD WAR II ANTI-AIRCRAFT TRAINING CENTER

The enlisted personnel stationed at the hospital were housed on the backside of the hospital area between Avenue "M" and Avenue "N". They had two mess halls (T-5762 and T-5726) had dimensions of 40' x 212' and 25' x 120' respectively.

WAC

The Women's Auxiliary Corps mess hall which was built sometime in 1943 part of the expansion was in area 12, adjacent to the main hospital area, just south of it on Avenue "H". The mess hall (T-5790) was an L-shaped building with dimensions of 40' x 160' and 12' x 24'.

African American Troops

Because during this time in the country's history the Army was still segregated, the African American or "colored" troops had a separate mess hall (T-3528) that was also part of their recreational facilities.

Recreation Halls/Day rooms

Each of the regimental recreation halls or day rooms provided reading materials, checker boards, ping pong tables, piano, a magazine rack, and bookshelves. It is doubtful that the first units occupying the camp had these amenities. Initially, the recreation

Typical WWII Dayroom
Source: Fine, L; Remington, Jesse (1989) the Corps of Engineers: Construction in the United States. Center of Military History: Washington DC.

halls were used as religious services before the chapels were built. Many of the day rooms in the regimental areas measured 25'x46'.

With the expansion of the topside area, the day rooms gave way to recreation halls that measured 20'x72' and 20'x100'. There is also evidence that I found that some of the recreational halls were re-designated for other purposes. For example, the recreational hall (T-7312) was converted to a post office building in 1943[110] and recreational hall (T-7615) was converted to a service club[111]

Outside of the recreation halls were the regimented sports areas with facilities for kittenball(softball), baseball, basketball, tennis, and volleyball which amounted to little more than a dirt field in the initial camp buildout. Later fences, bases, and, perhaps some grass were installed.

Topside recreation hall (T-7715) opened May 1, 1943. There was a large cafeteria in conjunction with the hall. The hall space was approximately 88'x112' feet in maple and was big enough to be used as a dance floor as well as a basketball court. This recreation hall could also be used as a theater, as it had a stage, dressing rooms, and was wired for sound. Mrs. Ruth Talbot and Mrs. Nina McCoy were in charge in the hall under the guidance of Capt. Benjamin Bosley, Special Service Officer.[112]

<u>Administrative and Supply Buildings</u>
All the regimental administrative buildings were built to the same specifications as the recreation halls and the dayrooms. The supply

Typical WWII administrative and supply building
Source: Fine, L; Remington, Jesse (1989) the Corps of Engineers: Construction in the United States. Center of Military History: Washington DC.

rooms were different in that they did not have wooden floors but three-and-a-half-inch concrete foundation on grade that was suggested by Lippincott and Bowen. This change was approved by the Construction Quartermaster. This was mainly due to the weight of supplies.

Latrines

Latrines during World War II served as both a restroom and a shower facility. Camp Haan had at least 221 latrines of varying size, based on the type of latrine was built. Many of the latrines were building that measured 25' x 48', but some measures 25' x 36', and 25' x 56'. The latrines for the staff in the Hospital Area had dimensions of 20' x 64'.

As you can imagine the latrines were built for functionality and not aesthetics. Inside the latrines the building was split in two; one side contained the shower room was communal and had a concrete floor with spigots protruding out from the walls on three sides, the other side had a line of sinks on one wall and a line of toilets on the other with no partitions for privacy.

Anti-aircraft Training Center (AATC) Headquarters

The AATC headquarters building (T-1) was in area 10, which today would be located just south of present day Van Buren Boulevard on land occupied by the Riverside National Cemetery. The building was u-shaped and had dimensions of 50'-3" x 108'-2". This building and associated buildings in the post headquarters area were among the first to be built when construction started.

The post headquarters provided all the command-and-control functions for the anti-aircraft training center.

Post Headquarters

Source: Camp Haan Map Project Map. Southern California Real Property Disposal Case Files, 1946-1962. RG 269 Records of the General Services Administration. Box 59; National Archives and Records Administration, Riverside, CA.

Post or camp headquarters buildings (T-6 and T-7) were in area 10, which today would be located just south of Van Buren Boulevard on land occupied by the Riverside National Cemetery. The buildings were essentially three 20' x 100' building in the shape of a "U".

The post headquarters provided all the command-and-control functions for the entire camp. Typical personnel that occupied these building included: Commanding Officer, XO, Adjutant, Control officer, food and mess supervisor, Mimeograph Section, Headquarters Duty Officer, Orders section, Dir. Personnel Division, Director of Supply Division, Mail and Records Section, Morale Services Branch, Orientation Section, Commercial Accounts, Contracting Section, Safety Officer, and the Storage Branch and Supply Group.

Brigade Headquarters

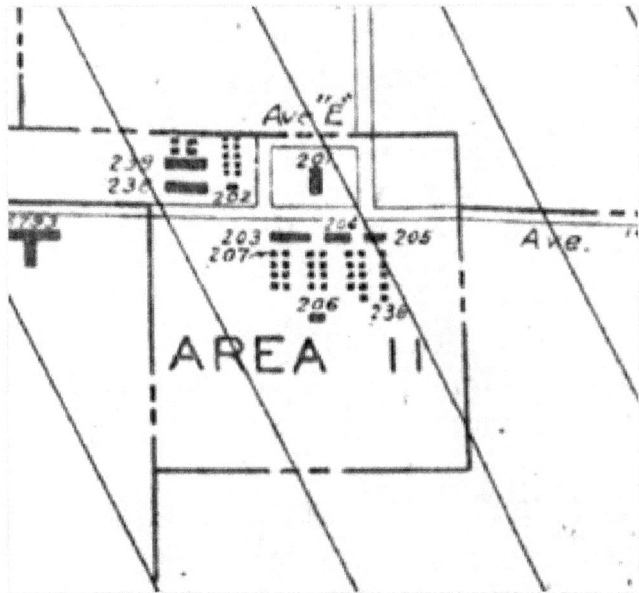

Source: Camp Haan Map Project Map. Southern California
Real Property Disposal Case Files, 1946-1962. RG 269
Records of the General Services Administration. Box 59;
National Archives and Records Administration, Riverside, CA.

Brigade Headquarters (T-201 and T-301) and located in areas 11 and 9, respectively. Building T-201 was the brigade headquarters for the 65th and 78th regiments, regular Army. Building T-301 was the brigade headquarters for the 215th, 216th, and 217th regiments, Minnesota National Guard.

The functions of the brigade headquarters were to provide command, control, and administrative function for two to five regiments.

Regimental Headquarters Buildings
The regimental headquarters buildings were in the regimental areas and arranged at the so-called head of the regimental area of camp. These buildings were u-shaped and were 50'-3" x 108'-2" and surrounded by roadways.

Each regiment scheduled for Camp Haan, at least in the plans, called for twelve batteries[113]:

1. Searchlight Battery
2. Gun Battery
3. Gun Battery
4. Gun Battery
5. Machine Gun Battery
6. 37 mm Battery
7. 37 mm Battery
8. 37 mm Battery
9. Medical
10. 1st Battalion Headquarters and Combat Training
11. 2nd Battalion Headquarters and Combat Training
12. Regimental Headquarters Battery

The regimental headquarters buildings provided all the command, control, and supervision for the entire regiment.

Headquarters Battery
Although not occupying a specific "headquarters" building on camps. Headquarters Battery occupied space in the regimental areas, typically in a non-descript building labeled "Administration and Supply." Each Battery had their own Headquarters Battery. For example, based on the camp layout for the Regimental area in Area 1, there were eleven Headquarters Battery (T-522, T-525, T-528, T-531, T-534, T-537, T-542, T-545, T-548, T-551, and T-554)

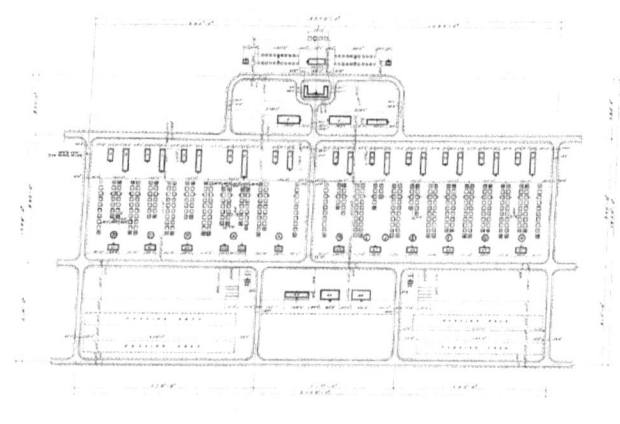

Typical regimental area of Camp Haan

and occupied building that were 25' x 51'.

The Headquarters Battery was responsible for the technical supervision of the Battery's maintenance operations, unit administration, food service activities, and support operations. Typically, the Battery Commander, First Sergeant, and a few enlisted staff worked in the building.[114]

Post Exchange
Part of the services that the Army provided for troop morale were the post/base exchanges. Prior to World War II, the Post Exchange was operated independently by the different camps and posts. It was not until 1941 when it was recommended that there should be an established Army Exchange Service. This led to the standardization of pricing and the ability to operate a central buying program.[115]

There was no camp post exchange (PX) in the early days of the camp. Instead, each regimental area was outfitted with a mini PX. The regimental PXs were said not to have all that much in them other than soft drinks, snacks, ice cream, and sometimes basic toiletries. In most cases, troops bought items and treats when they

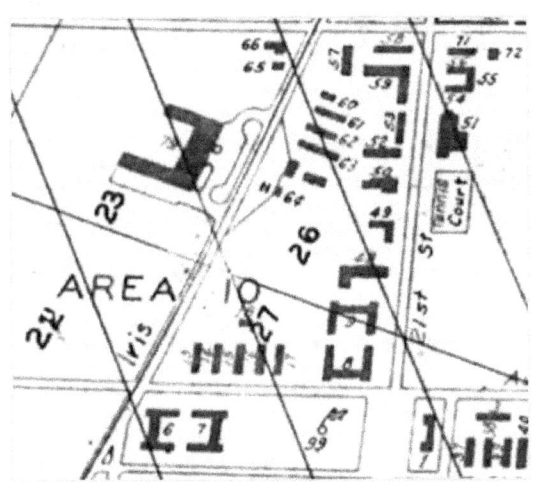

Source: Camp Haan Map Project Map. Southern California Real Property Disposal Case Files, 1946-1962. RG 269 Records of the General Services Administration. Box 59; National Archives and Records Administration, Riverside, CA.

went out to Riverside, Redlands, and San Bernardino.

The main camp Post Exchange (T-79) was in area 10 of the camp in what is called the Headquarters Support Area. The building was a U-shaped building with dimensions 20' x 80' and two 48' x 160'. The exchange also had a 20' x 48' warehouse and building labeled as an out-building with dimensions of 40' x 60' presumably to provide office space for the Exchange Officer, Asst. Exchange Officer, General Mgr., Purchasing manager, and Warehouse manager. This post exchange had a cafeteria and soda fountain, open from 7 am to 9 pm daily[116] and is said to have served delicious hamburgers (with meat)[117], an officers clothing shop and adjacent tailor shop, enlisted men's clothing department, and a barber shop where you could get a haircut for $.40[118]. In 1943, the PX had 15 full-time civilian employees[119]. The PX was even known to hire soldiers on occasion for Sunday and evening work stocking shelves[120].

Each regimental area also had a mini-post exchange. The post exchanges in these areas had dimensions of 37' x 99'. They included shopping space and storage space. As smaller versions of the main Post Exchange, the regimental post exchanges carried writing supplies, postcards, magazines, cigarettes, carbonated beverages/soda, and ice cream.

Commissary

The Commissary is a grocery store on camp or post. Commissaries have evolved over the years; however, a commissary on camp was a necessity due to the isolated location of Camp Haan to the amenities in Riverside at the time.

Camp Haan's Commissary (T-68) was in area 10 of the camp in what is called the Headquarters Support Area. The building was 20' x 140" and close to the Post Exchange

Camp Haan Commissary. Source: Picture Parade, circa 1943

Laundry

The laundry facility (T-4064) was in area 6 and sandwiched between the railroad and area 5 on Avenue "A". The building was 108'x 258' and generally rectangular. Adjacent to laundry building, 52 feet from the building, was a boiler house that supplied steam to the laundry building.

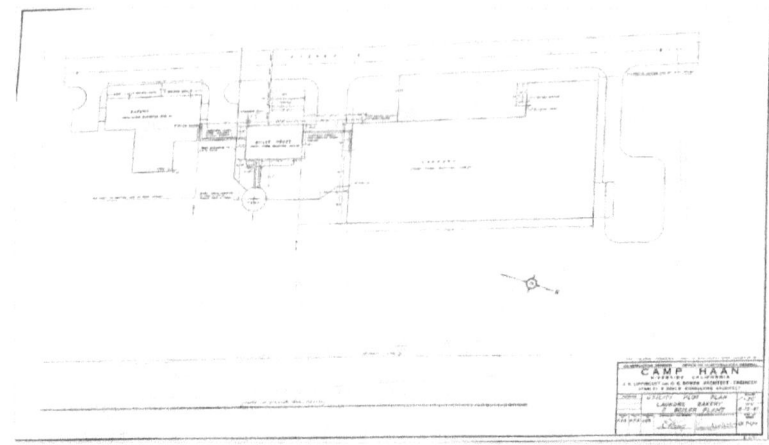

Camp Haan laundry facility building diagram. Source: Block Plans. Project Map. Southern California Real Property Disposal Case Files, 1946-1962. RG 269 Records of the General Services Administration. Box 59; National Archives and Records Administration, Riverside, CA.

The boiler house (T-4065) was a rectangular building with dimensions of 60' x 37' made of wood frame and corrugated steel. The boiler supplied steam to both the laundry and the bakery. The

Laundry Facilities.
Source: United States War Department. (1941). Citadels of Democracy: Camps and Plants for Men and Munitions. U.S. Government Printing Office, Washington.

CAMP HAAN
THE HISTORY OF RIVERSIDE'S WORLD WAR II ANTI-AIRCRAFT TRAINING CENTER

boiler house had a 1,340-gallon water storage tank that was 32'-3" from the building and buried 12,000 gallon oil and gas tanks 20' from the building.

The laundry had 8 stationary sleeve ironers purchased from the American Laundry Machine Company, 8 shoulder shaper tables purchased from the American Laundry Machine Company, 5 pedestal ironing tables, 4 sewing machines purchased from Singer Manufacturing Company, and 12 marking machines purchased from National Marking Machine Company[121].

Bakery

The bakery (T-4068) was an L-shaped building on the East side of camp in area 6 of the camp. The bakery was immediately adjacent to the railroad tracks and next to the boiler house. The building contained a three-oven bakery that nominally produced 17,000 loaves of bread per day. By 1943, the bakery was working 2-shifts

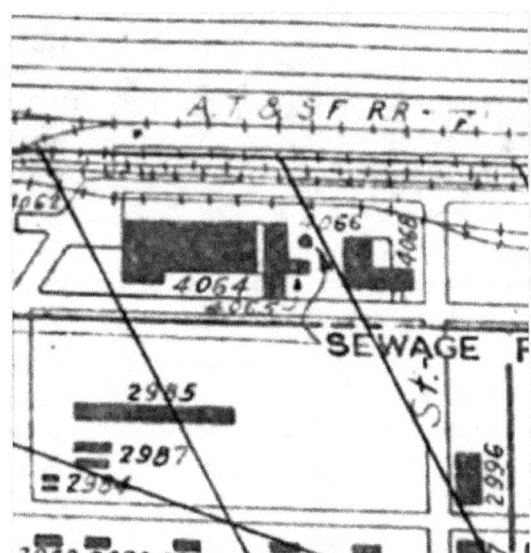

Source: Camp Haan Map Project Map. Southern California Real Property Disposal Case Files, 1946-1962. RG 269 Records of the General Services Administration. Box 59; National Archives and Records Administration, Riverside, CA.

and produced 25,000 loaves per day.

Baker at Camp Haan making rolls.
Source: Picture Parade.

Chapels

Chapels represented a staple in the camps and posts and provided an important service. On December 7, 1941, there were 1,487 chaplains on duty in either the regular Army, National Guard, or the Reserves. At their peak, this number surged to around 8,000. Chaplain ratios were used to aid in staffing camps and posts at a ratio of one chaplain per one thousand troops. So, if assuming the ratios held, then Camp Haan could have had upwards of 80 chaplains at the camp during the height of the training center's operational days.

CAMP HAAN
THE HISTORY OF RIVERSIDE'S WORLD WAR II ANTI-AIRCRAFT TRAINING CENTER

Camp Haan south chapel shown on a Fotone Postcard (The Ullman Company) circa 1942. Source: personal

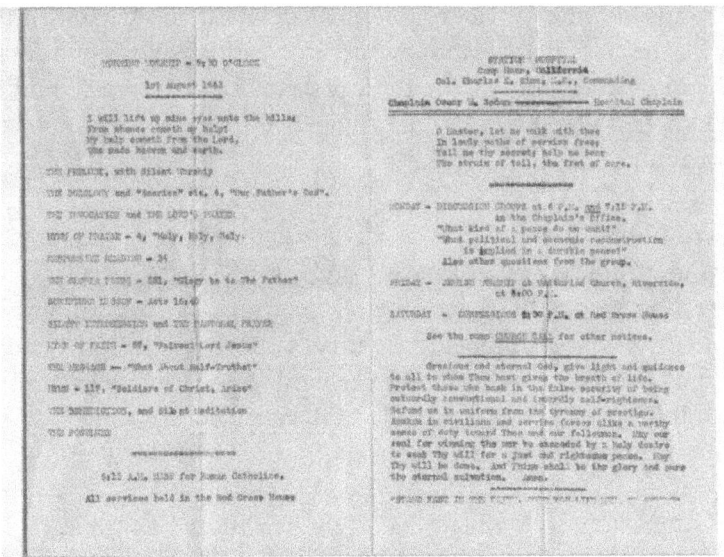

Worship phamplet from Camp Haan station hospital service, August 1, 1943. Source: personal

The chapels (T-518, T-1118, and T-2918) on Camp Haan had dimensions of 37' x 81' and each chapel was equipped with a $1000 (in 1941 dollars) electric organ. The main floor of the chapel was large enough to hold 300 soldiers using long bench style seating with kneelers. It included an altar, pulpit, and lectern that was movable so other denominations or events could take place in the chapel as needed. The chapels also included chaplain's rooms, consultation rooms, and a cloak or robe room. Upstairs was a gallery that held seating for 57 soldiers.[122]

Numerous media sources stated that there was a total of five chapels on Camp Haan; however, disposition records and subsequent Real Property Surplus Inspection reports reveal that there were only three chapels; North Chapel that had the Chaplain's office, a Central Chapel, and a South Chapel.

What probably had happened was the three chapels (North, Central, and South) along with services at the station hospital provided the bulk of the spiritual services; however, when the personnel population surged, other building, such as recreation rooms and theaters, were used to hold additional services. It is also very plausible that services were held down at the battery level as well in the regimental and battery recreation rooms. Southern California, being known for the excellent weather, you could also conclude that some services may have been held outside in areas or opportunity.

Guest House
The guest house was an Army-style hotel, located nearby and operated in conjunction with the service club. The guest house was designed to house family and friends of those soldiers in the camp hospital but also used for visitors and dignitaries who visit the camp. Rates in 1941 were $1/day for single rooms and $1.25/day for a room occupied by two persons.

The Guest House (T-52 and T-53) in area 10 of Camp Haan. They were wood framed structures 130' x 30'. The building looks almost exactly like the barracks of the cantonment. They were located on 21st street, across the street from the service club and tennis courts and adjacent to the civilian personnel office and the finance building. Eventually the buildings were covered in Stucco as part of camp beautification. The guest house opened in Jul 1941.

Camp Haan Guest House
Source: Picture Parade

Theaters

Theaters were used for movies but also were used for special programs and broadcasts. Theaters were also used extensively for mass training events, concerts, and lectures.

A theater was not included in the initial camp build, so by the time the 101st Brigade arrived it was realized that a large convening space was needed. A large circus tent with 8-foot plywood walls was built off C street. It was not a permanent structure, instead it was a large circus tent and olive drab green with two or three center poles that drape down over a walled structure made of plywood. The wood on the inside was painted black. This afforded the size that was needed and was lacked in the regimental recreation halls. Religious activities were also held in this tent until the chapels were built.

CAMP HAAN
THE HISTORY OF RIVERSIDE'S WORLD WAR II ANTI-AIRCRAFT TRAINING CENTER

Theater 1 was in an area 10 of the camp, in the area known as the service area. Because this was the first theater in the camp as it was being built. Theater one also held the theater officer's office.

Theater 2 was in area six of the camp and was just east of the hospital area. This was also a temporary structure; therefore, it was the same circus tentage as theater one. This theater would later be converted to a training auditorium sometime in 1942.

Theaters 3 and 4 both opened on May 1, 1943 in the newly expanded topside area. Theater three could hold approximately a thousand men and was available to both military and civilians in the original camp area as well as the topside area.

Theater 3 could hold 1,000 men and was available to both military and civilians of the original camp area and the topside area.

Theater 4 had a large stage with lighting arrangements and dressing rooms. It was designed to accommodate the U.S.O tour shows. It could hold 1,000 men and was available to both military and civilians of the original camp area and the topside area.[123]

In 1943, SSgt Delmer R. Jones and Sgt Dave Overbeck in charge of the theaters under the guidance of Capt. Leonard Stallcup, Theater Officer.[124]

Service Club

The service clubs were always a popular recreational location for both enlisted and commissioned officers. Service clubs usually included large halls, were dances, concerts, and other programs were arranged. Some service clubs included a complete cafeteria

serving hot food and evening meals and may include a soda fountain as well as a stocked library[125] holding recent newspapers from around the country and popular magazines. One such member was Lieutenant Fred Lockwald from Illinois. He joined in September 1940.. He was a Air Corp officer who was attached to Camp Haan or possibly March Air Field. He was sent over to the European theater and was subsequently shot down. He was captured and held as a prisoner of war at Stalag Lft 1 Barth-Vogelsang Prussia 54-12. He was later repatriated.[126] In July 1944 he married Maureen Moore in Oak Park Illinois. It appears they had four children. Fred died in June 1963 and Maureen died in July 1997. Both are buried next to each other in Queen of Heaven Catholic Cemetery in Chicago, Illinois.

CAMP HAAN
THE HISTORY OF RIVERSIDE'S WORLD WAR II ANTI-AIRCRAFT TRAINING CENTER

Camp Haan Officers' Club (aerial), November 20, 1944.
Source: March Air Field Museum

Officer's Club patio. Source: personal

CAMP HAAN
THE HISTORY OF RIVERSIDE'S WORLD WAR II ANTI-AIRCRAFT TRAINING CENTER

Many of the service clubs are furnished with comfortable chairs, powerful radio, and grand piano. Typical service club hours were from noon to 10 PM daily, with the library open the same hours except for Friday evenings, when it closed during Battalion dances. The library has available more than 8500 volumes, 100 periodicals, and some 25 newspapers from across the country Officers Club T-2 was a square shaped building in area 10 of camp Haan. The construction of the Officers' Club started in the early summer of 1941. Its square footage was 46,520 sq. ft. It had a bar, cafeteria, and dance floor. It also had recreation space, reading space, and a barber and beauty shop.

In November 1942, it received an upgrade; new appendages were being built that would provide space for a bowling alley, mess hall, and officer's sleeping quarters. A swimming pool was also added to the building.[127] The original Officers Club was destroyed by fire and was rebuilt. It was built of wood and adobe.

There were several enlisted service clubs on Camp Haan. The first, Building T-51 in area 10 of Camp Haan represented the Enlisted Service Club. Opened in Jul 1941. This club was a 2-story T-shaped building measuring 100-foot-long and 59-foot-wide and 80-foot-long and 50 foot wide. This building was on 21 Street across from

Camp Haan enlisted service club shown on a Fotone Postcard (The Ullman Company) circa 1942.
Source: Riverside Historical Society

the Guest house. The hostesses responsible for the guest houses were also responsible for the T-51 service club. The hostesses would schedule dances for enlisted men on the weekends and would invite civilian girls from Riverside.[128] One of the hostesses was Mrs. W. L. Colley.[129] The service club had a large dance floor, cafeteria, soda fountain, and terraces lounges.

Later Service clubs T-7616 and T-7716 were added for enlisted men in the Topside part of the camp after 1943. These clubs contained a cafeteria, dance floor, lounges, and a library.

There were separate service clubs for African American troops T-3527 and T-3528 on Avenue C in Area 6 of Camp Haan. They were located just east of the Prisoner of War compounds. Segregation was still prevalent during WWII.

Prisoner of War Buildings
Prisoner of war buildings in World War II was based on standardized plans, like all mobilization construction of the time. Each POW facility included prisoner barracks, guard barracks, administration, warehouse area, hospital compound, and recreation area within the stockade guarded by watch towers. In keeping with the provisions of the Geneva Conventions, POWs could be enclosed within a stockade but not confined or imprisoned in cells. The barracks and support buildings were built off the series 700

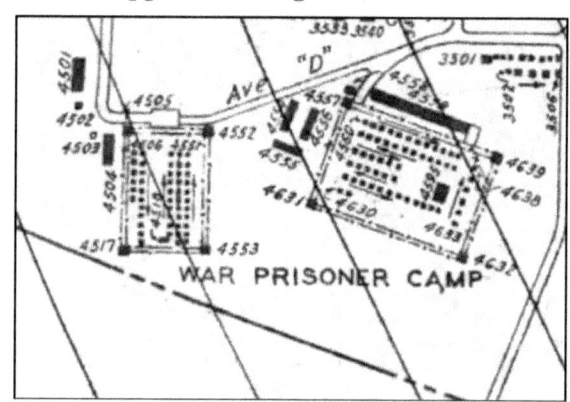

Camp Haan's Prisoner of War (POW) camp layout.
Source: Camp Haan Map Project Map. Southern California Real Property Disposal Case Files, 1946-1962. RG 269 Records of the General Services Administration. Box 59; National Archives and Records Administration, Riverside, CA.

plans.

Camp Haan's POW facility was in area 6 on the North side of camp and just North of the hospital area on Avenue "D". There were two separate compounds established. The smaller one on the left was the original stockade, and the larger one on the right could house 300 POWs. Although not specifically stated in documents, the author believes that the two different compounds were used to segregate the German and Italian prisoners.

The prisoners were housed in the wood-framed 16' x 16' tents and in compounds that were enclosed with double-rowed fences and concertina wire/razor wire. These tents may have been removed in exchange for hutments as many of the POW camps were transitioned to hutmants; however the Camp Haan's construction plans show the housing as tents and there is no record of sale of removal of hutments from this area.There were guard towers are all four corners.

Compound 1
    Guard towers – (T-4505, T-4552, T-4517, and T-4553) Towers were elevated eight to 10 feet in the air and 6' x 6'
    Latrine – (T-4518) measured 25' x 36'
    Mess – (T-4504) measured 25' x 94' and located outside of the fenced compound.

Compound 2
    Guard towers – (T-4557, T-4639, T-4632, and T-4631) Towers were elevated eight to 10 feet in the air and 6' x 6'
    Latrine – (T-4595) measured 20' x 40'
    Mess – (T-4559) measured 20' x 136' and located outside of the fenced compound.

Administration and Other Buildings
    Stockade Office – (T-4501)
    Isolation Cell – (T-4506) 8' x 12'
    Carpenter Shop – (T-4554) 22' x 102'

    Guard Barracks – (T-4555) 15' x 65'

Stockade Headquarters – (T-4556) 20' x 100'
Guard House – (T-4558) 18' x 27'

Camp Haan Station Hospital

The first official Camp Haan hospital plan drawings and specifications were approved and given to the contractors on October 21, 1940 but were recalled by the constructing quartermaster on October 28, 1940. This was due to the changes that were taking place on the 700 series drawings and specifications. While the plans were still being worked out, the contractors were given the go-ahead to start the foundations. The contractors started pouring concrete footing for the hospital group on October 31, 1940.

The hospital area was built to the West of the regimental area 5 and between the Quartermaster and Ordinance Area. It encompassed a four-block plot of land just south of 35th street and the buildings were built on Avenues "H", "J", "K", "L", and "M." It was

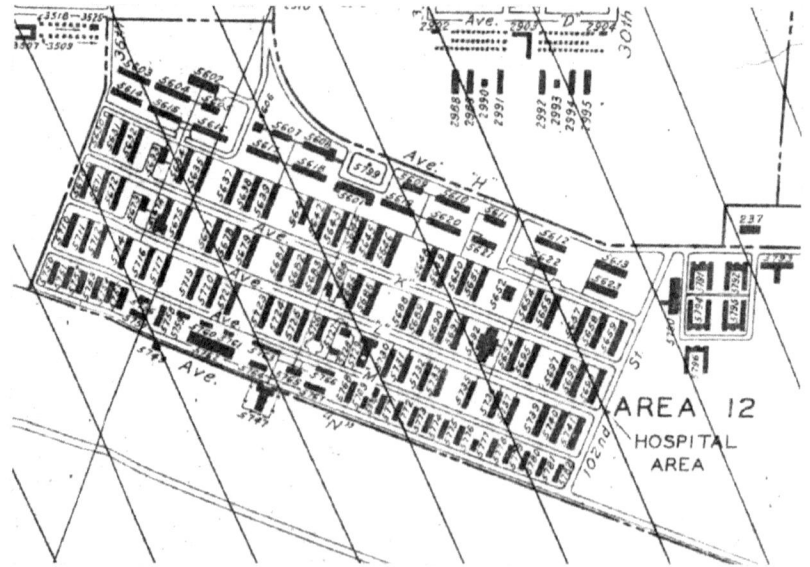

Camp Haan's station hospital layout
Source: Camp Haan Map Project Map. Southern California Real Property Disposal Case Files, 1946-1962. RG 269 Records of the General Services Administration. Box 59; National Archives and Records Administration, Riverside, CA.

situated near the Northwest property line of the camp in area 12.

Camp Haan station Hospital, March 1941
Source: personal

Camp Haan station Hospital, March 1941
Source: personal

CAMP HAAN
THE HISTORY OF RIVERSIDE'S WORLD WAR II ANTI-AIRCRAFT TRAINING CENTER

Camp Haan station Hospital, March 1941
Source: personal

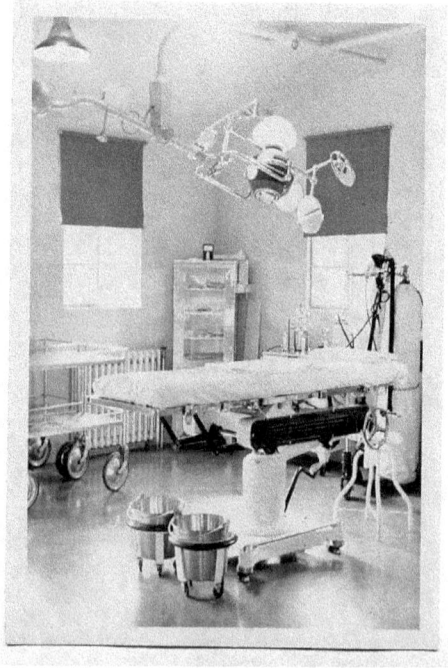

An Operating Room at Camp Haan
Source: personal

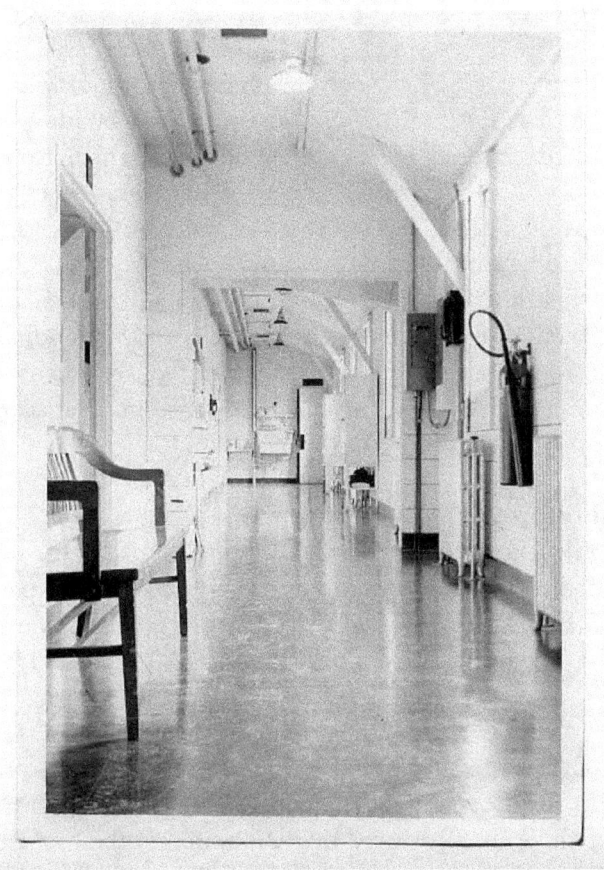

Hospital Hallway at Camp Haan
Source: Personal

By February 1941, the hospital was partially open even though the entire area was still under construction. During this time, if troops arriving to camp Haan arrived sick from the trains, depending on the severity, they were transported across the way to the March Field hospital. This very quickly placed the March Field hospital at capacity; it was decided tents were to be set up in the blacktopped parking areas around the March Field hospital to care for the sick troops. This only lasted a few months and by June 1941 the camp station hospital had a capacity of almost 500 beds. The units or wings of the hospital were divided into units of 33 beds each for the enlisted and the officer's wards held 22 beds each.[130] The personnel authorized to man this camp hospital would have been 37 officers, 60 nurses, and 275 enlisted men.

The boiler plant (T-5727) for the station hospital was used for heating, sterilization, and domestic use. The building itself was wood framed covered with corrugated steel which housed three Kewanee[131] boilers. Each boiler had 2,500 square feet of heating surface and 300 cubic feet of furnace volume; it operated at 125 pounds of operating steam pressure. Due to the proximity of March Airfield the boiler plant did not have a typical stack, instead it had induced draft fans and Venturi stacks only extending five feet above the roof line. The boilers ran off fuel oil and two 12,000-gallon storage tanks were installed underground adjacent to the building.

Hospital Improvements in 1941

One notable improvement to the hospitals was the installation of automatic fire-sprinkler systems in all the wards and patient care buildings. By December 1941, the installation in all the wards, except the detention wards, and kitchens were War Department policy.

In 1944, Camp Haan hospital had the capacity available, so they opened up the hospital to provide maternity and infant care for wives and children of enlisted men stationed in the San Bernardino and Riverside County area; Camp Haan, March Field, Camp Anza, Camp Irwin, Camp Young, and the San Bernardino Army Airfield. Although care was given at the hospital, all inpatient hospitalizations were taken over to Riverside Community Hospital under the supervision and care of medical officers assigned from Camp Haan.[132]

Hospital Train[133]

Hospital trains were used to transport large numbers of wounded or convalescing troops from the debarkation point to other areas in the Zone of the Interior.

Rail cars were 84-ft long, each car was equipped 36 beds in three-tier arrangement, a sterilizer room, utility room, and a kitchenette.

CAMP HAAN
THE HISTORY OF RIVERSIDE'S WORLD WAR II ANTI-AIRCRAFT TRAINING CENTER

Movements of patients being transported to or between medical facilities in the Zone of Interior, were regulated by The Surgeon General, who had to consider the medical needs of the patients and bed vacancies in the respective Hospitals. The Surgeon General supervised the maintenance of the medical equipment and the staffing of the cars with medical personnel.[134]

Camp Haan, despite little evidence, did have a Hospital Train Unit as a detachment to the station hospital.[135] The Hospital Train Unit was part of the Special Command Unit 1964[136]. It operated to and from the camp from 1941-1945. The only photographic evidence I have been able to find that the hospital train was at camp on was in

Camp Haan salvage yard, circa 1946
Source: Yeager Family Library, March Field Air Museum

this salvage picture of Susie Q the B-17, where you can see in the background, a hospital train in the railyard.

The hospital train normally had a capacity of 256 bed patients and usually consisted of 16 Ward Cars, 1 Utility Car, 1 Officer Personnel Car, 2 Orderly Cars, and 1 Kitchen, Dining and Pharmacy Car. Separate quarters, including bunks, latrine and shower facilities were available for Officers and Nurses, while Enlisted personnel also had similar facilities at their disposal. Electric and steam generators, storage lockers, food storage facilities, pharmacy, toilet facilities, sink, and medicine cabinets were on board. The Hospital Train was organized as follows:

- Train Headquarters
- Administrative Division (Mess Section, Supply Section, and separate Engine Crew)
- Professional Division (Surgical Section, Medical Section, Pharmacy Section)

Each of the Ward Cars was sufficiently equipped with pajamas, sheets, pillows, blankets, compartmented trays, bed pans, litters, medicine cabinets, catheters, and a complete Ward Case containing hemostats, scalpels, and other medical instruments. The Pharmacy was supplied with prescription balance, graduates, drugs, and medicine. According to T/O 8-520 dated April 1, 1942 personnel of a Hospital Train consisted of 4 Officers, 6 Nurses, and 33 Enlisted, subdivided as follows: 1 Major – 1 Captain – 2 Lieutenants – 6 Nurses – 1 First Sergeant – 1 Staff Sergeant – 1 Corporal – 1 Technician 3d Grade – 6 Technicians 4th Grade – 8 Technicians 5th Grade – 6 Privates First Class – and 9 Privates.

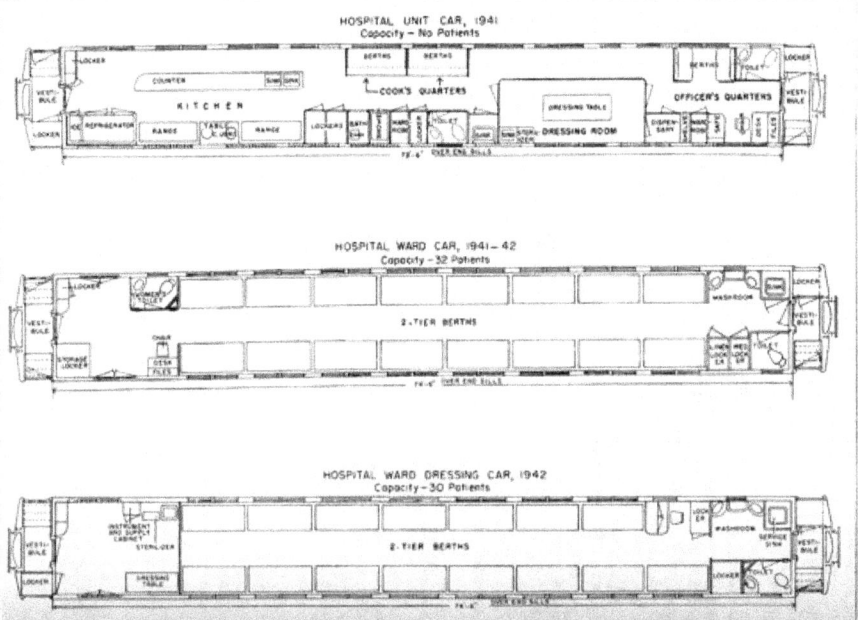

Basic plans for hospital trains, 1941-1942
Source: WW2 U.S. Medical Research Centre

Areas of Camp Haan

The regimental areas were very much planned out. The Quartermaster General established "Typical Regimental Area" block plans to assist the engineers and architect. Each area was approximately 2,048 ft. by 1,200 ft. and Regimental area consisted of three area: (1) Regimental headquarters, headquarters staff and services, (2) Batteries and companies, and (3) warehouses, shops, gas stations, and vehicle parking. Each of these areas were separated by roads 22 ft wide.

Regimental headquarters, services, and drill area

This area contained the regiment headquarters, a mess hall for officers, two lavatories for officers, a recreation building, an Exchange, and an infirmary. There was also dedicated space in this area for men to drill. The drill area was located adjacent to the headquarters area, if you orient the regimental area (pg. 105) where the headquarters building is up, the drill areas would be above the regimental headquarters.

CAMP HAAN
THE HISTORY OF RIVERSIDE'S WORLD WAR II ANTI-AIRCRAFT TRAINING CENTER

Artillery Batteries and Companies

This area contained thirty-four buildings that supported the different batteries and companies including battery office and supply buildings, latrines, and mess tents. There were also 374 "A" tents for enlisted men, and four "A" tents and 43 "D" tents[137] for

Camp Haan regimental tent area, circa 1941
Source: personal

officers. All the tents were aligned in a column formation off of the regimental headquarters.

If you orient the regimental area where the headquarters building is up, on the left side the Searchlight Battery is located in the area marked "D", the gun batteries are located in the areas marked "C","B",and "A", 1st battery headquarters and combat training is located in the area marked "K". The area on the right side (from left to right) were comprised of Area "M" which housed the regimental headquarter battery, "L" the 2nd battery headquarters and combat training, area, and "J" the medical company. Area "E" which the machine gun battery and area "F", "G", and "H" were the 37mm gun batteries.

In total, each regimental area was designed to be comprised of approximately 1,800 enlisted men and 74 officers.

CAMP HAAN
THE HISTORY OF RIVERSIDE'S WORLD WAR II ANTI-AIRCRAFT TRAINING CENTER

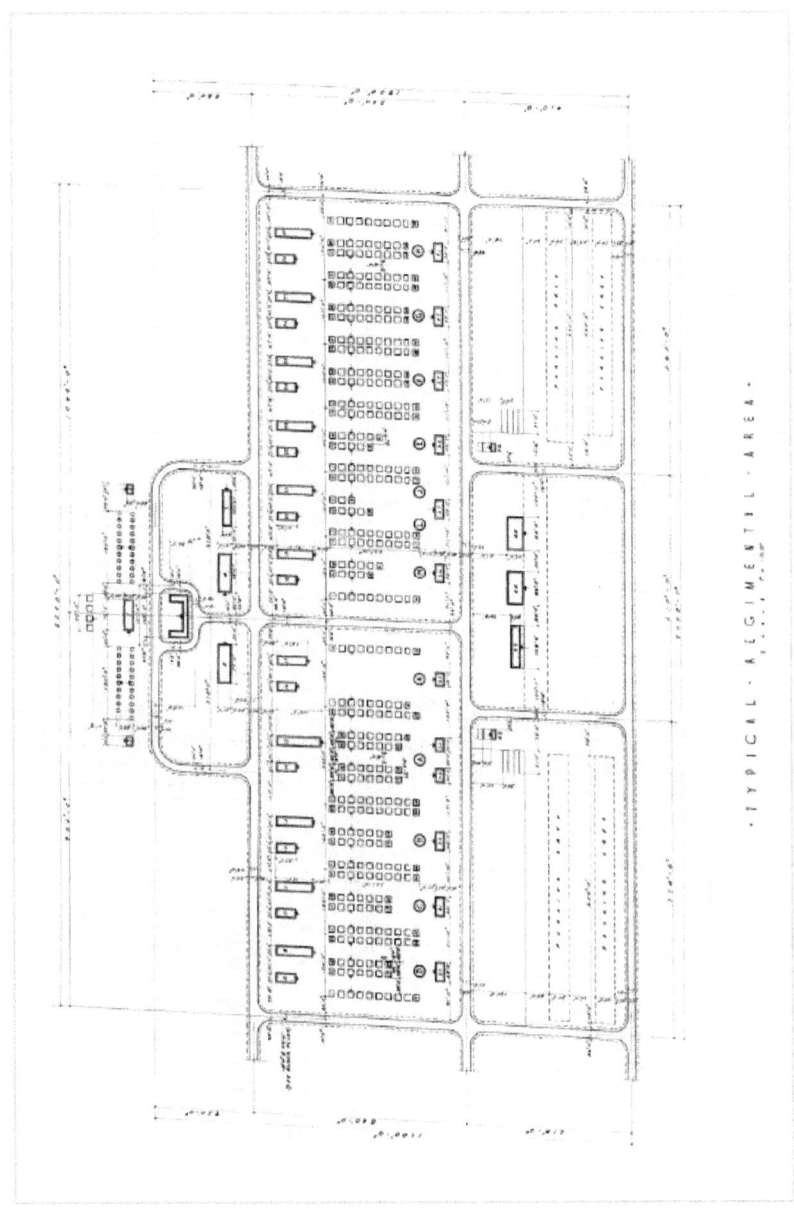

TYPICAL REGIMENTAL AREA

Warehouses, shops, gas stations, and vehicle parking

This area contained the various repair shops for regiment, warehouses for storage a gas facility, and vehicle parking for the vehicle assigned to the regiment.

Headquarters Areas

The headquarters area was the first area that was built during the initial build. During this time, the Quartermasters and representatives for the contracted companies had offices in this area which they would later vacate and relocate once the military command complement arrived. The post commander resided here. The Army Service Forces (ASF) managed the posts while the Army Ground Forces (AGF) managed the training. The post commander represented as the camp's business manager. The post commander and his support staff were responsible to the 10,000 to 60,000 personnel stationed there. This included services like laundries, service clubs, libraries, bakeries, mess halls, utilities, maintenance, and protection.

Areas 1, 2, and 3

Areas 1, 2, and 3 were regimental areas and were locate south of present day Van Buren Boulevard, where the Riverside National Cemetery is today.

Area 1 had the large mess hall mentioned earlier (T-517) and the south chapel (T-518). It also had a salvage yard close to the rail.

Area 2 had the central chapel (T-1118) and a fire station #2 (T-1119).

Areas 4 and 5

Areas 4 and 5 were regimental areas and were located north of present day Van Buren Boulevard, where the relatively new commerce and warehouse areas are located. Area 4 also had an aluminum salvage yard.

Area 5 had the north chapel (T-2918) and fire station #1 (T-2919).

Area 6

The camp service area was in the extreme north side of the camp from C street east to the U.S. 395 and continued south along the highway and the railway all the way through area 4 and ended at the salvage area.

The service areas contained a lot of warehouses for dry goods, equipment and supply, refrigeration warehouses, Quartermaster Ordinance, bakery, laundry, clothing equipment, salvage yard, and supplies issued by other service units such as the signal corps.

	Bldg. #	Uses
Warehouse 2	T-4038	Ordinance, fire control, small arms
Warehouse 3	T-4063	Armament parts, clothing retail
Warehouse 4	T-4035	
Warehouse 6	T-4052	Commissary cold storage
Warehouse 9	T-4047	Office of QM, incoming property, inbound supplies
Warehouse 10	T-4046	Commissary dry storage
Warehouse 13	T-4043	Classification of supplies and goods
Warehouse 15	T-4024	General warehouse
Warehouse 17	T-4062	General warehouse
PX Warehouse	T-79	PX goods and supplies
Shipping Warehouse	T-4068	Outbound supplies and goods
Warehouse G	T-4051	Automotive Parts

In area 6, the warehouses straddled the railway. A line of 8 warehouses on each side of the rail provided ample storage for the Quartermasters in addition for the warehouses off the immediate rail. There were also cold storage plants as well as butane plants and I storage buildings in this area as well. Each quartermaster warehouse generally had dimensions of 60' x 153' and usually had a platform on the rail side of the building. The railway was owned by the Santa Fe railroad company. There were also a couple loading ramps (T – 4033 and T – 4034) where goods and supplies can be stored in staged for pickup from the regiments. This area also had the two prisoner of war camps, a fire station (T-3549), and a large training auditorium (T-3548).

CAMP HAAN
THE HISTORY OF RIVERSIDE'S WORLD WAR II ANTI-AIRCRAFT TRAINING CENTER

In the 1940s the Army was still somewhat segregated, and because of this Camp Haan had separate barrack facilities.

Area 7
Area seven was another regimental area, although modified, it had a mix of tents asandutments.

Area 8
Area eight is also an unknown housing area that contained hutments. This area was between Avenue E and Avenue H, East to West and 10th St. to 8th St., North to South.

Area 9
Area nine held the brigade headquarters and support for the 215th, the 216th, and the 217th. Not only did hold the brigade headquarters in support functions. It also housed officers that were attached to that brigade. The brigade headquarters building (T – 301) was located at the corner of 10th and Avenue E.

Area 10
Area 10 contained the antiaircraft training center headquarters and the camp headquarters along with housing and facilities for all officers assigned to those functions. Area 10 was the first area to be built for the camp and was used as construction staging offices during the build out.

Area 10, also known as headquarters support area contained several of the important support functions of the camp. This included:
- Post exchange (T – 79) and gas station (T – 64)
- American Red Cross (T – 65 and T – 66).
- Dental clinic (T – 57).
- Post office (T – 58)
- Finance office (T – 59).
- Citizens National Bank (T – 60).
- Public relations (T – 62).
- Personnel office (T – 48)
- Service club (T – 51).

- Guesthouse (T – 52 and T – 53)
- Signal school (T – 54 and T – 56).
- Baker's and Cook's school (T – 61).
- Commissary (T – 68)
- Intelligence Office (T – 92).
- Theater (T – 74)
- Officer's Club (T – 2).

Area 11
Area 11 held the brigade headquarters and support for the 65th and 78th. Not only did hold the brigade headquarters in support functions. It also housed officers that were attached to that brigade. The brigade headquarters building (T –201) was located at the corner of 26th and Avenue E.

Area 12
Area 12 contained the hospital in its entirety, as well as the WAC area. In addition to the hospital, it contained all quarters, mess halls, and recreation for officers, nursing staff, and enlisted support. There is also evidence that there were quarters for the hospital train detachment between Avenues M and N on the backside of the hospital area. There was also an American Red Cross building on the backside as well (T – 5747).

Area 13
Area 13 on the southernmost end of camp Haan contained the main camp sewage treatment plant, holding tanks, and leaching fields. The incinerator (T – 5911) was located just to the west.

Area 14
Area 14 was on the southern western side of the camp. It was largely open space except for training areas that included the skeet range, the small arms range (T – 6006), the judo course, gas chambers (T – 6001 and T – 6002) and debarkation towers (T – 6000) located in the obstacle course area. The obstacle course was located just west of areas 15 and 16.

There was also the water treatment plant for the topside section of the camp as well as a million-gallon clean water tank, which coincidentally remains on-site today. The concrete shell of the remnants of the water treatment plants still exists today.

Areas 15 and 16
Areas 15, 16 were also regimental style housing areas for additional Army personnel. This area was just to the west of area 10, the headquarter support area. Notably, this area also contained the campus training swimming pool.

Area 17
Area 17 on the northern side of the camp was largely cold storage and large warehouses that were intersected by the railyard and railway. These warehouses (T – 6502, T – 6504, and T – 6508) measured 48' x 640'.

Areas 22-36
Areas 22 through 36 represented the topside area of the camp and was the last part of the camp to be built. This part of the camp had 700 series style buildings which included full barracks and associate buildings. This area was used to largely house the greatest number of drafted personnel assigned to the camps. A post office was also opened in building T – 7312 in area 25, in 1943 for the convenience of the men.[138]

In addition to numerous barracks, mess halls, latrines, and administration buildings. This area also held a training auditorium T – 8008), the service club (T – 7616), a fire station (T – 7614), and a large recreation hall (T – 7615).

There were 2 more skeet ranges located adjacent to areas 22 and areas 27. In later years of the camp, areas 30, 31 and 32 were turned into disciplinary barracks areas and were isolated from the other areas around it through use of guard towers and fencing.

Magazine area

The magazine area was located on the northern side of the camp and contained all the different underground magazines for holding a munition. The underground magazines (T – 15004 through T – 15016) were located away from populated areas in concrete style magazines. This area was cordoned off by concertina wire and had personnel acting in sentries 24 hours a day. This area was retained by March airfield at the closure of the camp and subsequently became property of March Air Force Base. This area is still used today by March Air Reserve Base.

CHAPTER 6
WORLD WAR II YEARS

Units

There were many units assigned to camp on over the six years it was in operation. A full list of known units can be found in the appendices.

For the purposes of this book, I would like to focus on the initial units assigned to camp on at its opening, which were two brigades: the 37th and the 101st Brigade.

The 37th Brigade consisted of the 78th and the 65th Coast Artillery.

65th Coast Artillery, all the batteries, including the headquarters battery was activated on June 1, 1938 at Fort Winfield Scott in San Francisco. Additional batteries were activated on October 11, 1939. The unit was transferred to Camp Haan on January 16, 1941.[139]

The 78th Coast Artillery, commanded by Lieutenant Colonel Robert H. Van Volkenburgh, issued special order no. 2 on August 5, 1940, to his adjutant, Lieutenant Maxwell M. Kallman, ordering the 78th Coast Artillery from Fort Roscrans to March Field. On August 13, 1940, all the batteries, including the headquarters battery was activated. 78th Coast Artillery was temporarily housed at March Air Field and moved over to Camp Haan in February 1941.[140]

Men from the 78th Coast Artillery at Camp Haan standing in front of a motor repair shop (T-2981 or T-2381), 1941.
Source: War Department (1941). 78th Coast Artillery Year Book

Men of the Medical Detachment from the 78th Coast Artillery at Camp Haan standing in front of a regimental infirmary building (T-2910 or T-2310), 1941.
Source: War Department (1941). 78th Coast Artillery Year Book

CAMP HAAN
THE HISTORY OF RIVERSIDE'S WORLD WAR II ANTI-AIRCRAFT TRAINING CENTER

Men of the 78th Coast Artillery at Camp Haan standing in front of a hand painted mural in one of the regimental dayrooms, 1941.
Source: War Department (1941). 78th Coast Artillery Year Book

The 101st Brigade consisted of the 215th, 216th, and 217th Coast Artillery comprised of Minnesota National Guard, the 47th Quartermaster's Corps, the 49th Quartermaster's Corps. The 216th searchlight battery called themselves the "moonlight Calvary." The 7th and 18th Ordinance Companies which were the Army's 7th and 18th Medium Maintenance Companies which were transferred from Aberdeen, Maryland to Camp Haan, California around June 20, 1941 to support the camp.[141] Two units of Nevada's National Guard were converted from the 40th Military Police Company and the 2nd battalion of engineers into the 121st Coast Artillery,[142] 121st arrived at Camp Haan on 9 July 1941.[143] They occupied an area south of the 101st Brigade in area 1. Finally, the core area support unit 1967 or commonly known as SCU 1967. Except for SCU 1967, these units were quickly trained and moved out to areas such as the Presidio area of San Francisco or Long Beach and Los Angeles areas Los Angeles for additional training and/or coastal defense protection. For the most part the initial units were moved out to other locations before the attack on Pearl Harbor in December 1941.

In December 1942, the War Department implemented a major reorganization of the antiaircraft units. Coast Artillery units (battalions, groups, and brigades were redesignated as antiaircraft artillery (AAA) battalions, groups, or brigades.[144]

WACS in Camp

Women served in World War II, not only backfill for the men who went off to war, but also in the Army. The Army initially established Woman's Army Auxiliary Corps (WAACS), in May of 1942;[145] it was later converted to active duty and renamed the Woman's Army Corps (WAC). November 1943 saw the first WAC to be assigned to Camp Hann. Lt. Emma W. Johnson of Corvallis, Oregon was assigned as the PX Chief's Aide at Camp Haan. Lt.

Lt. Emma Johnson (right) and Major Keith Shipley (left) as Lt. Johnson is welcomed to Camp Haan.
Source: Camp Haan Tracer, Tuesday November 9, 1943.

Johnson went through basic training in Des Moines, Iowa and then to Administration Specialist School. She then attended an 8-week Officers Candidate School. She was selected to Army Exchange School in Trenton, New Jersey and completed that assignment before she was assigned to Camp Haan, California.[146] She served as the assistant exchange officer to Major Keith Shipley.

Early on in 1944 saw the recruitment of 73 women directly to Camp Haan. Lt. Mary Eileen Ryan, WAC recruiting officer in San Bernardino was instrumental in enlisting these women. Under this program, women enlisted directly to Camp Haan, allowing them to stay close to home. "It enables women to enter the Army and still stay close to home," remarked Lt. Ryan. Positions that these women filled were clerk, general clerks, statistical clerks, draftsman, stenographers, personnel clerks, supply clerks, and administration inspector.[147]

Organization

Upon arrival at Camp Haan, military personnel were assigned to a brigade (regiment) and then into specific batteries. The brigade consisted of 3,000 to 5,000 men and was headed up by a commissioned officer, usually colonel, and then sub-divided into two to five battalions headed up by a lieutenant colonel. Each battalion had two to four batteries of approximately 150 to 280 men each, with a battery commander, usually a captain, in charge of each battery.

The battery was further divided into four platoons, each headed by a lieutenent, assisted by the sergeants, oversaw the quarters and barracks and responsible for basic training in drill formations and manual of arms. These noncommissioned officers comprise the cadre, a term used to designate the nucleus or framework of the battery.

It was the battery commander, assisted by other commission officers and a noncommissioned officer of the first sgt. grade, through whom came many routine orders and assignments.

<u>A typical day.</u>
Reveille sounded at 6 AM each day, except for on Sunday, on Sunday, it was 7 AM. At 615 AM each weekday morning, the men would fall out in front of their tents or barracks for roll call. And, usually, a short session of calisthenics. The men then had time for morning activities, making beds, and cleaning their tents and barracks. Breakfast was served in the mess halls within their own batteries between 6:45 AM and 7:30 AM.

At 7:30 AM, the actual program of the day commenced for the trainees. It usually started with an assembly to cover any important news over the camp's public address system and was followed by an hour of infantry drill formations in the manual of arms. The remainder of the day is spent in lecture courses in actual practice of theory taught in the class.

Retreat was called at 5:00 PM and supper immediately followed thereafter. Lights are out in the tents and barracks at 9 PM, and a bed check was performed at 11 PM.

On Wednesday afternoons, military training was put aside for mass calisthenics and participation in sports such as baseball, football, applicable, etc. on Saturdays, the workday ended at noon unless other duties or special details were assigned.[148]

Passes, leave, furloughs
During the initial weeks of training, the men were expected to remain in camp. After that initial period of training, men could go to Riverside after retreat (5 p.m.), Saturday afternoons, and Sundays. The men would still have to receive a pass from their battery commander and the number of available passes would fluctuate based on the needs of command. This type of pass was typically used. To go catch a movie, purchase civilian supplies, or just get away from the camp for a couple hours.

It was possible to receive an overnight pass for Saturday night, with permission of the battery commander by filling out an application and running it through the first sergeant. This pass allowed the soldier to be on pass, away from the camp from the mid-afternoon on Saturday to Sunday morning (5 a.m.). Overnight passes were extremely popular in Camp Haan; it allowed the men to go socialize, drink, have dates, and even travel beyond Riverside. Downtown Riverside was exceedingly popular for soldier stationed at Camp on including the Mission Inn Hotel and the Fox theater. Soldiers wishing to venture farther out would often find themselves in downtown Los Angeles or Hollywood area. The Hollywood Canteen was an immensely popular spot for entertainment for serviceman.

Still further, and perhaps only in exceptional cases, a 3-day pass was given. This type of pass was only given in emergencies.[149] three-day passes were rarely given, mainly since it impacted the soldier's training regimen and affected the teamwork aspect of antiaircraft training.

CAMP HAAN
THE HISTORY OF RIVERSIDE'S WORLD WAR II ANTI-AIRCRAFT TRAINING CENTER

Primary Training

During the mobilization leading up to the United States' involvement in WWII, Army training centers were being built all over the country. Camp Haan, being an anti-aircraft training center, was charged with taking civilians and indoctrinating them into the Army culture and becoming fully trained anti-aircraft units. Camp Haan acted as a boot camp for thousands that were stationed there. Since the camp housed both active duty and National Guard units that arrived at different times, the units were in various stages of

T.P Foster at Camp Haan standing in front of tent B-6 in regimental area 4. T.P. Foster was assigned to the three inch gun battery "B" while in the 65th Coast Artillery and the 37mm gun battery "F" while in the 78th Coast Artillery.
Source: picture courtesy of Lille Foster

training. This staggering of training became a very important tool for scheduling purposes at the height of the soldiers requiring training.

When the men arrived at camp. They were given military clothing, a rifle, a bayonet, canteen, gas mask, helmet, and certain other equipment to use while they are at the camp. Some of the National Guard units arrived with uniforms and equipment. T.P. Foster (regular Army, assigned to the 65th Coast Artillery) commented on the uniforms he was given at Fort Sheridan enroute to Camp Haan were wool and he was assigned to southern California, "Here we have been in the Army a month out in the state of California and we still haven't been issued a damn bit of clothes to fit the climate."[150]

For those newly indoctrinated to the Army, the regular training schedule started off with one week of orientation followed by thirteen weeks of preliminary training. Military personnel spent at least one hour daily on the drill ground and practice of formations a manual of arms. After the preliminary training was complete, a certain number of enlisted men, based on aptitude test, experience,

Pvt. David Frank Scott cleaninig his rifle before guard duty at Camp Haan, November 1943.
Source: Camp Haan Tracer, Tuesday November 9, 1943

and other qualifications were selected for enlisted specialist school. The school offered a wide variety of subjects designated to train cooks, clerks, automobile and artillery mechanics, bugler, telephone men, meteorologist, radio technicians, truck drivers, and many other mechanical and professional specialists.

Following the initial fourteen weeks, advanced training commenced and included target practice, field engineering, overnight camps, convoying, and other field activities. It is during these 14 weeks that the men got familiar with antiaircraft weaponry such as a 90

Bakers and Cooks School, building T-61, Camp Haan
Source:

mm gun, the 37mm gun, the 40 mm gun, the 50-caliber machine gun, the 30-caliber machine gun, and searchlights. Other equipment that the men were trained on included the director, which computed firing data for the gunners, power control units, sound locators, and other detecting devices and observation instruments.

This shows crew learning how to manipulate a medium anti-aircraft gun, a multiple machine gun suitable for use against such planes as the Stuka dive bombers.

Troops in the open ranges of Camp Haan learning how to set-up and maintain anti-aircraft guns.
Source: Los Angeles Times, Monday, March 10, 194, p. 3

CAMP HAAN
THE HISTORY OF RIVERSIDE'S WORLD WAR II ANTI-AIRCRAFT TRAINING CENTER

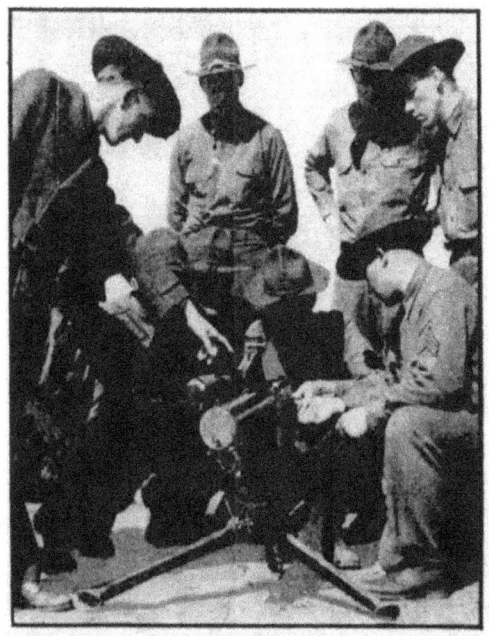

Here is group of soldiers getting instruction in the operation of the small anti-aircraft gun, virtually a machine gun for use against low strafing planes.

Source: Los Angeles Times, Monday, March 10, 1941, p.3

It was here camp Haan where US Army antiaircraft and Coast artillery antiaircraft were taught to bring down enemy planes. This was fitting since the camp motto was, "Keep 'em Falling."[151]

Garland Griffin, in a 1958 Press-Enterprise article, said this about the training at camp Haan,

> "We drilled endlessly on the flats of Camp Haan and crawled about on knees and elbows…We dug many gun pits and sat in them all night tracking March Field planes with our searchlights, radar, and gun barrels."[152]

CAMP HAAN
THE HISTORY OF RIVERSIDE'S WORLD WAR II ANTI-AIRCRAFT TRAINING CENTER

By 1943, advances in artillery technology were beginning to be seen and taught at Camp Haan. The 124th Coast Artillery Battalion was the first unit equipped and trained with radar controlled 90mm guns. The unit, after training, was shipped to the southern English coast where they were credited with shooting down 841 V-1 rockets destined for the heart of London, perhaps saving thousands of lives in London.[153]

Troops at Camp Haan learning how to set-up and function the anti-aircraft gun battery.
Source: Los Angeles Times, Monday, March 10, 1941, p. 3

CAMP HAAN
THE HISTORY OF RIVERSIDE'S WORLD WAR II ANTI-AIRCRAFT TRAINING
CENTER

Men training on the anti-aircraft gun batteryat Camp Haan, circa 1942
Source: March Field Air Museum, Yeager Family Library, Riverside, CA

Pioneering

Pioneering was another phase of training in which the men would construct temporary bridges to convoy trucks and guns. They did this out in the open fields of Camp Haan. This technique was used to get the men to think critically about getting vehicles and equipment from one location to another over rough terrain.[154] The areas surrounding Camp Haan had no shortage of difficult terrain and rocky outcrops to provide a rich environment to train in; the area still contains large rock outcroppings but are quickly disappearing due to development.

Pioneer Training at Camp Haan
Source: Coast Artillery Journal Aug-Sep 1941

Cultural Exchange

Because the United States was allied with many countries during WWII, it provided opportunity for some cultural exchange and joint training, especially in the waning years of the war. This was especially important for the public relations aspect for the President and the War Department since The U.S. had been at war for eighteen months and citizens were starting to question the prolonged campaign. The British War Office on the other side of the Atlantic also needed the help of the United States to keep pressing in the war, so a British Artillery contingent was sent to the United States to raise awareness and use the British military as ambassadors.

In September 1943, Camp Haan hosted a British anti-aircraft artillery unit. Captain R. Tedger, of First Company, antiaircraft demonstration battery, Royal Artillery commanded.[155] The British unit, consisting of 346 officers and men, demonstrated their tactical and training procedures.[156] Camp Haan and Riverside was just one stop on their tour and were in town only a few days. The aircraft demonstration battery toured 30 states during their 6-month tour in the United States.

This record of tour would be lost to time if it weren't for Clifford Cole, a radar expert assigned to the British Demonstration Battery.

CAMP HAAN
THE HISTORY OF RIVERSIDE'S WORLD WAR II ANTI-AIRCRAFT TRAINING CENTER

During his 6-month visit to the United States, he took meticulous notes of the entire visit. Major Cole's entire experience can be read in Invading America, by Loaghtan Books.[157]

> *A parade today in Riverside so out came the shorts and shirt. I went into Riverside with the colonel after first dashing around inspecting equipment. The drive into Riverside reminded me of the film country one see on Technicolor films. The sun blazed down in a clear blue sky, on country browned by continual sun. The mountains edging the plain on which Camp Haan and Riverside are situated, are of brown rock, sandy type, with the mountains rising sheer out of the plain.*[158]

Major Cole would go on to say that he was awe inspired by the large turn out of military, bands, and civilian services, and that he felt that the crowd was a little taken aback by the British working uniform and unique arm swinging. He commented that great attention was paid to the film stars and the shorts of the British Tommies.

Parade in downtown Riverside in 1943. Photo with Permission from Sara Goodwins
Source: Riverside Historical Society

CAMP HAAN
THE HISTORY OF RIVERSIDE'S WORLD WAR II ANTI-AIRCRAFT TRAINING CENTER

Parade in downtown Riverside in 1943. Photo with Permission from Sara Goodwins
Source: Riveriside Historical Society

Source: San Bernardino County Sun, October 3, 1943.

Mine and Demolitions School

Apart from Camp on being an antiaircraft artillery training center, the camp also housed many different types of schools; mining and demolitions school was just one of them. The school provided the men the opportunity to train, to detect and clear minds and minefields, assess for route clearance and reconnaissance, and the emplacement and clearance of landmines. The school was primarily used as an introductory course to help augment combat engineers/field engineers[159] in the field.

Demolitions training at Camp Haan.
Source: Picture Parade

Rigorous and highly specialized training for antiaircraft soldiers to provide education and practical knowledge in all aspects of forward area operations. Topics included how to deal with booby-traps and anti-personnel mines. The AATC at Camp Haan was receiving reports from the front regularly to provide the most realistic course as possible. The rocky outcroppings around Camp Haan provided a perfect backdrop for the course.[160] At the conclusion of each course, the graduates were expected to go back to their battalions and companies to act as instructors.

Combat Swimming

"Many of the casualties in this war, in which so much depends on ship-to-shore movement under enemy fire...have been caused by drowning rather than bullets."
Brigadier General Nichols

The Camp Haan swimming pool was built in late 1943 in area 15.[161]

Soldier training in the pool at Camp Haan, circa 1943
Source: Coast Artillery Journal, Volume 86 No. 1
United States Coast Artillery Association, 1943, Pg. 77

CAMP HAAN
THE HISTORY OF RIVERSIDE'S WORLD WAR II ANTI-AIRCRAFT TRAINING CENTER

In 1944, While Brigadier General Nichols was in command, he established the precedent that all men in his command would be able to swim 50 yards clothed and carrying a full gear complement. This camp-wide course was established in conjunction with the American Red Cross after a report that upwards of 60% of men entering the Army couldn't swim and another 30% considered not proficient in swimming.

Aerial of Camp Haan Pool (empty) on November 20, 1944. This was in Area 15.
Notice the antiaircraft pieces just south of the pool.
Source: March Air Field Museum, Yeager Family Library, Riverside, CA.

The program was divided into three phases, based on the starting aptitude of the men. The first two phases were swimming basics including floating and basic swimming methods. The final phase of the program called the aquatic warfare course, was held offsite some miles from Camp Haan at Railroad Lake and dealt with the practical aspects of swimming in combat. There trainees learned how to descend a Jacob's ladder (rope ladders down the sides of ships), tactical swimming through wreckage or burning oil, and learned how to utilize equipment and clothing as life-saving equipment.

Judo

When the war in the Pacific started to heat up, the Army realized that its men needed additional training in hand-to-hand combat. The Army developed Judo at its training centers as a defense

ARMY DEVELOPS JUDO DEFENSE AGAINST JAP ATTACK—Backing out of a trench to force their opponents to jump the barrier and thus be off balance when attacked, these anti-aircraft artillery trainees at Camp Haan, Calif., learn a new type of Judo defense developed to overcome Jap Ju Jitsu tricks. The new system is intended to give the Yanks advantage in all types of hand-to-hand encounters.

Source: Monrovia Daily News-Post (Monrovia, California) Thursday, February 11, 1943, pg. 6

technique to combat the Japanese hand-to-hand Ju Jitsu.[162] Judo in hand-to-hand combative techniques were used in World War I as well.

Camp Haan had a large amount of space dedicated to the instruction of Judo. It was an important part of the basic training component of the training at the camp. Located in area 14 of the camp, southwest side, it was adjacent to the small arms range.

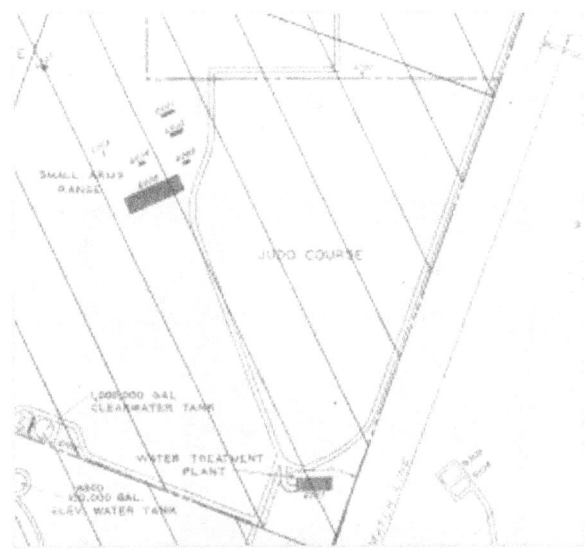

Judo course in area 14 of Camp Haan.
Source: Camp Haan Map Project Map. Southern California Real Property Disposal Case Files, 1946-1962. RG 269 Records of the General Services Administration. Box 58; National Archives and Records Administration, Riverside, CA.

The Dogs of War...

1943 saw the addition of canines on Camp Haan for the first time. Under the watchful eye of dog trainer Mr. Lee Duncan, 11 dogs spent three months going through their own basic training. The German Shepherds, Great Danes, and Doberman were trained as guards, disarming men, locating the wounded, rescuing down men, and carrying loose ends of telephone wire. They were trained to carry telephone wires from a forward advance listening post back to the rear control stations.[163] The canines were intensely trained to

Canine Training at Camp Haan, circa 1943.
Source: Coast Artillery Journal, Volume 86, May-June, 1943.

commands and placed near gunfire at various points in their training to get used to the sounds. It was not just the dogs that got trained, it took almost as long for men to get trained to properly command and care for the canines.

Canine Training at Camp Haan, circa 1943.
Source: Coast Artillery Journal, Volume 86, May-June, 1943.

Overall, there were 10,425 dogs trained during World War II, hundreds of military installations were issued dogs; nearly 90% of them were trained for sentry duty.[164]

Canine Training at Camp Haan, circa 1943.
Source: Coast Artillery Journal, Volume 86, May-June, 1943.

Field Exercises

Field exercises and field training was, perhaps, the most important phase of antiaircraft training that the men would undergo while at camp Haan. The ironic thing was… it was not held at camp Haan. Part of the reason why Camp Haan was chosen for Riverside California was its proximity to the Mojave Desert.

On August 8, 1940, President Roosevelt established a 1,000 sq mile range in the Mojave Desert and named it the Mojave Anti-Aircraft Firing Range (MAAFR). The area was chosen because of its remoteness and allowed the U.S. Army to train on anti-aircraft weapons that would become the first line of defense if Japan attacked the U.S. mainland. First desert drills first started in April 1941.[165] The first exercises at the Mojave anti-aircraft firing range were beyond primitive. Once the convoys arrived at Barstow, they needed to be refueled. The process seems innocuous enough, but with over 100 vehicles in the convoy and only two gasoline tankers, the process took a while.

In a letter received (Sharon Anthony Papers, Riverside Library) from former Lt. Ryan, Ryan commented on the trek to the Mojave firing range:

> *"From there it was another 40 miles across the desert; at that time there were no paved roads, only dust and heat. The dust got into everything and coated everything."*

It was common for units training at the Mojave antiaircraft fire range to be out in the field for long periods of time, including length of stays as long as 10 days. This was a necessary part of training as many objectives and milestones needed to be completed, including setting up camps, bivouac, setting up field services, field security and protection. This was in addition to the artillery practice.

Bicycle Lake range was the firing point for Camp Haan an area North of Barstow California in the Mojave Desert. 30 caliber anti-aircraft guns mounted on the carriages of 37-millimeter weapons. Night maneuvers, searchlights filling the sky from their positions 15 miles away along the rim of the range. Bombers towing target sleeves 1,000 yards behind them allows the searchlight and gun batteries to practice targeting.[166] Day time at Bicycle Lake were brutal as one of the officers recalled to the San Bernardino County Sun, "Temperatures of 140s in the daytime…I'll never be afraid of

Anti-Aircraft Guns to Roar Near Barstow

Anti-aircraft gunfire will echo across the vast Mojave range south of Barstow the next two weeks as nearly 1,500 Camp Haan soldiers conduct service fire of three-inch and 50-caliber ordnance.

The entire 65th coast artillery anti-aircraft unit, moving by truck convoy with all baggage and equipment necessary for a short stay, left Camp Haan Sunday night and opened its new headquarters at the firing center Monday night.

While at the Mojave range the men will live in tents with the same facilities provided for them that are used in Camp Haan. Water will be provided from a 524-foot well sunk into the desert sands to reach a subterranean spring of fresh water.

After the fortnight of target practice the unit will return to Camp Haan.

Source: San Bernardino County Sun (San Bernardino, California) Thursday, June 5, 1941. Pg. 6

Hades again." But heat was not the only thing the troops had to overcome out at Bicycle Lake, besides the heat, sudden dust storms and rattle snakes kept the troops on their toes.[167]

When training was complete, the convoys returned to Camp Haan, each of the vehicle needed an overhaul because of the pervasive nature of the gypsum dust in all the working parts, filters, and brake drums. The same had to be down with the anti-aircraft and personal weapons and other equipment. After that first trip, once word got out on the conditions there was a run-on gun and rifle covers in Riverside at the local sportsmen store.

In August 1941, the 216th convoyed out to Washington State, with the longest/largest and fastest convoy the Army ever maneuvered to date regimental size or larger; 1,000 miles in less than 5 days.[168]

In 1942, the Mojave antiaircraft firing range was renamed Camp Irwin as more permanent infrastructure began to be built at location.[169] Eventually, the road was paved, and training was near constant with the different battalions taking their turns on the range. Occasionally the entire brigade convoyed up. This provided an opportunity for different batteries to compete. The winner took home the target and bragging rights until the next opportunity. It was a real morale booster.[170]

Despite Camp Irwin closing in 1944 and being placed on surplus status, Units from Camp Haan still used the training center because it became part of the California-Arizona Maneuver Area (CAMA) otherwise known as the Desert Training Center (DTC). Its mission was to train United States Army and Army Air Forces units and personnel to live and fight in the desert, to test and develop suitable equipment, and to develop tactical doctrines, techniques, and training methods. The DTC is where General Patton famously trained his armored divisions for the North African Campaign.

Pilot Training

March Army Air Field, between 1941 and 1946 was training pilots to master the B-17, B-24s, B-29, P-40s, P-51s, and P-38s. March Air Field also became the home of the WASPs (Women's Army Service Pilots) whose job was to ferry airplanes and cargo to and from bases.

CAMP HAAN
THE HISTORY OF RIVERSIDE'S WORLD WAR II ANTI-AIRCRAFT TRAINING CENTER

Because Camp Haan was located next to March Field, it was not all that uncommon to see aircraft in and out of the field at all hours of the day. Aircraft manufacturers from Los Angeles and Long Beach area would fly the newly built aircraft from the factories to March as a shake down flight. One Lt., On duty, caught a rare sight of a B-19 trying to land in March Air Field. "I recall that its vertical stabilizers were four stories high from the ground to the top. It was escorted by A-20s and P-38s - it reminded me of a mother hen and her chicks.[171]" He recalled that the plane didn't land on the first and second attempts but made it down on the third. The plane was on display on the weekends and drew large crowds from Riverside and Camp Haan.

Source: San Bernardino County Sun (San Bernardino, California) Thursday, August 7, 1941. Pg. 9

Camp Haan's Combat Reports[172]

World War II was fought on the other side of the world from Camp Haan. The only access to the war news for the soldiers was the reel at the beginning of the movie or what the soldiers hear from letters from loved ones. Life a Camp Haan, or any other training center could be isolating. Brigadier General Handwerk's headquarters decided to initiate the Camp Haan Combat Report. The Combat report consisted of young antiaircraft soldiers telling their story and experience from the forward locations via electric transcription (mostly vinyl records at that time). Each recording consisted of a basic lesson; in first person narrative, just like a conversation. This presentation style was key, because it presented the material without giving the men the sense they were being talked at.

Presenting these stories were the same young soldiers that passed through the training center at the beginning. It was not just US soldiers, Handwerk's headquarters cumulated over 50,000 words of informal interviews from the British Composite Artillery Battery. All veterans of Narvick, Dunkirk, Malta, and the Battle of Britain.

Handwerk believed that there was value and fundamental principles of military training that could be vividly impressed on the young soldiers going through initial training. He believed that by making the connections between the tasks that soldiers will face in forward locations, would show the importance of the smaller tasks they are learning at the training center.

The combat reports were used all over Camp Haan, in the day rooms, the mess halls, and even the firing range and were intensely popular by the troops because the stories were presented with no fancy words, no flowery Army jargon. To the soldiers, these reports were speaking their language and provided a possible glimpse into their own future after training.

Firing Range

The range was designed by Lt. Col. Paul B. Nelson (AATC Plans and Training Officer). Rifle range construction started in April 1941 and completed sometime May 1941. This project was constructed by Army troops assigned to Haan and worked under civilian foremen. It had 64-targets and could accommodate pistols, rifles, automatic rifles, and machine guns and was used full time not only by men at Camp Haan but other units within a 25-mile radius. The range was a reinforced concrete structure with a concrete overhead shelter, walls and pillar supports, and concrete and earth fill backstop. The bays were separated by concrete, bullet-proof walls. At its completion, the range was the only one of its type in the US Army; modern, weatherproof, and designed for night firing.

Camp Haan Rifle Range.
Source: Riverside Historical Society.

Camp Haan Rifle Range.
Source: Riverside Historical Society.

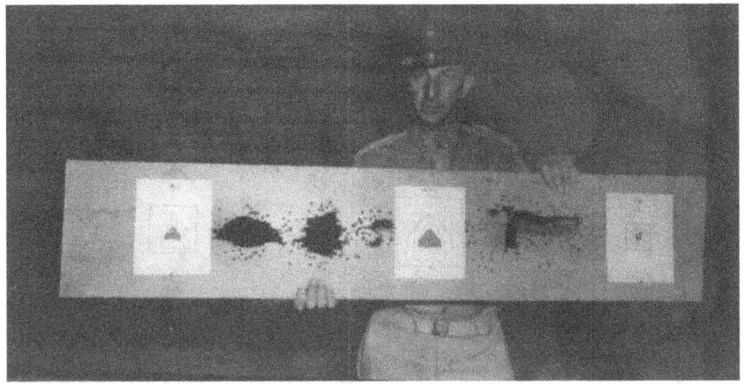

Soldier holding shooting score cards at Camp Haan rifle range.
Source: Riverside Historical Society.

Open House Army Day

On April 7, 1941, just months after the first troop arrival to Camp Haan, Brigadier General Colladay opened the gates and held an open house for the public to demonstrate how soldiers live and show them typical military activities. Exhibits included: three-inch antiaircraft guns, searchlights, .50-caliber machine guns, mobile radio truck, 37 mm guns, telephone switchboards, and other vehicles.[173] Demonstrations included: formal guard mount, drills in sighting in the big guns, aiming searchlights, establishing field communications, and a review of troops. The camp opened up certain mess halls, recreation halls, and tent rows were available to the public for inspection.[174]

Review of Troops

August 1, 1941 was the first full motorized review of soldiers at Camp Haan. Included in this was a ring of 45 searchlights illuminated the parade ground.[175] Festivities started at 1815 and high-ranking military officials and civilian officials from neighboring communities were in attendance. Lt. Col. James B. Brown, a brigade executive officer, organized the event.

Pass in review at Camp Haan shown on a Fotone Postcard (The Ullman Company) circa 1941.
Source: Riverside Historical Society.

September 28, 1941 review of troops from both the 37th and the 101st Brigade, numbering approximately 10,000 paraded by the Maj Gen Gardner, the new commander.[176] Massed bands from the 216th and the 217th regiments set the rhythm for the review.

October 2, 1941, the first public review of troops at Camp Haan occurred. 10,000 troops paraded for over 5,000 spectators that attended. It was the largest military demonstration ever staged in the Inland Empire at the time.

Source of News for the Troops

Since Camp Haan was so large and so many military and civilian personnel were working at the camp, all personnel were kept informed about life on camp, riverside, and nationally through the camp newspaper the "Post Beacon." This was later replaced in 1943 by the "Tracer". The Camp Haan Tracer included Camp Irwin as well. It was written, edited, and published by personnel from both camps every Tuesday. As you would expect, the Tracer looked and read like a regular newspaper at the time. It included sections for headline news and features, had a sports section, comics, editorials, and had updates to what the units were doing. It regularly sold in the camp PXs for two cents, but could be found lying around in all the recreation halls and many of the tents

Source: Riverside Historical Society

Sports

Sports and recreation were not considered on the initial Camp Haan buildout. The early troops to Camp Haan did not have a

Men playing baseball in the dirt at Camp Haan, circa 1941
Source: personal

swimming pool, tennis, basketball, or volleyball courts, and no baseball, or football fields, only bare dirt. Intramural sports were held in Perris and surrounding areas. To some degree, every soldier at camp Haan was an active participant in one or more athletic activities. Commissioned officers oversaw each battery's athletic program and arrange competitive play between the different organizations. Many platoons organized into teams for the minor sports activities, that included horseshoe tournaments, bowling, ping-pong, tennis, boxing, wrestling, rifle, and pistol team competitions. This was possible because each battalion had its own fully equipped recreation hall. Upon arrival at Camp Haan, the new trainees became a member of the YMCA; every Camp Haan soldier was afforded free membership privileges.

The soldiers also played sports at March Field and in Perris, CA. As the camp was built out and expanded, baseball fields were added. Because many of Camp Haan's first units came from Minnesota, hockey was a popular sport. The camp contracted with the Orange Belt Ice Gardens to allow intramural hockey to be played. Camp

Game Program from Camp Haan vs. Fresno State football, 1941.
Source: personal

Haan's football and baseball team even had the opportunity to play professional and college athletes on occasion. The Los Angeles Angels traveled to Camp Haan for a twilight game on June 22nd, 1943. The Los Angeles Angels won 12-0[177]. The football team, on occasion played UCLA Bruins football team in November 1941 and Fresno State on October 4, 1941[178].

City Entertainment

In 1941, Riverside County had just 103,000 resident - less than 4 percent of its current population. Residents of Riverside County, while initially skeptical of the presences of military in the cities, would eventually develop a kind of kinship with the men in uniform. Special bus routes were created to take military from March field, Camp Haan, and Camp Anza into the cities of Riverside, San Bernardino, and Perris. The Riverside Civic auditorium was open daily for the enlisted men and served as a place for them to unwind with activities such as the pool, ping pong, writing materials, lounges, showers, and restrooms.[179]

Colonel Ryan in recounting his off time, "Generally the weekends allowed the troops to decompress from a hard week of drill and other duties. If the soldier was not on duty during the weekend, they descended into Riverside and San Bernardino. The Mission Inn's Lea Lea Room was a popular destination for dancing on a Saturday night. The Victoria Country Club was also popular for Sunday brunch and social functions".

Lea Lea Room Sign on display at the Mission Inn Museum. Photograph by K. Beaulieu

"Bars like Circus-Circus were popular. Soldiers got nickel-a-draft Lucky Lager, Hamm's and Pabst Blue Ribbon beer. If they got drunk, they could sleep it off at the Hunt's Rubidoux theater or at the YMCA building on Eighth Street in Riverside.[180]"

CAMP HAAN
THE HISTORY OF RIVERSIDE'S WORLD WAR II ANTI-AIRCRAFT TRAINING
CENTER

There was even a men's store in Riverside called Sweet's that many of the Camp Haan men regarded as the best men's store in Riverside.

Riverside and San Bernardino residents took part in acts of patriotism by inviting soldier into their homes. If not just for dinners, many opened their homes to the soldiers all weekend to give some respite to Army camp life. This went on all through the

Source: The San Bernardino County Sun. Friday, Aug 22, 1941

southland.

In 1941, Riverside and San Bernardino represented the largest cities close to Camp Haan for recreational purposes. During longer

146

furloughs soldiers ventured out to Los Angeles, Long Beach, Huntington Beach, Newport Beach, and Hollywood in search of escape from camp life. On weekends, it was not uncommon to see Camp Haan Soldiers on the LA and Orange County beaches.

ny Restricts Sale Of Liquor to Troops

Riverside county liquor establishments were instructed yesterday to sell liquor to March field and Camp Haan soldiers only between the hours of 6 and 10 p.m. and to refuse sale to any March field and Camp Haan soldiers carrying firearms.

A joint bulletin issued by the commandants of the two camps said:

"Effective this date liquor will be sold to soldiers of Camp Haan and March field only between the hours of 6 p.m. and 10 p.m. No liquor will be sold to soldiers of Camp Haan and March field who are armed with any type of fire arms."

Source: The San Bernardino County Sun. Thursday, December 25, 1941

On occasion, the soldiers of Camp Haan were discouraged from going into the city.[181] The cities of San Bernardino and riverside were never officially list as out of bounds for army soldiers, but there was a reputation of ramped prostitution activities going on in both cities at the time.

By 1943, Riverside was used to the infiltration of soldiers boasting the local economy and for the soldier it was a welcome break from the camp. Gallagher remarked that; "Riverside was a small beautiful southern California town with a small mission to identify it as a historical site. Most of the homes and even the railroad station had those architectural features of white or pastel-colored stucco walls with red roof tiles."[182] For the longer weekends or three day passes, the Los Angeles and Hollywood area was a favorite destination. During this period, churches and schools would set up makeshift dormitories to house soldiers on leave. One popular spot was the Hollywood Canteen.

Hollywood Canteen
A favorite spot in the LA/Hollywood area for servicemen in 1943 was the Hollywood Canteen. The canteen was located at 1451 Cuhuenga Boulevard. It operated from 1942-1945 as a club offering food, dancing, and entertainment for servicemen. The price of admission was the uniform, and once inside everything was

Hollywood Canteen, c. 1943
Photo of the Hollywood Canteen - by J.H. Elder Jr.

free. The canteen was run by volunteers all from Hollywood; stars, directors, grips, dancers, musicians, writers, etc....

Servicemen could dance with Betty Grable, be served a sandwich by Shirley Temple, and watch performances by Bob Hope and Carmen Miranda. Roy Rogers even rode his horse, Trigger, right onto the stage for some prancing tricks.[183]

It was reported in the first 6 months of its opening, service men consumed more than 20,000 loaves of bread, 7,500 pounds of coffee, 12,500 pounds of meat, more than 50,000 pieces of cake, 750,000 sandwiches, and 375,000 packs of cigarettes.[184]

This canteen was so popular with servicemen that Warner Brothers studios made a movie entitle Hollywood Canteen, and starred many of the real volunteers.

By the time the canteen closed its doors, it had estimated that it serviced almost 4 million servicemen.[185]

Noted Celebrity Volunteers

Abbot and Costello	Bing Crosby	Laurel and Hardy
Don Ameche	Bette Davis	Ann Miller
Louis Armstrong	Doris Day	Glenn Miller
Jean Arthur	Olivia de Havilland	Donna Reed
Fred Astire	Cecil B. DeMille	Roy Rogers
Lauren Bacall	Walt Disney	Mickey Rooney
Lucille Ball	Tommy Dorsey	Frank Sinatra
Jack Benny	Duke Ellington	Red Skelton
Humphrey Bogart	Faye Emerson	Three Stooges
George Burn	Errol Flynn	Mae West
Gracie Allen	Eva Gabor	Esther Williams
Gary Cooper	Ava Gardner	Jane Withers

Hollywood Palladium

Another popular venue in Hollywood during WWII was the Hollywood Palladium. Constructed and opened in 1940, the Palladium was a dance forum that could hold 3,500 people on the dance floor.[186] Gallagher would describe this venue as, "Stepping into another world: a world of excitement and anticipation. It could only be compared to one of today's giant rock concerts."[187] Indeed the Palladium was a world of excitement, entertainers such as Tommy Dorsey and Frank Sinatra played opening night and had many big-name headliners over the years.

Community Partners

The view of the military and World War II post Pearl Harbor was very much different than before the Japanese attack. The country went from a period of legislative isolationism to being fully supportive of military action and the men and women who served. This was clearly evident from the number of offerings and support the local cities like Riverside, San Bernardino, Perris.

Troops from March Field and Camp Haan were honored guests at the Orange Show in celebration of Army Day. All troops were convoyed in. Soldiers showed off some drills and formations. As an added feature, Paramount Motion Pictures sent cameramen to film and photograph the troops.[188] Sent An excess of 10,000 troops from Camp Haan assembled in the National Orange Show stadium[189], San Bernardino for a demonstration and a football

Parade Marks Opening of Bond Drive

Squadron of armored cars from Camp Haan is shown moving along E street yesterday as San Bernardino opened its participation in the Seventh War Loan drive with a parade of 2,000 troops, Wacs, Navy hospital corpsmen and nurses. Three Army bands were included in the procession.

Source: The San Bernardino County Sun, Wednesday, May 16, 1945.

game with Camp Ord.[190] October 1941.

900 gift boxes were presented to soldiers from students at Riverside High School in December of 1943. Also, during Christmas week, the soldiers were admitted to the movies for free.[191]

AAA battalion presented an open-air concert and exhibition in downtown San Bernardino on Dec 2, 1944. Various equipment from the 195th AAA was set up and 29-piece band entertained residents for four hours. The event was set up in conjunction with the sixth war loan drive.[192] A similar exhibition occurred for the seventh war loan drive but included WACs, and hospital staff from Camp Haan.[193]

Private citizens even were encouraged to do their part to support the troops and their morale stateside before heading overseas. Citizens of the surrounding areas routinely opened their homes for meals, entertainment, and conversation. The public even opened their homes to servicemen during the holidays.

Citizens Are Asked to Entertain Soldier Lads At Their Homes Thanksgiving Day; 600 Army Men From Camp Haan Here for Maneuvers

Source: The Desert Sun, Friday, November 14, 1941.

Residents of Banning had Camp Haan soldiers over the weekend in August 1941.[194]

Even the Army reciprocated toward the community, the Army lent Huntington Park twelve 2.5 ton pickup trucks to the postmaster to help deliver Christmas parcels to residents,[195] and in July 1945, 600 soldiers from the camp help the forest service battle a brush fire 15 miles northeast of upper Santa Ana canyon.[196]

Repatriating soldiers transiting through Camp Haan. Date Unknown.
Source: Kansas Historical Society

Repatriating soldiers transiting through Camp Haan. Date Unknown.
Source: Kansas Historical Society

CAMP HAAN
THE HISTORY OF RIVERSIDE'S WORLD WAR II ANTI-AIRCRAFT TRAINING CENTER

Repatriating soldiers transiting through Camp Haan. Date Unknown.
Source: Kansas Historical Society

Source: Picture Parade

CAMP HAAN
THE HISTORY OF RIVERSIDE'S WORLD WAR II ANTI-AIRCRAFT TRAINING CENTER

A holiday feast, date unknown. Source: Picture Parade

Source: Picture Parade

CAMP HAAN
THE HISTORY OF RIVERSIDE'S WORLD WAR II ANTI-AIRCRAFT TRAINING CENTER

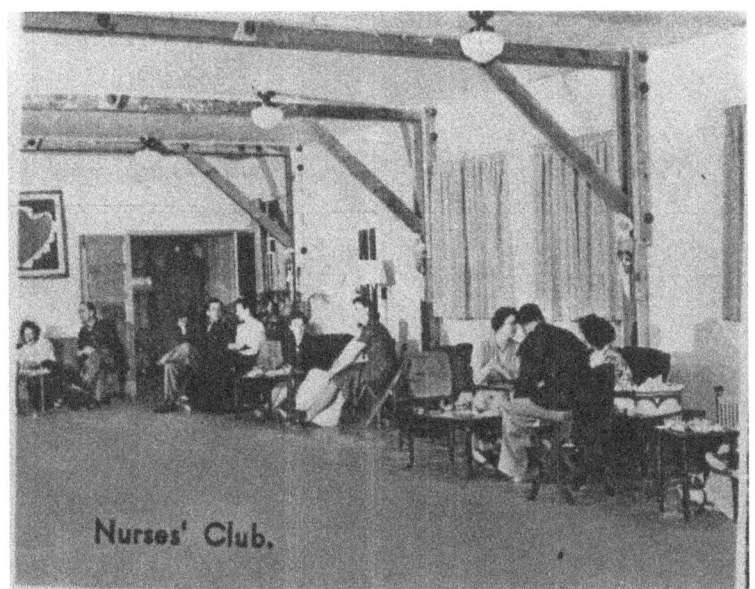

Source: Picture Parade

Group photograph at Camp Haan, date unknown. Source: personal

Soldiers taking some downtime in one of the regimental recreation rooms at Camp Haan, date unknown. Source: Picture Parade

CAMP HAAN
THE HISTORY OF RIVERSIDE'S WORLD WAR II ANTI-AIRCRAFT TRAINING
CENTER

Camp Haan station Hospital, March 1941
Source: personal

Unknown soldier and his date, circa 1941
Source: personal

Marriage in Camp

Although the chapels were erected for spiritual purposes, Camp Haan, on occasion, performed matrimonial affairs once permission was obtained. One such wedding, the Freeberg-Haskins wedding was held in the North chapel (building T-2918) and was decorated properly for the occasion. The date was November 10, 1942. Lieutenant Hazel Ida Freeburg, a nurse stationed at Camp Haan, and Lieutenant Walter Alphonso Haskins joined in matrimony. Service was read by Chaplain S. D. Masante. Following the ceremony, the reception we held in the Nurses' Recreation Hall (building T-5606).[197] After the war, the couple moved to Salem, Oregon, and by all accounts lived a rich and happy life. Records indicate that Hazal passed on January 7, 2002 and Walter passed on June 30, 2002. Both are buried at Belle Passi Cemetery, Woodburn, Oregon.[198]

Col. Bowen "Bo" Smith, mentioned earlier, and many other servicemen stationed at Camp Haan, met their future wives while at Camp Haan. Smith proposed to his wife Diana on Mount Rubidoux. Bo entered the Army as a recruit at the beginning of World War II and attended officer's candidate school. During WWII, he led his anti-aircraft battery in five European ground combat campaigns. He was awarded the Bronze Star and Purple Heart. Bo left the Army at the end of WWII and married Diana Lilley, whom he met while stationed in Southern California. Realizing his true calling was to be a career Army officer, Bo returned to the service, spending more than 30 distinguished years in the service of his country. While in the Army, Bo graduated from the University of Maryland and attended the Army War College. Bo served two tours of duty at the Pentagon and another tour in the South Pacific, where he was involved in atomic weapons testing. He also served as commanding officer of the 21st Artillery Battalion in Schofield Barracks, Hawaii. As a colonel, he was the inspector general of the Eighth Army in Korea and received the Army Commendation Medal. During the Vietnam years, he was professor of military sciences and commanding officer of the ROTC program at the Claremont Colleges in Southern California.[199] For Bo and many other veterans, bonds that would stand the test of time were made at Camp Haan. The artillery unit he was assigned to at Camp Haan used to gather for a reunion at a nearby Riverside hotel and reminisce about history that few would understand. The group has a memorial plaque on the walls of the Riverside National Cemetery Amphitheater. Col. Bowen Smith, passed away in 2009.

Riverside National Cemetery Amphitheater.
Photo courtesy of K. Beaulieu

Aircraft Accidents Near Camp Haan

Aircraft flying overhead was a way of life at Camp Haan, not because there were aircraft stationed there, but because the camp was adjacent to March Army Airfield. Not only were planes flying at all hours of the day and night from the airfield, but because of the proximity to the aircraft factories on the coast, March Army Airfield provided a nice "shakedown" flight. The vast availability of aircraft in the air also provided ample targets for the men to train sighting in at the camp.

During the time that Camp Haan was an active camp, there were several aircraft accidents that occurred near the camp.

May 27, 1942

In May 1942, a P-38F Lightning aircraft (Serial number #41-2303)[200] crashed in the hills just west of Camp Haan. The best approximation of the location would be west to where the Ben Clark Training Center is today. The pilot Lieutenant Richard Oliver Whyman was killed[201], aged 23. He enlisted in the Army Air Corps as an Air Cadet on October 2, 1941.[202]

> **PLANE CRASHES, BURNS**
> March Field, Cal., May 27-- (UP)—A P-38 interceptor plane crashed and burned in the hills west of Camp Haan today.

Source: The Hanford Sentinel, Wednesday, May 27, 1942

Lt. Richard Oliver Whyman's WWII draft card.

Source: The National Archives in St. Louis, Missouri; St. Louis, Missouri; WWII Draft Registration Cards for Arizona, 10/16/1940-03/31/1947; Record Group: Records of the Selective Service System, 147; Box: 135.

June 8, 1943

On June 8, 1943, a B-24 "Liberator" Bomber en route from

Four Burned To Death As Big Bomber Falls

March Field, Cal., June 8—(UP) —Four men were burned to death early today when a large bombing plane, enroute from Sacramento to March Field, crashed and burned a short distance southwest of Camp Haan. Names of the occupants of the plane were withheld temporarily by the Army Air Force.

Source: The Hanford Morning Journal, Wednesday, June, 9, 1943.

Sacramento to March Air Field crashed a short distance southwest of Camp Haan. The bomber crashed on final approach to March Air Field runway. Four men lost their lives.[203] Lieutenant Robert Lee Alexander, 2lt. Leroy Ellsworth Webb, SSgt Jimie T. Cauley, and SSgt Aulton A. Collins.[204] Records indicate that all of the crew except SSgt Collins died in the crash; he was transported to March Field hospital where he died of his injuries.[205]

Source: Applications for Headstones for U.S. Military Veterans, 1925-1941. Microfilm publication M1916, 134 rolls. ARC ID: 596118. Records of the Office of the Quartermaster General, Record Group 92. National Archives at Washington, D.C.

Lt. Robert Lee Alexander (1919-1943)
Source: Findagrave.com

Sgt. J.T. Cauley (1918-1943)
Source: ancestry.com

July 26, 1943

On July 26, 1943, a B-24E "Liberator" bomber from the 38th bomb squadron crashed in the ditch at the far end of the runway. all of the aircrew members escaped with minor injuries. Four first responders received minor burns while trying the save the crew; six men from Camp Haan were awarded the Soldier's Medal for their acts in saving the crew:

Captain David M. Miller
Captain Arthur H. Walters
2Lt Albert A. Alop
2Lt James E. Frick
WO Kenneth S. Berger
PFC Raymond F. Hartzel

About an hour later another B-24E Liberator bomber crashed (Serial number #42-7262) from 38th bomb squadron stationed at March Field. This time the crew wasn't so lucky; three crewmembers lost their lives; Lieutenant Robert H. Mack (pilot), Lieutenant William W. Walton,[206] (copilot) and Corporal Merle E. Detwiler (engineer).[207] Both bombers crashed on takeoff near camp Haan.[208]

According to eyewitnesses, the bomber took off and attempted to get altitude from the runway immediately after another bomber had taken off and crashed in a ditch at the far end of the field; the wreckage from the previous crash was still smoking. Before the plane reached the end of the runway one of the engines went dead, and the pilot, was faced with the alternatives of joining the other bomber in the ditch, possibly killing or injuring that crew and the first responders or attempting to complete the take off. The pilot chose the latter alternative; the plane struggled to gain altitude and struck the power lines above the field, causing it to explode and crash in flames.

There were reports that there was a third B-24 Liberator bomber crashed shortly after the first two.

William H. Towner was the captain in charge of the fire department on Camp Haan for much of the camp's operational existence. In an article to the San Bernardino County Sun, he recalled the plane crashes and fires.

> "Once three B-24s from March Field crashed at Camp Haan within a period of 30 minutes...then there were several blazes at the officer's club, and a P-38 caught fire 1,000 feet over camp, crashing into a ward at the hospital."

The War department recognized him for meritorious civilian service for rescuing a flyer from one of the downed B-24s. Towner was a World War I veteran that served in France in a machine gun battalion with the first army. After the Camp Haan posting, he took over as Chief of the Fire Department at the San Bernardino Army Airfield.[209] William died on December 30, 1967 in Long Beach California aged 73 years.

Later, the investigation into the cause of the bomber crashes were determined to be bad/stale fuel that was put into the planes.

March 7, 1944

On March 7, 1944 a twin engined P-38 caught fire in flight and crashed into one of the hospital buildings at Camp Haan. The plane was on a routine flight when it developed engine trouble, The pilot was Lieutenant Gene Hickok. Luckily the plane hit a relatively unoccupied ward. Lieutenant Hickok bailed out his plane and landed uninjured. The initial reports said that three were killed but those couldn't be confirmed early as the burning plane prevented searchers from gaining access to the building.[210] It was later

Lieutenant Gene Hickok's WWII draft card.
Source: The National Archives in St. Louis, Missouri; St. Louis, Missouri; WWII Draft Registration Cards for Washington, 10/16/1940-03/31/1947; Record Group: Records of the Selective Service System, 147; Box: 77

confirmed that four were killed, two x-ray technicians and two patients.

Blaine Street Housing complex[211]

With the buildup before World War II, thousands of military personnel flooded into the Riverside area for both Camp Haan and March Field. This caused the need for additional family housing. The Blaine Street Housing complex (later called Canyon Crest Family Student Housing) was created to fill that need. The site was located in an area that's now part of the University of California Riverside campus, was bound by Blaine Street to the north, Linden Street to the south Canyon Crest Dr. to the west, and on the east by UC Riverside's corporate yard. The site comprised of 51 acres and had 180 residential dwellings, a couple of support buildings, and park space.

Construction started concurrently with Camp Haan in 1940 by the Army Corps of Engineers, and the primary architectural style used was late 1930s minimalist. Several types of buildings on the site

Blaine Street Housing (Canyon Crest Family Student Housing) as seen in September 2009.
Source: Google Earth

included single dwellings and duplexes.

The residential units consisted of two basic designs; a flat roof design and units where the exterior walls rise above the flat roof system, creating a low parapet encircling the roof line. The single residential units were approximately 30 feet long by 25 feet wide (750 sq. Ft.). Each building was poured concrete walls set on a pour concrete foundation. In later years, the walls were covered in semi-rough concrete stucco. Additionally, at some point, the units with the parapet roofs were modified and given a replacement medium pitch gable roof system.

There were also variations of the duplex residential units. The smaller of the duplexes were rectangular buildings approximately 55 feet long by 25 feet wide (1,375 sq. Ft.). The building construction was the same as the single dwellings with concrete walls on poured concrete foundations. Consistent with the single dwellings, all the duplexes had flat roofs and those with parapets were, at some point, given the medium-pitched gable roof system.

The site had offset duplex units. These units were comprised of two rectangular 55 feet long by 25 feet wide (1,375 sq. Ft., together 2,750 sq. Ft.) structures combined together but offset by approximately five feet. Tese units were also concrete structures sitting on poured concrete foundations. At some point, all of the offset duplexes had the pitched roof modification applied.

The two-bedroom duplexes comprised a rectangular structure measuring approximately 65 feet long by 25 feet wide (1,625 sq. Ft.). The building was concrete resting on a concrete foundation. These building also had the pitched roof system modification at some point.

Over time, several of the residential units were converted for other uses after UC Riverside took ownership. The Building that houses KUCR radio is a former duplex residence. Other buildings were tuned into maintenance buildings, carpentry shops, and a laundry facility.

CAMP HAAN
THE HISTORY OF RIVERSIDE'S WORLD WAR II ANTI-AIRCRAFT TRAINING CENTER

Additional Construction

In 1943 a nursery school was added at 756 Linden Street. This was a much-needed addition to the community since there was a large number of women entering the workforce to help the war effort. It serviced approximately 30 children between the ages of two and five.

In 1964 a park and a playgound was added to the site along with a picnic pavilion near the intersection of Cherry and Florida Street.

The areas around the site saw growth as well as families moved in. Grocery stores opened, and there was a community hall nearby that showed motion pictures, housed the local newspaper and activities such as Boy Scouts, Girl Scouts, and a women's club.

According to Steve Lech, a Riverside County local historian, the name of the housing complex has changed over the years[212]. What was originally the Blaine Street Housing Complex was later deemed Married Student Housing (mid-1980s) and finally the Canyon Crest Housing Complex (CCH).

Administration

Almost immediately after being built the U.S. Army turned over administrative control of CCH to the Federal Public Housing Authority (FPHA). In 1942, the control was passed to the Housing Authority of the County of Riverside (HACR).

With the drawdown of World War II, CCH was scheduled for disposition, just like many of the World War II buildings; however, with the hostilities in Korea government retained the property. The HACR managed the site until 1954 when after two years of negotiation with the U.S. Government and HACR, the property and buildings were sold to UC Riverside for $600,000.

Part of the arrangement in the sales was that UC Riverside would allow the current tenants to stay as long as they needed.

Blaine Street Housing Complex Today

For many years, UC Riverside used the complex for housing and other functions. The complex was evaluated for listing on the

National Register and the California Register and was deemed that the complex, located away from military bases merely played a supporting role in the war effort by providing housing and did not meet the criteria to be considered historical to the region, coupled by the fact that UC Riverside made improvements to the buildings after assuming ownership like doors and windows, and gabling the roof.

As of this writing, the entire complex has been razed in favor of newer, modern student housing buildings on the UC Riverside

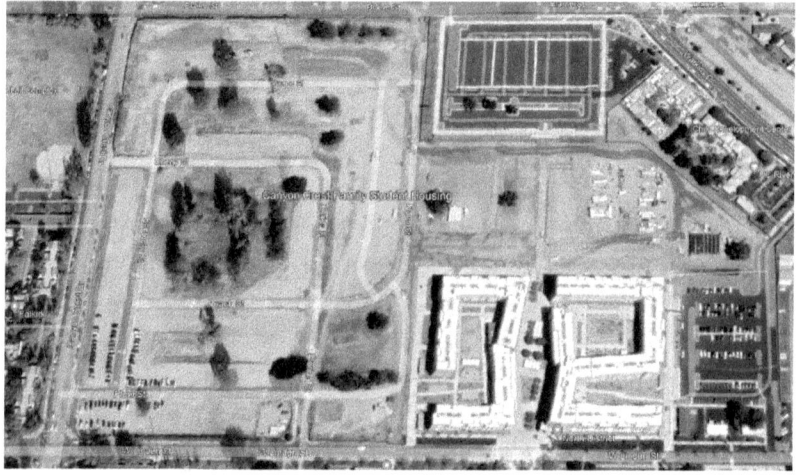

Blaine Street Housing (Canyon Crest Family Housing) in April 2021. Notice all the structures have been removed and housing buildings for UC Riverside are being added.
Source: Google Earth

campus. The UC Riverside developmental plan calls for residence halls for 3,000, apartments complex for 2,000, recreation fields, and a parking structure.[213]

Disciplinary Barracks

After World War I, many of the disciplinary barracks used during the war were turned over or leased to the Department of Justice. In 1940, the Army brought back the disciplinary barracks with one major shift, instead of just housing prisoners, there was more emphasis placed on rehabilitation to return them to duty. During this period of U.S. Disciplinary Barracks, more emphasis was placed on school than ever before. In some cases, prisoners were allowed to attend school during the day rather than work and "earn their keep."

With the United States' entry into the war and the increase of Army troop strength, brought with it an increase in the prisoner population. The Army required more prisons to house the demand. By July 1944, three branches were designated[214] and 13 more by the end of the war. Camp Haan would be one of these 13. Designated as the southwestern branch of the U.S. Disciplinary Barracks for confinement of general prisoners on Friday, May 26, 1945.[215] Colonel E. A. Everitt arrived to take command of the

Source: Los Angeles Times, Sunday, June 24, 1945

southwestern branch of the U.S. Disciplinary Barracks on June 23, 1945.[216]

The prisoners were closely supervised and required to work 44 hours per week to "earn their keep." They wore blue fatigue uniforms with the letters USDB marked on the back. Throughout the war, the camp Quartermaster General would guide a lot of the prisoners' work. It was not uncommon to see USDB prisoners working in the various machine and electrical shops, the salvage yards, carpenter shops, laundry, and in the case of California-based USDBs, working for the forestry service.[217]

U.S. Disciplary Barracks layout, Camp Haan, 1945-1946.
Source: Camp Haan Project Map. U.S. Engineer Office. August 1948. Camp Haan Map Project Map. Southern California Real Property Disposal Case Files, 1946-1962. RG 269 Records of the General Services Administration. Box 58; National Archives and Records Administration, Riverside, CA.

CAMP HAAN
THE HISTORY OF RIVERSIDE'S WORLD WAR II ANTI-AIRCRAFT TRAINING CENTER

A portion of Camp Haan's Topside was cordoned off with double fencing for the disciplinary barracks. The U.S Army added guard towers around the perimeter This was undoubtedly a cost saving effort and made sense since training was wrapping up due to V-E Day a few weeks before the camp was designated a disciplinary barracks. The areas that were used were 30-32. Since these areas we used for soldiers assignd to the AATC for training, the disciplinary barracks had all the ameneities that regular Army soldier had such as; barracks, mess halls, latrines, administrative and supply areas, a training auditorium, recreational auditorium, and day rooms.

Expansion

In a 3103 audit in May of 1950 that listed all the land purchased or leased under the since the 1943 expansion, notably 32 properties were purchased through declaration of taking, War Powers Act (WPA)[218], 7 properties were donated by the landowners.

The topside area of Camp Haan was built as an expansion in 1943 to further expand the anti-air training. The area would be referred to as the "Topside" area of Camp Haan because this area was built on the southwest side of Camp Haan on an elevated plateau west of Regimental Area 1. The Topside area would add 13 more battalion areas to the camp's infrastructure. The Topside area was such a major expansion that the existing electrical into the camp could not support the expansion, so the Topside part of the camp was fed from an entirely separate electrical substation.[219]

CAMP HAAN
THE HISTORY OF RIVERSIDE'S WORLD WAR II ANTI-AIRCRAFT TRAINING CENTER

Camp Haan "Topside" building layout
Source: Camp Haan Project Map. U.S. Engineer Office. August 1948.
Camp Haan Map Project Map. Southern California Real Property
Disposal Case Files, 1946-1962. RG 269 Records of the General Services
Administration. Box 58; National Archives and Records Administration,
Riverside, CA.

Topside Pool

Pool was complete in 1943, could accommodate nearly 500 men. It was a popular spot after an afternoon on the obstacle course. It would be used for training during the week and allowed for recreational use on the weekend from Saturday afternoon and all-day Sunday.

Prisoner of War Camp

Since before the U.S. entered the war, Great Britain had been housing prisoners of war in the various theaters of operation. In fact, by the time the United States entered the war, Great Britain held 23,000 German and 250,000 Italian prisoners.[220]

Once the U.S. entered the war, the decision was made to transport the prisoners of war back to the U.S. (Zone of the Interior). Once ships made the Atlantic crossing with U.S. military troops, then the ships would return back to the U.S. with wounded and POWs.

Once captured, in the field by combat troops, POWs started a journey that ultimately end with them in POW camps in the Zone of the Interior. Combat troops would advance the POWs up through the echelons to the Corps level. At that point the POWs were screened by Army intelligence and then custody was handed off to Army Military Police. From this point, POWs were held in theater, in what the Army called enclosures, and placed into labor companies as needed. They were then sent to a port or control point, where they were transported to the U.S.

CAMP HAAN
THE HISTORY OF RIVERSIDE'S WORLD WAR II ANTI-AIRCRAFT TRAINING CENTER

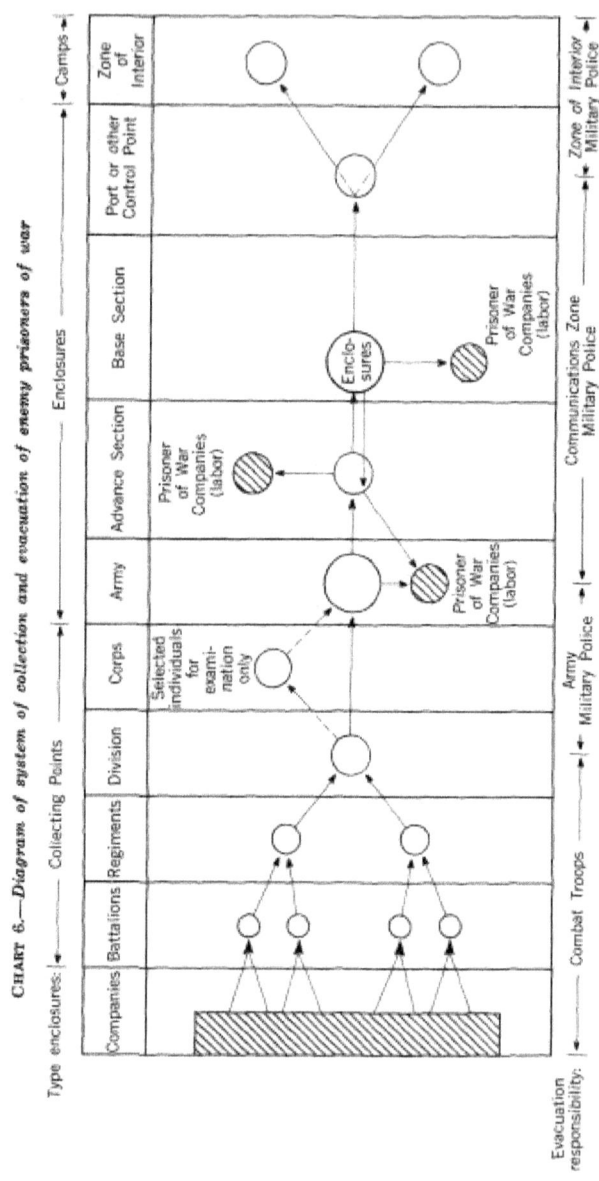

Flow of enemy prisoners of war during World War II.
Source: AMEDD Center for History & Heritage. Preventive Medicine in World War II. Vol. 9. 1969. Ch06p353.jpg (640×398) (usgovcloudapi.net)

CAMP HAAN
THE HISTORY OF RIVERSIDE'S WORLD WAR II ANTI-AIRCRAFT TRAINING CENTER

By Early 1943, the detention of 425,000 enemy prisoners of war in the United States forced the Army to separate the camps into multiple separate camps.

Prisoners were segregated out by nationality and category: Italian prisoners, Japanese prisoners, German Anti-Nazi prisoners, German Nazi prisoners, German Anti-Nazi Navy prisoners, and German Nazi Navy prisoners. Russian soldiers captured wearing German uniforms were considered German Nazi prisoners.[221]

Standards for housing prisoners of war was governed by the Geneva Conventions of 1929 stated that POW camps provide, "housing that was sanitary, healthful, and adequately heated and lighted." Every POW camp in the United States initially met and then exceeded the Geneva Convention requirement.

By 1943, there was a shortage of manpower due to the number of fighting age males actively involved in World War II, this led the Army to begin to use the prisoners as labor manpower. Prisoners who worked were given a daily wage of $0.80 in canteen credits in addition to the $0.10 per day that the Geneva Conventions required to be used for necessities. Enlisted prisoners were required to work if they wanted to be paid; however, the officer prisoners were not required to work and still received regular pay. If the officer prisoner decided to work, they had the opportunity to earn wages above the regular rate. As high as 95% of the enemy prisoners, who could work, were employed by private building contractors of in military installations.[222]

The wages received by the POW was deposited into the POW's account, and the POW would receive a check at time of repatriation for the full amount of account balance. POWs could withdraw funds from their account for the purpose of purchasing items from the canteen using coupons, or "chits".

POW Chit, Camp Haan, 1944-1946
Source: personal

Items that could be purchased included: stationery and postage, soap and shaving supplies, cigarettes, and tobacco, and even beer.

Designated as a POW camp in April 1944, built and established September 9, 1944 initially as a branch camp of Camp Florence, AZ. It was not long before Camp Haan POW camp became a base camp and POW separation center. Other POW camps that were designated branch camps of Camp Haan:

Camp Phoenix, AZ
Camp Anza, CA
Camp Lockett #1, CA
Camp Locket #2, CA
Camp Palm Springs, CA
Santa Ana Air Base, CA

POWs also contributed to the Victory Chest Drive in 1945. The Chino Champion, a local newspaper at the time, reported that German prisoners from Camp Haan received permission and contributed $519.47 to the Victory Chest Drive (Otherwise known as the Eight War Loan ran from October 29 - December 8, 1945)[223] specifically for the Young Men's Christian Association.[224]

Originally there were 1 guard to every 10 prisoners, but later this was expanded to 1 guard to 32 prisoners. Commanders also had the leeway to source guards from the civilians in the event there was not enough Army personnel. Guards supervised the prisoners during movement armed with carbines and rifles. At several camps, canines were also used.

Camp Haan operated a prisoner of war camp on the northern end of the camp, north of the hospital area.

Generally, the food that the prisoners had was equivalent to what the American servicemen were receiving. Some substitutions were made for ethnic preferences. The Italian POWs, of example, had an increase in pasta and noodles and a decrease in meat. Meals were served three times a day and there were special meals prepared on all major holidays.

The POWs all wore uniforms with distinctive "PW" stenciled on both the front an back.

Some POW camps had their own theaters and recreation areas. From camp layout maps of Camp Haan, it does not appear they had separate theaters and recreation. In this case, the POWs were scheduled to use the theaters when the military and civilian personnel on the camp were not using the buildings. The same

Typical POW dress in WWII. This photograph is from a POW housed at Camp Gruber, Oklahoma, 1945. Source: Oklahoma National Guard

process occurred with the chapels.

There was not an abundance of German and Italian translators, so typically the translators travelled from camp to camp on a recurring basis to provide services.[225]

Prisoner of War Camp, Camp Haan, 1944-1946.
Source: Camp Haan Project Map. U.S. Engineer Office. August 1948. Camp Haan Map Project Map. Southern California Real Property Disposal Case Files, 1946-1962. RG 269 Records of the General Services Administration. Box 58; National Archives and Records Administration, Riverside, CA.

The prisoners did all sorts of activities on camp Haan as well as March Field. "It was a familiar site to see prisoners of war doing household chores," Stated Technical Sergeant John Williamson, March Air Force Base Historian in a May 1995 article in The Press-Enterprise.[226]

Prisoners from Camp Haan labor jobs for the community. One of the many recurring jobs that the prisoners took part in was in the various citrus fields and vineyards for both harvesting and pruning in and around Riverside. Many of the local grower welcomed the extra hands and commented highly on the quality of work they produced. They were also used as a labor force to expand Camp Haan. Prisoners were sent to Mitchell Convalescent Hospital, Camp Lockett, Campo, California to work.

There are records that Camp Haan housed 248 German and 213 Italian prisoners. These POWs worked in local citrus orchards.[227] It is estimated that the work the prisoners provided save an estimated $157 million dollars over the course of the war.

Escapes from the camps was expected, and several did occur. In fact, an average of 55 POWs a month began fleeing the camps after VE-day once it was announced that the prisoners would be returned to Europe, many into Russian-occupied zones.[228]

On April 13, 1946, A German prisoner, Ruldoph Soelch, escaped while working the citrus fields near Pomona.[229] German sympathizers James and Lydia McBride picked up Soelch, a former Hermann Goering Bodyguard and Nazi. After they picked up Soelch, they fled to Detroit. Soelch was ultimately recaptured in Detroit, Michigan after being harbored by Lydia McBride. According to the Detroit Free Press, while being harbored, Soelch and Mrs. McBride fell in love. Dismayed, James left moved to Pennsylvania. After a somewhat lengthly court battle of "he said/she said," eventually, both James and Lydia McBride were charged with harboring a prisoner of war and were sentanced to four years each[230] by Judge Arthur F. Lederle. Soelch was deported

German POW and escapee, Rudolph Soelch
Source: Detroit Free Press, Wednesday, January 8, 1947

back to Germany on January 23, 1947.

Wife Says Husband Aided POW

Denies Any Role of Escape Plot

Mrs. Lydia Joan McBride, 42, testified in Federal Court Friday that her husband, James, 40, aided the escape of a 24-year-old German prisoner of war without her knowledge.

"I didn't know what it was all about," she said. "My husband drove me to a secluded spot near the California prison camp after ordering me to put some old clothes in the car.

* * *

"HE PICKED up Rudolph Soelch, a German war prisoner whom I knew. It was the first I knew that he had escaped."

In a voice choked with emotion, blond, German-born Mrs. McBride told the jury of 12 women:

"I fell in love with Hugo Dorn Soelch's alias when we arrived in Detroit. I lived with him after my husband left me. I would have married him if I had been free."

* * *

THE McBRIDES are accused of aiding Soelch's escape last April 12 and subsequently of harboring him in Detroit.

Soelch, named as a co-conspirator, has been placed in contempt of court for failure to tell who aided his escape. He has claimed protection of the Geneva Convention.

The Government sought to reopen its case, announcing that Soelch wished to purge himself of contempt. Judge Arthur F. Lederle overruled the motion.

* * *

IN PLACING full blame for aiding in the escape on her estranged husband, Mrs. McBride contradicted an alleged confession signed when arrested by FBI agents with Soelch in a rooming house at 74 Edmund Place Sept. 13.

"I took full responsibility for the escape of Hugo, because I didn't want my husband or my relatives to get into trouble," she said.

The trial will continue Monday.

Source: Detroit Free Press, Tuesday, January 28, 1947

CAMP HAAN
THE HISTORY OF RIVERSIDE'S WORLD WAR II ANTI-AIRCRAFT TRAINING CENTER

James McBride's WWII Draft Card
Source: The National Archives in St. Louis, Missouri; St. Louis, Missouri; WWII Draft Registration Cards for Washington, 10/16/1940-03/31/1947; Record Group: Records of the Selective Service System, 147; Box: 77

Couple Gets Four Years for Aid to POW

Source: Detroit Free Press, Tuesday, September 17, 1946

MRS. JOAN McBRIDE
Accused of harboring POW

JAMES McBRIDE
'She betrayed my country'

Source: Detroit Free Press, Saturday, June 11, 1947

By 1946, a lot of the branch camps were winding down operations and prisoners were being re-assigned to base camps. The prisoner of war camp at the Los Angeles Fairgrounds was being vacated and the a few hundred prisoners were re-assigned to Camp Haan.[231]

Italian Service Units
In 1943, Secretary of War Henry Stimson proposed the idea of organizing POWs into units to provide labor like the Civilian Conservation Corps (CCC). In 1944 a group of Italian prisoners was formed into an "Italian Service Unit (ISU)" to provide vehicle and other maintenance for the camp. ISUs had increased responsibilities resulting in increased privileges. It is estimated that 65% of Italian POWs signed up for ISU. The men selected for this unit are thoroughly screened by Army Intelligence to ensure they were not pro-Nazi or pro-Fascist. Intelligence screening remained continuous and the Italian POW could lose their privilege at any point and returned to the Prisoner of War compound. Typically, men in the ISU were segregated from the rest of the POWs, this was the case at Camp Haan also. The members of the ISU are house in similar housing to house used by the regular army, 16 x 16 pyramidal huts and have the freedoms of the camp's recreational and worship facilities. On weekends these men also received permission go beyond the gates, in small groups with escorts.[232]

The reception to the POW camps in the United States, in general, was received with caution, but eventually most cities came to appreciate the additional labor that the POW camps brought.

Repatriation
Eventually all the POWs were returned home in accordance with the Geneva Convention. Several departure points were utilized to repatriate the POWs, the same points of departures that were used to ferry U.S. troops to the European and Pacific theaters; Los Angeles, New York, Boston, San Francisco, and New Orleans were among the ports. As ships were returning U.S. troops home, the ships were turned around and loaded with POWs. The last of the POWs were repatriated by June 30, 1946 thus marking an end to stateside POW camps for World War II.

CAMP HAAN
THE HISTORY OF RIVERSIDE'S WORLD WAR II ANTI-AIRCRAFT TRAINING CENTER

The maximum number of German POWs held by the United States was 371,683. The maximum number of Italian POWs reached 51,156. In total, there were 1,193 POW camps, ISU camps, and POW hospitals.[233] There were POW camps in every state except Nevada and Vermont.

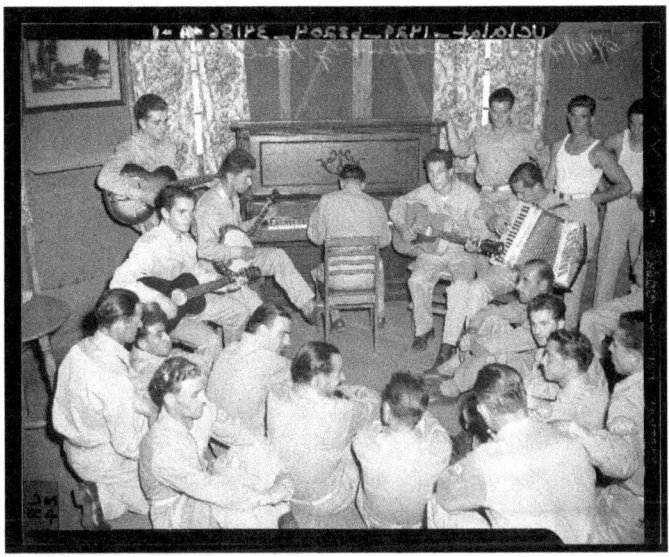

Title: Italian war prisoners playing music at Camp Haan, Calif., 1944
Collection: Los Angeles Times Photographic Archives
Owning Institution: UCLA, Library Special Collections, Charles E. Young Research Library

Separation Center

August 16, 1945, Army designated Camp Haan as a separation center

> **Camp Haan New Separation Center**
>
> Camp Haan, near Riverside, yesterday was designated as one of five additional army separation centers which probably will be added to the 22 already in existence throughout the country to speed the discharge of personnel.

Source: San Pedro News, August 17, 1945

Even prior to this, in October 1944, Camp Haan designated am Army Service storage and separation center to support the Los Angeles port of embarkation (31 Oct 1944 - San Bernardino Sun) Class I Army installation.

The War Department performed analysis on holdings and looked at the utilization of facilities owned or leased by the War Department throughout the war, and as the war was drawing down, certain installation that were declared "excess" by the War Department were prime locations for other uses.

By April 1945, the War Department canceled contracts for additional construction at ports, training centers, and depots, except for the programs that were adding additional hospital and separation center capacity.[234]

Debarkation Center

Initially, Camp Anza was designated as a debarkation center in Early June 1945 and was quickly moved to Camp Haan. June 28, 1945, Army announced that Camp Haan would be a debarkation center.[235] Operations started on July 9, 1945 and U.S. Troop returnees would spend no more than 48 hours at the camp awaiting transportation to personnel centers across the country.[236]

Birmingham General Hospital (Los Angeles) was designated as an evacuation hospital and the Surgeon General did not like the hospital performing dual roles as an evacuation and debarkation hospital and attempted to limit the use of general hospitals as debarkation hospitals. At that time, it had 800 beds dedicated to debarkation. At the same time across the United States (both East and West Coast) there were a total of 22,332 total hospital beds, 10,365 were strictly for debarkation.[237]

In June 1945 Camp Haan regional hospital also took over the processing of patients debarked at Los Angeles from Birmingham General Hospital. Wounded and sick GIs from the hospital ships were also processed at Camp Haan.[238] One notable patient that was known to come through Camp Haan was Major. Winthrop Rockefeller, grandson of John D. Rockefeller.[239]

Once Japan surrendered in September 1945, the Army started to transition many of the support units for returning soldiers and wounded. The Camp Haan hospital once again was directed to transition and was named a prisoner survey hospital on September 19, 1945.[240]

Shortly thereafter, the camp began to downsize and was utilized as a storage center and collection point for equipment and supplies.
The total troop capacity of the posts and camps during the war was 2,450,000 personnel, by May 31, 1946 the personnel capacity had been reduced to 995,000. Along with this reduction in capacity, 35 general hospitals, 26 post installations, and 45 prisoner of war camps were also place in "surplus" category. Personnel assigned to the Army Service Force (ASF) was reduced to 50%, 1,227,000 to 638,000.

On June 11, 1946 the Army Service Force (ASF) ceased to exist and the major functions were returned back to the War Department General and Special Staff.[241]

CHAPTER 7
POST-WORLD WAR II

After the surrender of Germany and Japan, military personnel demobilized in a process called Operation Magic Carpet. This was a slow process to not only get military personnel back from the theaters of war, but then they had to be processed. In 1945, as the defeat of Germany and Japan were realized, the United States had 12 million military personnel overseas; through demobilization and out processing, by mid-1947, that number dropped to 1.5 million, a reduction of almost 90%.

Even with all the functions that Camp Haan had transitioned to since the antiaircraft training center, Camp Haan's days were numbered, and Camp Haan was officially closed on August 31, 1946.[242] With exception of the laundry facilities. Camp Haan had rather large laundry facilities and that remained open so the ath quartermasters could utilize the resource for March Field and the remaining personnel at the facility.

CAMP HAAN
THE HISTORY OF RIVERSIDE'S WORLD WAR II ANTI-AIRCRAFT TRAINING CENTER

> Reproduced from the holdings of the *National Archives at Riverside*
>
> WAR DEPARTMENT
> The Adjutant General's Office
> Washington 25, D. C.
>
> AGAM-PM 602 (27 Aug 46)   6 September 1946
> AO-I-MDGSP/C2
>
> SUBJECT: Surplus - Camp Haan, California
>
> TO: Commanding Generals:
>   Army Air Forces
>   Army Ground Forces
>   Sixth Army
>   Chief of Engineers
>
> 1. Effective as of 31 August 1946, Camp Haan, California, is placed in the category of surplus, with the exception of the quartermaster laundry which is classified as a class III activity and placed under the jurisdiction of the Commanding General, Army Air Forces. It is, therefore, desired that action be initiated to dispose of this installation, with the exception noted above, in accordance with applicable laws, directives, and regulations.
>
> 2. Additionally, it is desired, that all appropriate agencies be notified of the last date for transmission of mail to this installation which does not concern action to be taken in connection with its closing.
>
> 3. Agencies concerned with the furnishing of supplies and equipment to this installation will cancel all back orders for such supplies and equipment and will furnish only those required by the station to efficiently fulfill any action required in its orderly closing. The provisions of ASF Manual M 706, 30 April 1945, will apply.
>
> BY ORDER OF THE SECRETARY OF WAR:
>
> B. M. FITCH
> Brigadier General
> Acting The Adjutant General

Source: Southern California Real Property Disposal Case Files, 1946-1962. Region 9. RG 269 Records of the General Services Administration. Box 58; National Archives and Records Administration, Riverside, CA.

Salvage

Following the end of World War II, unneeded fighters, and bombers, such as the P-40, B-25, B-24, and B-17, were quickly phased out and retired.

CAMP HAAN
THE HISTORY OF RIVERSIDE'S WORLD WAR II ANTI-AIRCRAFT TRAINING CENTER

Flight crews ferried the bombers back across the Atlantic and Pacific to the United States where the majority were sold for scrap and melted down at disposal depots and desert boneyards such as Kingman Army Airfield in Arizona. While not on the scale of Kingman, Camp Haan operated a salvage yard at the end of the war.

Camp Haan always had a salvage area in areas 4 and 1. Area 6 salvage area was created in 1945 just prior to closure, between area 4 and the railyard; on Avenue A and 24th Street and had parceled off some additional space for aluminum salvage as early as 1945. Salvage proved dangerous as well, when on July 15, 1946, civilian contractor Robert L. Carpenter from Grand Ridge, Florida, while working salvage, was killed when he came in contact with a high-tension wire carrying 33,000 volts. He left behind his wife, Grace which he married in 1922. Also injured were Ivan Glidewell and Simeon Rosson.[243]

WWII draft registration card of Robert Carpenter
Source: The National Archives in St. Louis, Missouri; St. Louis, Missouri; WWII Draft Registration Cards for Florida, 10/16/1940-03/31/1947; **Record Group**: Records of the Selective Service System, 147; **Box**: 72

The War Assets Administration (WAA) contracted with the Metal Reserve Company to use some land on the north end of Camp Haan for a salvage depot for industrial scrap aluminum. The permit was signed on November 27, 1946 and was valid for a 5-year period. The salvage yard was used as a dismantling and staging facility for aircraft aluminum and other aluminum awaiting to be melted down. Camp Haan certainly burned miscellaneous trash and refuse at the salvage yard; however, all the smelting operations took place off site in the nearby cities of Corona (Northeast side) and Ontario (South of the Santa Fe pre-cooling plant[244])[245] and operated by the west coast branch of Aluminum-Magnesium Inc. after the city of Colton disapproved of the smelting plant.[246]

Salvage at Camp Haan, circa 1946-1948. Note the Speery ball turrets from B-17s or B-24s in the foreground.
Source: Yeager Family Library, March Field Air Museum

Salvage at Camp Haan, circa 1946-1948. Note the wing piece with the US insignia.
Source: Yeager Family Library, March Field Air Museum

Salvage at Camp Haan, circa 1946-1948.
Source: Yeager Family Library, March Field Air Museum

Salvage at Camp Haan, circa 1946-1948. These appear to be aircraft fuel tanks.
Source: Yeager Family Library, March Field Air Museum

Salvage crews loading the remains of B-17 "Suzy-Q" 1946-1948. These appear to be aircraft fuel tanks.
Source: Yeager Family Library, March Field Air Museum

CAMP HAAN
THE HISTORY OF RIVERSIDE'S WORLD WAR II ANTI-AIRCRAFT TRAINING CENTER

The remains of B-17 "Suzy-Q" (41-2489) before being scrapped at Camp Haan. Records indicate that this picture was taken on/near July 15, 1946. Unknown male and female in the picture. This is likely one of the last pictures of the famous B-17.
Source: Yeager Family Library, March Field Air Museum
Source: R. Freeman & D. Osbourne (2000) The B-17 Flying Fortress Story. Arms & Armour, ISBN-13: 978-1854095220

CAMP HAAN
THE HISTORY OF RIVERSIDE'S WORLD WAR II ANTI-AIRCRAFT TRAINING CENTER

Note about B-17 "Suzy-Q"
The B-17 was known for taking far more punishment than any other plane in the air. The R.A.F only signified their bombers by numbers, whereas the Fortress crews had a variety of names they personalized. Because the bomber could take more damage and remain airworthy, the B-17 started to accumulate records that were published and used in newpapers and stories during the war. Perhaps the most famous was the Memphis Belle…still being remembered 70 + years after the war. Suzy Q was another one of those planes that had a significant history itself.

One of the fightinest fortresses to ever get in newspaper print in two continents was a lady called Suzy Q. This member of the nineteenth Bombardment Group…had been in action since the outbreak of the war. On her nose was painted an astonishing list of places she had visited, and on her side was a panel bearing twenty-six rising suns, to tell the world that Suzy's gunners had knocked off twenty-six Japanese planes.

Along the sides of her graceful fuselage, in her tail, and on her wings were many patches. They covered bullet holes she had received in battles over Macassar Straits, Java, Borneo, the Celebes, Rabaul, and New Guinea. She had logged more that 2,000 hourse in the air and had been hit more time than you could count; yet not one of her crew had been killed or injured. Some of the tales told of Suzy Q are unorthodox for even a well-trained bomber. On one occasion, she ran out of fuel and had to be brought down in a small clearing in northern Australian bushland. The spot was isolated, and there were no means of assistance near by. The crew went four days without food while they waited for gasoline to be dropped. They filled the time by building a runway so Suzy Q could take off after fuel arrived.

Cont'd

CAMP HAAN
THE HISTORY OF RIVERSIDE'S WORLD WAR II ANTI-AIRCRAFT TRAINING CENTER

> *Suzy's commander, Lieutentant Colonel Felix Hardison, opened up the motors with the brakes still on. Suzy Quivered like a racehorse and then, as the brakes were released, she tore into the air as if she were shot out by a rubber band.*
> Excerpt from Bombers by Keith Ayling
>
> After returning to the U.S., Lt. Col. Hardison said, "You know, there are three beautiful things in this world – a woman, a thoroughbred horse, and a flying fortress."
> The crew also commented that, " Suzy Q should be awarded the Congressional Medal of Honor. She never failed us. She crossed the equator four times, and flew thirty-five thaousand miles around the world."

The remains of B-17 "Suzy-Q" (41-2489) before being scrapped at Camp Haan. Records indicate that this picture was taken on/near July 15, 1946. This is likely one of the last pictures of the famous B-17.
Source: Yeager Family Library, March Field Air Museum

1940s era salvage equipment at Camp Haan
Source: Yeager Family Library, March Field Air Museum

With exception of the salvage yard and remaining command staff, a few security guards, and logistics personnel, Camp Haan remained almost vacant the remainder of the year. The entire camp was declared surplus by the War Assets Administration (WAA) on January 20, 1947.[247]

The Great Sell Off

Camp Haan's fate was sealed on February 28, 1947 when the commanding general officially turned over command to the War Assets Administration (WAA), Los Angeles District Engineers [248] and approved its permanent closure; declared that all assets were to be removed from the camp. All personal and installed property was transferred from the Sixth Army to the WAA; this included property necessary for maintenance, fire protection, and guarding. Not included in the surplus declaration were certain tracts of land, easements for runway operations, the laundry facilities, and the utilities such as the electric stations, sewage, and water treatment plants. March Field took over all utility contracts of Camp Haan and invoiced back the WAA for utilities that the scant staff used throughout the selling process. Telephone contracts were also terminated.[249]

CAMP HAAN
THE HISTORY OF RIVERSIDE'S WORLD WAR II ANTI-AIRCRAFT TRAINING CENTER

Because of the proximity of March Airfield, the Army retained 672.89 acres[250]. the WAA, in coordination with March Field, started the transfer of real and installed property to March Field occurred in 1947 through 1949 as the War Assets Administration determined that the buildings were needed; that amounted to 192 buildings. Even so, there was still many assets that needed to be dealt with and as early as December 1946, the WAA began placing advertisements in the local papers.

Also, during this time, the incinerator (T-5911) was dismantled and destroyed. A large pit was created next to the building and it was bulldozed into that hole along with landfill materials and covered. This area was included on the Defense Environmental Restoration Program for Formally Used Defense Sites (DERP-FUDS). Today this area is part of the Riverside National Cemetery service area.

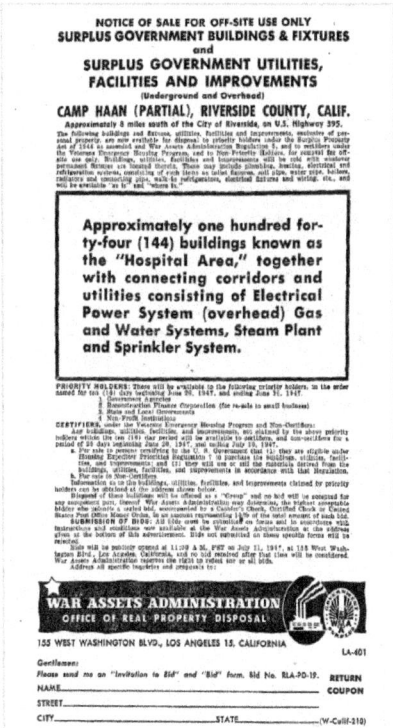

WSA advertisement for the sale of Camp Haan hospital buildings and fixtures.
Source: Southern California Real Property Disposal Case Files, 1946-1962. Region 9. RG 269 Records of the General Services Administration. Box 58; National Archives and Records Administration, Riverside, CA.

CAMP HAAN
THE HISTORY OF RIVERSIDE'S WORLD WAR II ANTI-AIRCRAFT TRAINING CENTER

Reproduced from the holdings of the *National Archives at Riverside*

NOTICE OF SALE
(FOR OFF-SITE USE ONLY)

SURPLUS GOVERNMENT BUILDINGS AND FIXTURES

CAMP HAAN (PARTIAL)
RIVERSIDE COUNTY, CALIF.

Approximately 8 miles east of the City of Riverside on U.S. Highway 395.

The following buildings, fixtures and utilities, exclusive of personal property, are now available for disposal to priority holders under the Surplus Property Act of 1944, as amended, and War Assets Administration Regulation No. 5, and to non-profit holders for removal for off-site use only. These may include plumbing, heating, electrical and refrigeration systems, etc.

Approximately 134 buildings or structures, more or less (temporary military type) and 12 items of residual utilities consisting of:

Hutments	Bomb Shelters	Sewer Collection System
Officers Quarters	Supply Rooms	Water Distribution Systems
Recreation Halls	Mess Halls	Electrical Distribution Systems
Hospital Buildings	Dayrooms	Railroad and Turnouts
Hospital Boiler Houses	Latrines	Gas Distribution Systems
Gas Stations	Warehouses	Fuel Oil Storage & Dispensing
Administration Bldgs.	Sentry Houses	System.
Fencing & Miscellaneous type buildings.		

All of the above offered as individual items; and
One Group of 73 buildings together with connecting open and enclosed walkways, sprinkler system and steam distribution system contained therein; and
One Group of 7 buildings; and
One Group of 2 buildings with connecting walk-ways.
No bid will be accepted for any component part where these buildings are offered as a "Group".

PRIORITIES: This offering is subject to priorities in this order:
1. Federal Agencies
2. Reconstruction Finance Corporation (for re-sale to small business)
3. State and Local Governments
4. Non-Profit Institutions
These priorities expire at 4:45 P.M. PST January 26, 1948.

SPOT BID SALE AT THE SITE
Buildings unclaimed by priority holders will be open for inspection to all interested persons commencing February 1, 1948, and ending February 10, 1948, Monday through Friday 9:00 A.M. to 4:00 P.M.
Buildings unclaimed by priority holders will be offered for "Spot Sale" at the Officers Club, Camp Haan, Riverside County, California at 9:00 A.M. PST on February 10, 1948. Bidders can purchase buildings for cash at this time and receive permission to commence removal operations within five days.
All bids must be submitted on "Bid Cards" which will be furnished to bidders at the time of the "Spot Sale".
War Assets Administration reserves the right to reject any and all bids and to withdraw from sale any buildings offered hereunder.
Write to the address shown below for catalog describing buildings and giving terms and conditions of sale.

WAR ASSETS ADMINISTRATION
Office of Real Property Disposal
Mail Address:
Camp Haan, Route #4
Riverside County, California
Telephone: Moreno 7261

WSA advertisement for the sale of Camp Haan buildings and fixtures. Source: Southern California Real Property Disposal Case Files, 1946-1962. Region 9. RG 269 Records of the General Services Administration. Box 58; National Archives and Records Administration, Riverside, CA.

In 1947 March Field moved their bomb storage facilities over to former Camp Haan ammunition magazine area. This gave March Field an additional safety zone area for the airfield.[251] Shortly thereafter in 1947, the United States Air Force was created, and March Airfield was renamed March Air Force Base.

Throughout this process, the WAA maintained a field director (Ralph Merritt), property manager (H.H. Moore), a stenographer, a typist, 3 guards (who also served as firefighters), a carpenter, and 11 other laborers on site until the site was cleared in summer of 1948.[252] The staff occupied some of the remaining staff houses, warehouses, and dormitory space during that time, totaling 27 buildings,[253] and set up a sales office for the Real Property Division in Camp Haan's vacated Officer's Club (building T-2).[254]

The advertisements caused an initial high demand, as all the buildings were being sold for a fraction of what it cost to build them a few years earlier. Schools, school districts, religious organizations, state organizations, non-profit organizations, and private individuals all placed bids on the surplus buildings. 460 building were sold in the week of August 20, 1947 with over 1,000 buildings remaining. The state of California placed a large bid in July 1947 for the entire lot of 144 buildings in the hospital area (area 12) for $151,460 (equivalent to $1.7 mil in 2020) to be used for the California's Veteran Housing Program. In a telegram to the Office of Real Property Disposal, from Robert Alford, Deputy Regional Director of Real Property Disposal on August 20, 1947, recommended the California bid be approved. He also cited his concern that approximately 450 buildings from former Camp Anza were going up on the market. He also cited that the hospital building had passageways and corridors installed, which further complicated disposition.[255] He did not overtly state it in the telegram, but the tone of the telegram suggests that he was concerned that if the state did not purchase the hospital area buildings, then the buildings would become exceedingly difficult to off-load given that Camp Anza was also off-loading its buildings at the same time. In the end, the hospital area was sold to the State of California. There was even an instance where the owners of, what is now known as Flabob Airport in Riverside, posed as farmers to purchase a few office buildings.[256]

The War Assets Administration were selling everything including an airplane mockup, a complete obstacle course, concrete isolation shelters, guard towers, 10-ton incinerator, wires, streetlights, and even manhole covers.[257]

Approximately 4,600 buildings were sold and moved.[258] The remaining scrap was carted over to the salvage yard on the other side of camp. By September of 1948, all the buildings that were sold were gone and the site was bare except the structures that remain that were transferred to March Air Force Base.[259] All of the paved and gravel roads remained along with the sidewalks and concrete foundations. The 16" water main coming into Camp Haan from the Iowa pumping station, the contract with the City of Riverside was canceled on January 15, 1947 and was removed completely sometime in early 1948 though 20" water main coming into the west side of Camp from Lake Matthews to Camp Haan and March Field remained in place. Electricity, sewer, gas, and telephone remained functional on the Camp Haan site for the remaining buildings that March Field acquired.

Hospital Cars

20 hospital cars were placed on sale at Camp Haan during the Camp sale. As stated previously, although no such register of Camp Haan hospital having a hospital train detachment attached, certainly hospital trains were used to transport injured and wounded military personnel to various places in the country. Camp Haan would have been one of those places. It is plausible and almost certain that a hospital train was used from LA debarkation center to the Haan hospital. Moreover, since Camp Haan was used as a salvage yard, this would be an ideal location to store the hospital cars awaiting purchase or dismantling.

By 1947, most of the hospital trains mission were complete and the Army, through the War Assets Administration, began to sell off the trains. Circus Entrepreneur Ringling Brothers Barnum and Bailey Combined Shows Circus initially purchased 25 cars, Army wide, to begin to replace old World War I train cars they had acquired. They took possession in January 1948. Ringling used the train cars heavily until 1956, when the organization went to highway trucks as a primary mode of transportation.

Most of the WWII hospital train cars were out of service by 1972, many of which sold off for scrap metal. Some still exist today in various places, still their story was not over -- fifteen of them quickly came out of retirement to serve as structures within Ringling's Circus World theme park (1974-1986) near Orlando, FL. Many of them served three more years within its successor park, Boardwalk and Baseball (1986-1990). Two of those went on to serve for decades as Grandpa's Steakhouse in Cocoa, FL (1992-2018).[260]

Possible Air Force Academy Location

The Camp Haan site briefly saw some possible life in 1950, A group of Army engineers toured the site and surrounding areas on January 10, 1950, headed by Lt. Col. Jackson Graham of the Los Angeles District for the Army Corps of Engineers.[261] In November, General Carl Spaatz, engineers, and surveyors toured the site and added it to list of possible suitable locations to establish an air academy that would function as West Point and the Naval

Air Academy Group To Visit Site Today

RIVERSIDE, Dec. 12 — The Camp Haan-March A.F.B. area's future as the site of a projected West Point of the Air Force may be decided tomorrow when an A. F. Academy site selection board headed by retired A. F. Gen. Carl T. Spaatz visits here.

The board will fly into M.A.F.B. from a tour of northern California sites to be met by members of the Southern California committee for the A. F. Academy, local civic leaders and educators, and M.A.F.B. officials.

They'll be taken on an immediate tour of the vast Camp Haan area, and then return to M.A.F.B. where the area's advantages as a site for the Air Force Academy will be presented to them.

Source: The San Bernardino County Sun, Wednesday, December 13, 1950.

Academy for the Air force. The Camp Haan site was one among 350 sites across the country were designated as potential sites.[262]

In December of 1950, a group of engineers and surveyors again came to the Camp Haan site to evaluate the area, and local new affiliates they, "were favorably impressed."

Ultimately, on March 9, 1951, the Air Force decided March Air Force Base-Camp Haan area did not make the cut, in fact, all of the

Air Academy Site

San Bernardino county lends its support to Riverside county, and the rest of Southern California, for the Camp Haan site for the proposed Air Academy. The Camp Haan site is immediately adjacent to March field. It was an Army camp during World war II and most of the property is still owned by the United States government.

Camp Haan is the only Southern California site which met the qualifications set up by the selection board. Three northern California locations also qualified in the preliminary investigation.

Under the leadership of the Los Angeles chamber of commerce all of Southern California has been united in support for the Riverside county location.

The movement for a Pacific coast location for the proposed Air Academy has been underway for years. The Atlantic coast has the Navy Academy at Annapolis and the Army Academy at West Point. The Pacific coast therefore contends that there should be recognition for this great and growing section of the nation. Probably that argument will not be the basis upon which the decision is made by the selection board.

Certainly, however, Southern California has elements that must be taken into consideration in the selection of a site for the principal training base for the future officers of the Air Force. First are the flying conditions. The interior of Southern California—of which Camp Haan is a part—has far more flying days than most other sections of the country. Second, is the proximity of Camp Haan to the airplane manufacturing industry and to the technical schools that could be of assistance in scientific training.

Then come the great air fields which would be needed in the training of cadets. March field and Norton field in San Bernardino are operated by the Air Force. Then there is the great naval experimental station at Inyokern, less than an hour's flying time distant.

Life at the Air Academy would not be all work and no play. Easily accessible are such great natural attractions as the San Bernardino mountains, the desert and the ocean. U. S. Highway No. 395 serves Camp Haan and it in turn connects or will soon connect with great state freeways leading to all parts of Southern California. All of the colleges and universities of Southern California have pledged their cooperation to the Air Academy, and in all of them are scientists who are closely associated with the development of aviation. All of the airplane manufacturing companies of Southern California have offered their cooperation in the training of the Navy's aviation experts of the future.

San Bernardino county has, of course, a direct interest in urging the selection of the Camp Haan site, for it is in close proximity to this county.

Representations have already been made to Congressman Harry R. Sheppard that his constituents would be pleased to have him join in whatever arguments are necessary at Washington in behalf of the Riverside county location.

Source: The San Bernardino County Sun, Thursday, January 4, 1951.

Army Eliminates Camp Haan Site as Air Academy

Almost two years of county promotion apparently went by the boards this week when an announcement from Washington, D.C. indicated that the Camp Haan-March Air Force Base area is out of the running for the Air Force Academy site.

Air Force Secretary Thomas K. Finletter said that possible sites for the Academy had been narrowed to seven. The only one of the seven in California is Camp Beale near Marysville.

The announcement came as a blow to Riverside county and Southern Californians who had united to promote the local site.

IN DECEMBER, an Air Force Academy site selection board toured the area and heard presentations by leading Southern California businessmen and educators. The presentations were under the direction of Donald Stevning of Riverside, member of the Southern California Air Force Academy committee and chairman of the Riverside Chamber military affairs committee and Oscar Trippet, chairman of the Southern California committee and president of the Los Angeles Chamber.

At that time the site selection board refused comment on the local site and on other sites they surveyed in California.

THE HAAN-MAFB area became an official contender for the Academy after January 1950 when U.S. engineers visited it and were "favorably impressed." At that time, the local site was one of 354 under consideration. On Nov. 17, the field was narrowed to 29 and the local site was still in the running. Later the local site became the only Southland contender and all Southern California interests rallied to promote it.

Stevning, who with other Riversiders has been boosting the Haan-MAFB site since the fall of 1949, was not available for comment on the announcement.

Source: The Desert Sun, Friday, March 9, 1951.

California sites were out of the running except for Camp Beale in Yuba County.

Once the Air Academy plan fell through, the WAA did not have any immediate plans for the Camp Haan site, so it enacted an erosion control plan which reseeded the barren camp areas with Sudan grass and domestic rye grass to provide erosion control and to keep dust down.

On April 5, 1951, Air Force Chief of Staff General Vandenberg transmitted General Order number 22 stating that Camp Hann was designated a part of March Air force Base and Camp Haan would no longer be referenced.

CAMP HAAN
THE HISTORY OF RIVERSIDE'S WORLD WAR II ANTI-AIRCRAFT TRAINING CENTER

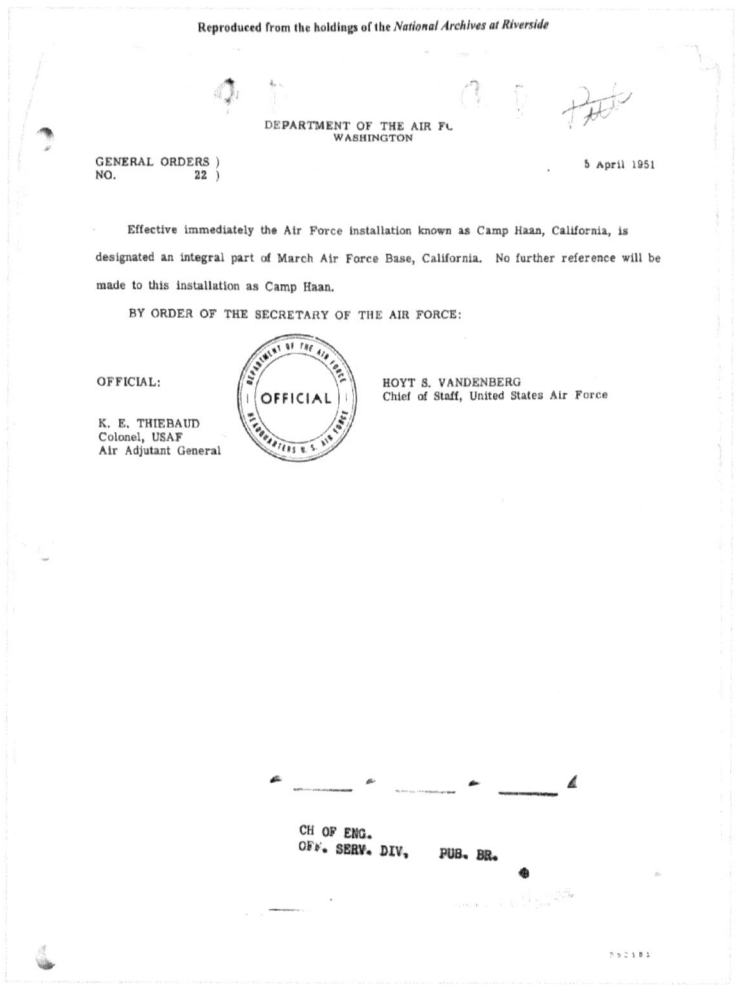

General Order 22
Source: Southern California Real Property Disposal Case Files, 1946-1962. Region 9. RG 269 Records of the General Services Administration. Box 58; National Archives and Records Administration, Riverside, CA.

CHAPTER 8
CAMP HAAN TODAY

As of this writing, no structures from the camp currently exist on site. There are some remnants of concrete pads from the buildings of Camp Haan were built upon, none of which were deemed historical by Riverside County. Many of the building were sold and moved to the local surrounding areas. One of the chapels was purchased by Woodcrest Church. This chapel still stands today at the corner of Van Buren Blvd. and Porter Ave.

Re-purposed Camp Haan church (T-518) in Woodcrest. Photograph by Google Maps.

CAMP HAAN
THE HISTORY OF RIVERSIDE'S WORLD WAR II ANTI-AIRCRAFT TRAINING CENTER

The American Legion Post 595 in the city of Perris, CA is a former Camp Haan building[263]. Midland School in Moreno Valley accumulated a few of the camp's barrack buildings. According to the Moreno Valley Historical Society, the old Camp Haan mess hall building from the Midland School were sold to the Edgemont Women's Club in 1954. The building was moved to its present location on Cottonwood Avenue near the old I-215. The building now is the Edgemont Community Center.

On the corner of S. Perris Blvd. and E 6th Street at the Greater New Hope Missionary, there is a 25'x87' Camp Haan structure still being used. Records show that it was sold to the Congressional Church of Perris in November of 1947[264]. During disposition, the building was listed as a postal office, but there is evident that the camps's teletype and telegraph chief operator's office was also in this building.

Re-used Camp Haan post office at 177 E 6th St, Perris, CA 92570. Photograph by K. Beaulieu

Thousands of buildings, fixtures, and equipment were sold to various schools and religious organizations. The State of California purchased much of the hospital complex.

A partial list of where some of the buildings were disposed top can be found in the Appendix.

Foundation remnants a mess hall (T-7844) in the Topside area from Camp Haan. This building was included in the disciplinary barracks area. Source: K. Beaulieu

CAMP HAAN
THE HISTORY OF RIVERSIDE'S WORLD WAR II ANTI-AIRCRAFT TRAINING CENTER

Foundation remnants of recreational auditorium (T-7715) in the Topside area from Camp Haan. This building was included in the disciplinary barracks area. Source: K. Beaulieu

Foundation remnants of latrines (T-7855, T-7856, and T-7857) in the Topside area from Camp Haan. These buildings was included in the disciplinary barracks area. Source: K. Beaulieu

CAMP HAAN
THE HISTORY OF RIVERSIDE'S WORLD WAR II ANTI-AIRCRAFT TRAINING CENTER

Multiple foundation remnants in the Topside area from Camp Haan. The foundations near the center of the picture (5 total foundations) were mess halls. These buildings were included in the disciplinary barracks area. Source: K. Beaulieu

Multiple foundation remenents in the Topside area from Camp Haan. These buildings was included in the disciplinary barracks area. Source: K. Beaulieu

CAMP HAAN
THE HISTORY OF RIVERSIDE'S WORLD WAR II ANTI-AIRCRAFT TRAINING CENTER

Foundation remanent of a training auditorium (T-8008) in the Topside area from Camp Haan. This buildings was included in the disciplinary barracks area.
Source: K. Beaulieu

March Air Force Base (then March Field) took ownership of several infrastructure facilities on Camp Haan to include the munitions storage, water treatment, rail facitilies, and maintenance facilities.

Many areas in and around Riverside and Moreno Valley areas have re-purposed cantonments buildings of US Army designs, but without records, it is difficult to discern the buildings of Camp Haan to those of nearby Camp Anza. To confound this even further, March Field also had 476 temporary buildings as of January 1943[265]. One has to assume that a portion of those buildings were also sold off around the the same time period.

When March Air Force Base turned into March Air Reserve Base due to the Base Realignment and Closure (BRAC) in 1993, the base size decreased by almost one-third and the U.S. government turned most of the land back over to the municipality.

The previous Camp Haan site remained somewhat barren for years following the closure except for some services. The Arnold Heights Housing area was still being used, the ammo dump and mutions magazines were being used by March Air Reserve Base along with a few buildings for small arms and an NCO academy. As the years passed on, the land slowly has become developed to include a retirement community, a regional training center for first responders, a national cemetery, a golf course, and commercial expansion.

Air Force Village West

Air Force Village West started as a pet project of General Curtis LeMay and was modeled after the first Air Force Village West in Texas (now called Blue Skies of Texas). Initially built upon 221 acres, Air Force Village West (AFVW) retirement community was built on the southwest side of the Camp Haan property, west of I-215 and south of Van Buren Blvd. This would have been the open areas between the Camp Haan's main camp and the topside area; just south of the obstacle course (The east side Amazon warehouse currently on site).

Source: Air Force Village West Specific Plan, Amendment No. 1. 2007

AFVW was opened in 1989 to care specifically for retired or honorably separated military officers and surviving spouses. It was open to all uniformed services who were at least 55 years of age. This age requirement has crept up a bit since its opening.

Perhaps the most famous resident at Air Force Village West was General Curtis LeMay himself. He retired in 1965 and moved to Newport Beach. In 1989, he moved to Air Force Village West to live out the rest of his days. He died on October 1, 1990, of complications from a heart attack in the 22nd Strategic Hospital on March Air Force Base.

General Curtis E. LeMay (1906-1990) Source: https://www.britannica.com/biography/Curtis-E-LeMay

Through various expansions in 1997 and 2007, the complex has since expanded to 660 acres. The entire community was brought into the March Joint Powers Authority in 2004. Name was changed in 2015 to Alta Vista Village; that company filed for bankruptcy in March 2019, and as of Jan 2021 it is now called Westmont Village.

CAMP HAAN
THE HISTORY OF RIVERSIDE'S WORLD WAR II ANTI-AIRCRAFT TRAINING CENTER

Westmont Village (Air Force Village West). 2023
Source: Google Maps

Ben Clark Training Center

In November 1995, the Joint Powers Authority (JPA) identified acreage in the western portion of the base as "…reserved to create a Riverside County Sheriffs Training Academy." The area encompasses approximately 400 acres and includes buildings and facilities which were home to the former non–commissioned Officers Academy and the 15th Air Force Headquarters[266]; prior to that, it was the western most portion of the Camp Haan property. March Air Force Base used the area to house the Non-Commissioned Officer Academy (NCOA), incidentally, it was the first NCOA the Air Force opened in the United States dating back to 1952.[267]

The location was designated the Ben Clark Public Safety Training Center (BCTC) by resolution of the Riverside County Board of Supervisors on September 24, 1996. CALFIRE/Riverside County Fire Department and Riverside County Sheriff's Department training programs were moved to the BCTC in the same year.
The BCTC has become a centralized training center facility that offers, Sheriff training, Fire Academy, Emergency Medical Technician courses, Paramedic Training and Recertification, and emergency management course. It is also the location of the majority of State Fire Marshal FSTEP and CSFTES course offerings in Riverside County.

Today the Ben Clark Public Training Center has classrooms, burn towers, burn props, scenario buildings, an equine complex, student housing, physical training facilities, a shooting range, and administrative offices.

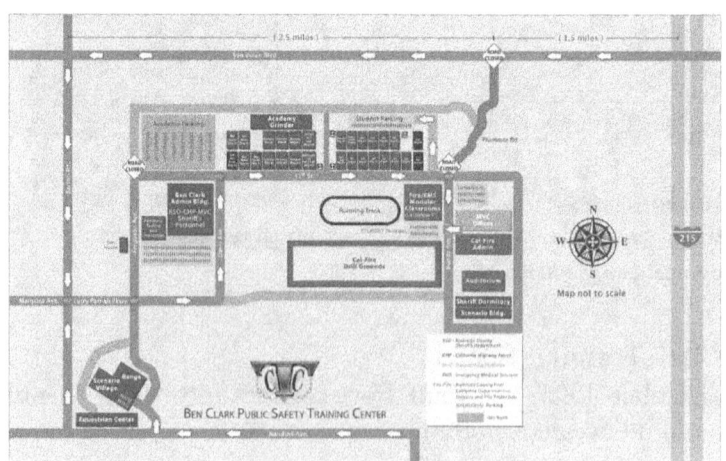

Ben Clark Public Safety Training Center. Source: https://www.rctoa.training/ben-clark-training-center.html

Riverside National Cemetery

Riverside National Cemetery (RNC) was established in 1976 through a transfer of 740 acres; however, this did not happen overnight. Lobbying for a cemetery began as early as the 1960s with base officials and the Riverside Chamber of Commerce. The roots of the cemetery begin in 1971 when the Military Officers Association petitioned for a national cemetery in the West.

At some point between 1971 and 1974, the exact date is unknown, a delegation advising the Veteran's Administration visited March Air Force Base and were bussed to a hilltop to look at the old Camp Haan site to see if it would be suitable for a national cemetery. The delegation was led by Navy Admiral John McCain, father of late Senator John McCain (R-Ariz.) The delegation was greeted and toured by Lt. General William Pitts, 15th Air Force Commander, and Colonel Stanford E. "Stan" Brown, base commander. By all accounts the admiral was impressed; however, it was noted that the other members of the delegation were displaying a more skeptical posture concerned about the availability of water for irrigation. Colonel Brown assured the delegation that the water would be reclaimed from the base's treatment plant and that there was plenty of water for the cemetery. A bonus to this was much of the water and sewage infrastructure from Camp Haan was largely in place. This would later play an important part in the decision.

There were also concerns about the highway traffic and noise to which Col. Brown suggested an earthen berm using concrete and other miscellaneous rubble from the demolition of the Camp Haan. "Brown said he had no idea how the delegation would judge the Camp Haan site when they departed but sensed the admiral like what he saw.[268]" Local efforts continued largely behind the scenes with civic leaders and lobbying in Washington until unofficially on April 8, 1975, John Mahan, VA Cemeteries Director, leaked that the Riverside site was the site chosen. It would be another three months before the House subcommittee on veteran cemeteries would endorse the site and recommend it be approved by Congress. In February 1976, Congress approved, and the VA announced that it would be awarding a $900,000 contract within a short few month, began work in June 1976 on the first 94 acres.

Groundbreaking and dedication was held on June 27, 1976 where more than 4,000 people gathered in the sweltering 105-degree temperatures.

Contract was awarded to a joint venture comprising of the KDH Corporation of Riverside and Equinox, a Malibu firm.[269]

Up until that time, a national cemetery had not been built since 1943.[270] Through lobbying and politics, t[271]he National Cemeteries Act of 1973 was enacted placing the national cemeteries under the responsibility of the Veteran's Administration. In the first decade of the National Cemeteries Act, the operation under the VA saw it greatest expansion, almost doubling its acreage portfolio. A national cemetery in Riverside was one such expansion.

The Administrator of the Veteran Affairs at the times; Mr. Richard L. Roudebush, said that California 3.2 million veterans - largest in the nation - was a major factor in his selection of Riverside as the location.[272] There were two other sites in the running; a site in western Merced County near the San Luis Dam and the White Wolf Valley, Southeast of Bakersfield.

The entrance to the cemetery is located of Van Buren Boulevard.
Riverside National Cemetery was dedicated and opened for burials Veterans Day, November 11, 1978. During some unseasonal cold rain and gusty winds RNC's first burial was Army Staff Sgt. Ysmael Villegas, who was awarded the Medal of Honor for bravery at the cost of his own life at Villa Verde Trail on the island of Luzon in the Philippines, March 20, 1945. Present that day were fifteen fellow Medal of Honor recipients, including General James Doolittle along with 1,000 other base and city officials and Riverside residents. Joe Foss, United States Marine Corps flying ace was the featured speaker. Having this as his final resting place was fitting since Staff Sgt. Ysmael Villegas' widow and son were invited to Camp Haan and presented Staff Sgt. Villegas' posthumous Medal of Honor on October 19 1945.

CAMP HAAN
THE HISTORY OF RIVERSIDE'S WORLD WAR II ANTI-AIRCRAFT TRAINING CENTER

World War II Hero's Reinterment Will Open National Cemetery

BY JOHN KENDALL
Times Riverside-San Bernardino Bureau

RIVERSIDE—The new Riverside National Cemetery will be dedicated in Veterans Day ceremonies today marked by the reinterment of a local World War II hero killed in the Philippines.

Graveside ceremonies with full military honors for Staff Sgt. Ysmael Villegas, a native of Riverside's Casa Blanca district, will mark the first burial in the 740-acre cemetery.

Villegas was posthumously awarded the Congressional Medal of Honor after he was killed March 20, 1945, leading an attack on fortified Japanese positions along the Villa Verde trail.

Urging his men forward, Villegas, a squad leader, rushed forward under heavy fire and wiped out five positions but was killed at the sixth. His body was brought home and buried at Olive Wood Cemetery.

More than 100 members of the Villegas family are expected to attend the reinterment service.

When fully developed, the new facility will become the largest national cemetery in the West. The main entrance is on Van Buren Blvd., about a half mile west of U.S. 15E.

Officials expect more than 6,000 persons to attend today's dedication ceremony, which is scheduled for 11 a.m.

Source: Los Angeles Times, Saturday, November 11, 1978.

An Additional 181 acres transferred to the VA in 2003 for additional expansion. Today, Riverside National Cemetery and its future expansion land covers much of the Camp Haan property south of Van Buren Boulevard close to interstate 215 (Old interstate 395). The area encompasses Camp Haan's Headquarters area and Regimental areas one, two, and three.

A newspaper add highlighting the new Riverside cemetery. Source: Times-Advocate, Tuesday, November 7, 1978

General Old Golf Course

Original built in 1955 as the March Airfield golf course, opened in 1958. Comedian Bob Hope hosted celebrity tournaments there that included guests such as Frank Sinatra, Dean Martin and Desi Arnaz.

The golf course was renamed the General Archie Old Jr. Golf Course sometime after 1984 in honor of Lieutenant General Archie

Old Jr. General Old was a bonafide war hero from the second World War, flying 43 combat missions against Germany in the B-17. He was later instrumental in as a Strategic Air Command officer and leader; in 1951 he was hand-picked by General LeMay to activate SAC bases in England and French Morocco[273]. He flew the first B-52 to circum-navigate the globe non-stop in 1957[274].

Lieutenant General Archie J. Old Jr. (1906-1984)
Source: https://www.af.mil/About-Us/Biographies/Display/Article/106026/lieutenant-general-archie-j-old-jr/

General LeMay pins the Distinguished Flying Cross on Lt. General Archie Olds Jr. after his circumnavigation flight in a B-52. Source: https://www.afgsc.af.mil/News/Photos/igphoto/2000884771/

He went on and commanded the Fifteenth Air Force at March Air Force Base for 10 years before his retirement. He retired in 1965 and died at the base hospital on March 24, 1984.

March Joint Powers Authority [275] took over the golf course from the military in 1996. The golf course opened to the public in 1998 as an 18-hole, par 72 golf course managed by the Donovan Brothers Golf LLC.

In 2018, the VA National Cemetery Administration proposed to acquire the General Old Golf Course for future gravesite expansion, this would amount to an additional 315 acres.[276]

In January 2019, the National Cemetery Administration announced that it had purchased the 315 acres from March Joint Powers Authority for 12.5 million but had no immediate plans to close the golf course[277]. With the purchase of the golf course, Riverside National Cemetery consists of 1,236.77 acres, making it the largest national cemetery managed by the National Cemetery Administration[278].

As of this publication, the general Old Golf Course is still operating next to Riverside National Cemetery.

March Joint Powers Authority/Commercial Expansion

Since 1988, the federal government has closed or realigned military installations throughout the United States. The California State legislature authorized the formation of the joint powers to regulate the disposition and redevelopment of the closed or realigned military installations.

In 1993, March Air Force Base was listed on the realignment list for a substantial reduction of military use. March Air Force Base was redesignated March Air Reserve Base in April 1996. At this time, the local communities of Riverside, Moreno Valley, and Perris formed the March Joint Powers Authority (JPA) under Article 1, Chapter 5, Division 7, Title 1.

The March JPA set out and prepared several planning, policy, and redevelopment documents.

The March JPS is governed by the March Joint Powers Commission (JPC) and is the decision and policy making body for the authority. The JPC consists of eight elected officials (two from each of the jurisdictions)[279].

Over the years, March JPA has cleared the Camp Haan site and prepped it for redevelopment. The Arnold Heights Housing area closed and in 2018 the whole area, representing the north part of Camp Haan, from Alessandro Blvd. to Van Buren Blvd. was to be developed for industrial, business park with mixed use commercial development.

Today much of the land has been developed or in current development. The Camp Haan site north of Van Buren Blvd is a mix of commercial, industrial and office buildings. The areas surrounding the Ben Clark Training Center are being developed for industrial and commercial.

CAMP HAAN
THE HISTORY OF RIVERSIDE'S WORLD WAR II ANTI-AIRCRAFT TRAINING CENTER

Summary

During the period surrounding WWII, only 270,000 out of a total of 6 million troop were housed in "permanent" buildings[280]. Cantonments played a pivotal role stateside and in the theater of war. Over the three years that the cantonment construction program existed, the War Department's Construction Division designed, directed, and erected army cantonments for which to provide facilities and shelter to over 5-million soldiers.

Overall, a small portion of the military personnel were billeted in tents, most troops were lodged, fed, trained, and supplied from temporary wooden buildings[281].

Post war, these same cantonment buildings provided much needed infrastructure for the post-war economy for local and state agencies. Even veteran home purchasing programs were established to use the building. In 1983, the Army was directed to dispose of all World War II temporary buildings and replace them with current Army specifications and building codes[282]. The Army may be getting rid of the old cantonment buildings, but they still exist, many disguised or modified since the late 1940s.

World War II mobilization marked a time in history when things were built at remarkable speed. Techniques in manufacturing were developed during this period that included standardization of building plans, prefabrication, and assembly-line approach were all new construction at that time. More so than the historical significance of the buildings and structures themselves, cthe cantonments of World War II are significant in planning, design construction, and innovation.

Besides the remarkability of the mobilization program and the cantonment construction, Camp Haan's legacy is rooted in the Riverside community as the largest west coast artillery training center, but even more so, it was also the number of soldiers routed through there. Originally only scheduled for 15,000 at a time, at its maximum 80,000 soldiers were trained and passed through the camp. It also was not just one group of 80,000 but waves of 80,000 soldiers, in processed, completed basic training, and trained with live ammunition in nearby Fort Irwin.

Despite this rich past, Camp Haan's history only remains in the historical records. None of the Camp Haan property or infrastructure were deemed significant to be added to the historic register because of demolition and development on the site at the time of the survey. The only physical remains of the camp are some crumbling concrete pads that are rapidly disappearing due to time and commercial development. Even more so, the history and the stories of the men that passed through Camp Haan's gates have died or are an old age. A few artifacts and pictures of the camp remain along with some passed down stories; hardly a legacy fitting of a camp that was the biggest anti-aircraft artillery training center on the west coast the country had and the thousands of men that were trained there.

CAMP HAAN
THE HISTORY OF RIVERSIDE'S WORLD WAR II ANTI-AIRCRAFT TRAINING CENTER

MISCELLANEOUS PICTURES

CAMP HAAN
THE HISTORY OF RIVERSIDE'S WORLD WAR II ANTI-AIRCRAFT TRAINING CENTER

Cover of a Camp Haan informational phamlet, circa 1941-1943. Source: personal

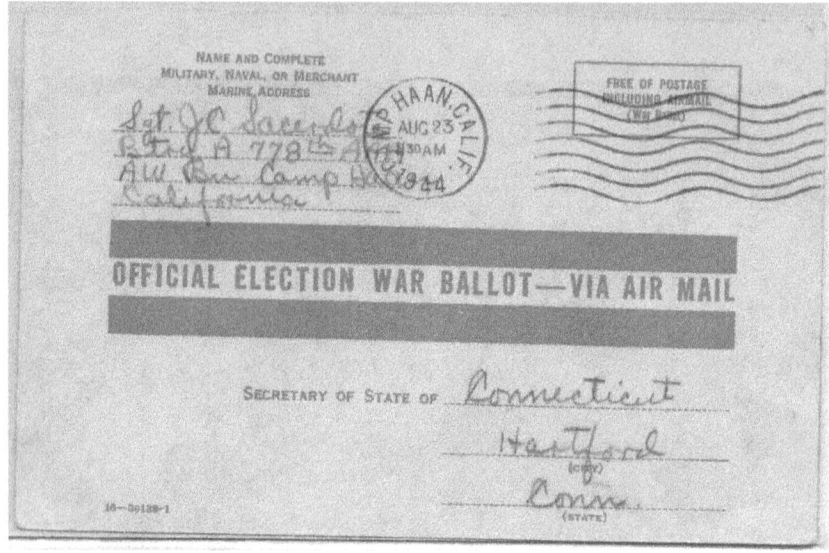

Official war ballet envelope, dated August 23, 1944. Source: personal

Letter envelope, dated July 9, 1943. Source: personal

CAMP HAAN
THE HISTORY OF RIVERSIDE'S WORLD WAR II ANTI-AIRCRAFT TRAINING CENTER

Letter envelope, dated August 6, 1943. Source: personal

Camp Haan matchebooks, circa 1941-1946. Source: personal

CAMP HAAN
THE HISTORY OF RIVERSIDE'S WORLD WAR II ANTI-AIRCRAFT TRAINING CENTER

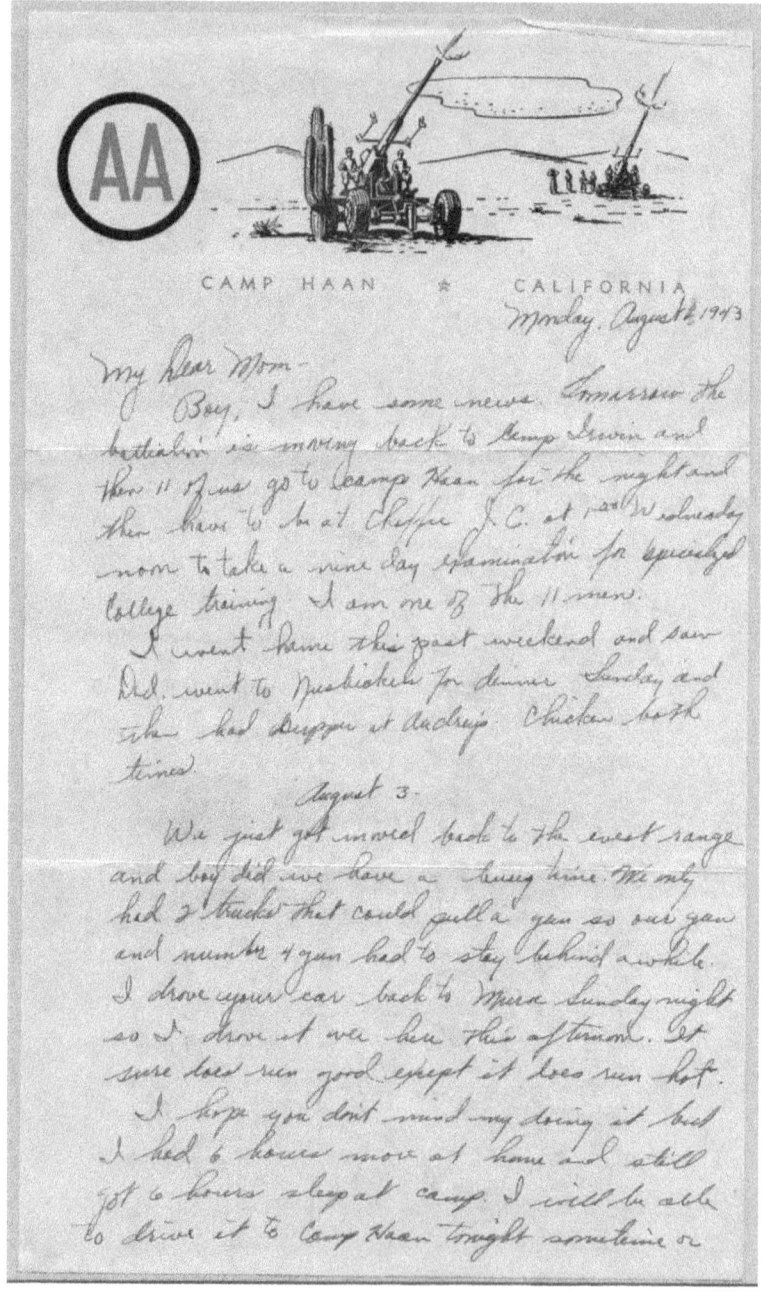

A letter home to mom, dated August 2, 1943. Source: personal

CAMP HAAN
THE HISTORY OF RIVERSIDE'S WORLD WAR II ANTI-AIRCRAFT TRAINING
CENTER

Title: Tracking on Planes, Camp Haan, California
Date: 1941
Collection: Frasher Foto Postcard Collection
Owning Institution: Pomona Public Library

Title: Officer, Camp Haan, California
Date: 1941
Collection: Frasher Foto Postcard Collection
Owning Institution: Pomona Public Library

CAMP HAAN
THE HISTORY OF RIVERSIDE'S WORLD WAR II ANTI-AIRCRAFT TRAINING
CENTER

Title: 1943: "The Fabulous Five":Dave Brubeck, Frances Glenn, Wes Cope and, Ralph Gephardt. Camp Haan, Riverside, CA
Collection: Brubeck Collection Medley
Owning Institution: University of the Pacific

CAMP HAAN
THE HISTORY OF RIVERSIDE'S WORLD WAR II ANTI-AIRCRAFT TRAINING CENTER

Camp Haan during construction, Early 1941
Resource: Riverside: Then and Now

The reading room in the officers club (T-2). Source: personal

CAMP HAAN
THE HISTORY OF RIVERSIDE'S WORLD WAR II ANTI-AIRCRAFT TRAINING CENTER

Sylveria "Vera" Graves (August 26, 1906 - August 3, 1996) at Camp Haan
Photo courtesy of Mary Graves

CAMP HAAN
THE HISTORY OF RIVERSIDE'S WORLD WAR II ANTI-AIRCRAFT TRAINING CENTER

Sylveria "Vera" Graves (August 26, 1906 - August 3, 1996) (L) and an unknown nurse (R) at Camp Haan
Photo courtesy of Mary Graves

KP Duty at Camp Haan. Circa 1941-1946. Identify Unknown
Source: Personal

CAMP HAAN
THE HISTORY OF RIVERSIDE'S WORLD WAR II ANTI-AIRCRAFT TRAINING CENTER

Theodore Pattengill Foster at
Camp Haan, circa 1941.
Photo courtesy of Lille Foster

Unknown Sergeant at Camp Haan, circa 1941
Source: personal

CAMP HAAN
THE HISTORY OF RIVERSIDE'S WORLD WAR II ANTI-AIRCRAFT TRAINING CENTER

Brigadier General Edgar B. Colladay was Camp Haan's first training center commander. He along with a small contingency of staff were among the first to occupy Camp Haan during construction. He was in command at Camp Haan from December 1940 to October 1941. He then went on to command an antiaircraft camp in Alaska.

San Bernardino County Sun (Sep 4, 1941)

Source: FindaGrave.com

Unknown Soldier at Camp Haan, circa 1941
Source: personal

CAMP HAAN
THE HISTORY OF RIVERSIDE'S WORLD WAR II ANTI-AIRCRAFT TRAINING CENTER

Unknown Camp Haan soldiers taking a bio-break during field training at Camp Irwin. Source: Yeager Family Library, March Field Air Museum

Unknown Camp Haan Soldier with companion
Source: Yeager Family Library, March Field Air Museum

CAMP HAAN
THE HISTORY OF RIVERSIDE'S WORLD WAR II ANTI-AIRCRAFT TRAINING CENTER

Unknown Camp Haan Soldiers during field training at Camp Irwin
Source: Yeager Family Library, March Field Air Museum

CAMP HAAN
THE HISTORY OF RIVERSIDE'S WORLD WAR II ANTI-AIRCRAFT TRAINING CENTER

Unknown Camp Haan Corporal field stripping his rifle during field training at Camp Irwin
Source: Yeager Family Library, March Field Air Museum

CAMP HAAN
THE HISTORY OF RIVERSIDE'S WORLD WAR II ANTI-AIRCRAFT TRAINING CENTER

Unknown Camp Haan Soldiers during field training at Camp Irwin
Source: Yeager Family Library, March Field Air Museum

Unknown Camp Haan Soldiers during field training at Camp Irwin
Source: Yeager Family Library, March Field Air Museum

CAMP HAAN
THE HISTORY OF RIVERSIDE'S WORLD WAR II ANTI-AIRCRAFT TRAINING
CENTER

Unknown Camp Haan Soldiers during field training at Camp Irwin
Source: Yeager Family Library, March Field Air Museum

Field training at Camp Irwin
Source: Yeager Family Library, March Field Air Museum

CAMP HAAN
THE HISTORY OF RIVERSIDE'S WORLD WAR II ANTI-AIRCRAFT TRAINING CENTER

Unknown Camp Haan Soldiers during field training at Camp Irwin
Source: Yeager Family Library, March Field Air Museum

CAMP HAAN
THE HISTORY OF RIVERSIDE'S WORLD WAR II ANTI-AIRCRAFT TRAINING
CENTER

Unknown Soldiers at Camp Haan
Source: Yeager Family Library, March Field Air Museum

Unknown Soldiers at Camp Haan
Source: personal

CAMP HAAN
THE HISTORY OF RIVERSIDE'S WORLD WAR II ANTI-AIRCRAFT TRAINING CENTER

Unknown soldier wearing a Camp Haan t-shirt in Riverside, CA, May 1943. Picture labeled "Bro."
Source: personal

CAMP HAAN
THE HISTORY OF RIVERSIDE'S WORLD WAR II ANTI-AIRCRAFT TRAINING CENTER

Unknown soldier getting in some rage time at Camp Haan, circa 1941-1945.
Source: Riverside Historical Society

THANKSGIVING DINNER 1941

Menu

Fruit Cocktail
Roast Turkey   Salt Wafers
Baked Ham   Giblet Gravy
Cranberry Sauce   Oyster Dressing
                      Asparagus
        Sweet Potato Birds
Celery   Mixed Sweet Pickles
Olives   Radishes
Hot Rolls   Butter
Mince Pie   Apple Pie
Ice Cream   Milk
Assorted Fruits   Mixed Candies
Cider   Coffee   Cigarettes

78th Coast Artillery AA Thanksgiving Dinner Menu, 1941
Source: Lille Foster

CAMP HAAN
THE HISTORY OF RIVERSIDE'S WORLD WAR II ANTI-AIRCRAFT TRAINING CENTER

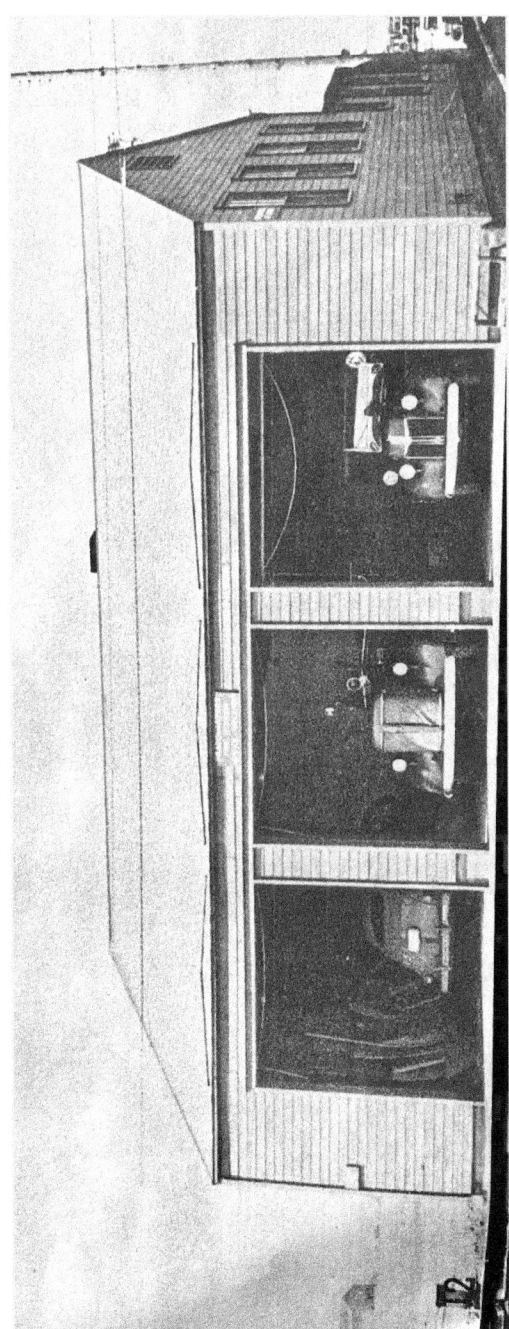

Headquarters Fire Station (T-50) at Camp Haan. Located in area 10. Circa 1941.
Source: Picture Parade

CAMP HAAN
THE HISTORY OF RIVERSIDE'S WORLD WAR II ANTI-AIRCRAFT TRAINING CENTER

Camp Haan band playing outside of the AATC headquarters building (T-1), circa 1941-1946.
Source: Picture Parade

CAMP HAAN
THE HISTORY OF RIVERSIDE'S WORLD WAR II ANTI-AIRCRAFT TRAINING CENTER

Band from Camp Haan performing at the Hollywood Canteen, circa 1941-1946.
Source: Picture Parade

Red Cross volunteers at Camp Haan. Believed to be the Red Cross recreation building (T-5729) in the hospital area, circa 1941-1945.
Source: Picture Parade.

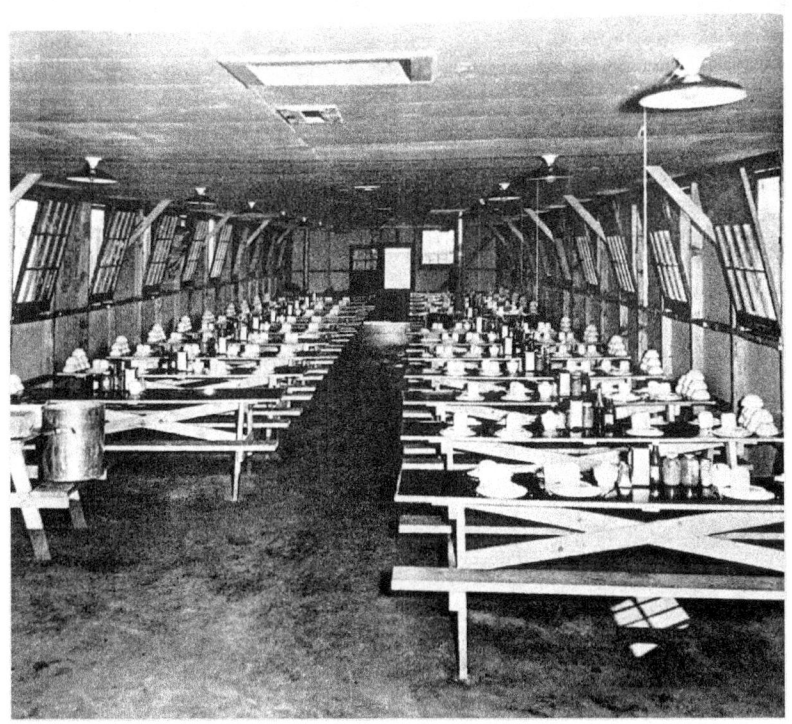

Typical enlisted regimental mess hall at Camp Haan.
Source: Picture Parade.

CAMP HAAN
THE HISTORY OF RIVERSIDE'S WORLD WAR II ANTI-AIRCRAFT TRAINING CENTER

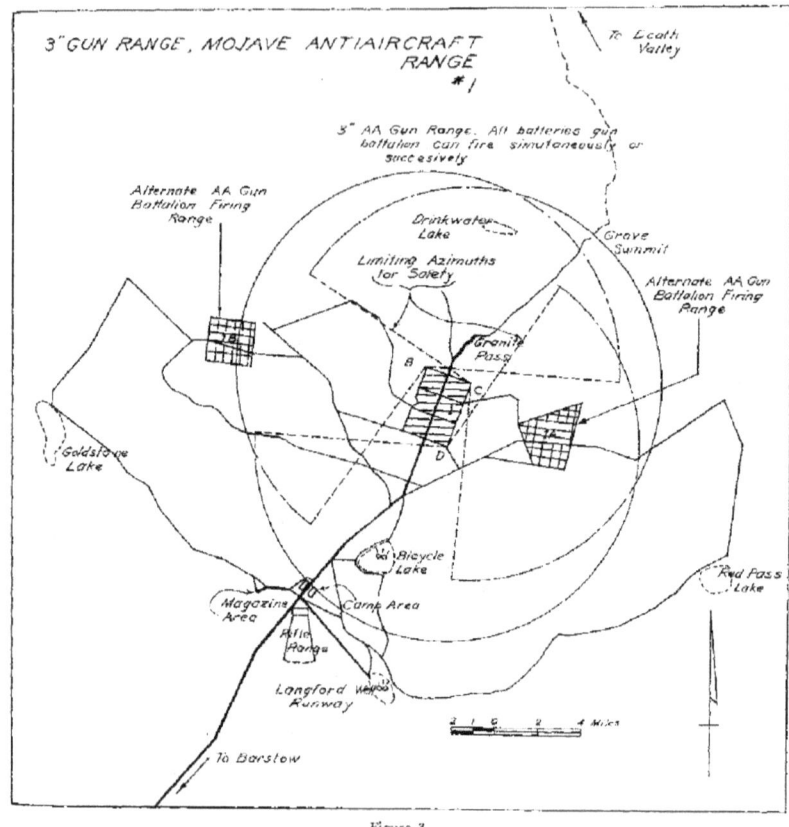

Figure 3

Hand drawn map of the Camp Haan anti-aircraft firing positions
Source: Coast Artillary Journal, September-October 1941

CAMP HAAN
THE HISTORY OF RIVERSIDE'S WORLD WAR II ANTI-AIRCRAFT TRAINING CENTER

Lt. Col. Harry W. Stark, Commanding Officer, 78th Coast Artillery, Camp Haan, circa 1941
Source: 78th Coast Artillery Antiaircraft year book, Sharon Anthony Papers, Riverside Public Library

Major Harry S. Aldrich, Executive Officer officer, 78th Coast Artillery, Camp Haan, circa 1941
Source: 78th Coast Artillery Antiaircraft year book, Sharon Anthony Papers, Riverside Public Library

CAMP HAAN
THE HISTORY OF RIVERSIDE'S WORLD WAR II ANTI-AIRCRAFT TRAINING CENTER

JANET BLAIR is no newcomer to the men of Camp Haan. She visited us last November if you recall. But we thought you might like to see her as she is today—a rising star in Hollywood—currently working before the cameras of Columbia Studios.

Source: Camp Haan Tracer, May 4, 1943
Courtesy of Riverside Historical Society

CAMP HAAN
THE HISTORY OF RIVERSIDE'S WORLD WAR II ANTI-AIRCRAFT TRAINING CENTER

WILLIE SHORE, that serious looking individual, is booked as a comedy dancer tonight at War Department Theater No. 1. Willie is a star of "The Band Wagon," hilarious USO-Campshow here to entertain you enlisted men. Contact your organization commander for free tickets.

Source: Camp Haan Tracer, May 4, 1943
Courtesy of Riverside Historical Society

THEATER No. 1

Today—USO Campshow: "The Band Wagon."

Wednesday and Thursday: Jon Hall, Maria Montez and Sabu in "White Savage."

Friday: Charles Laughton, Maureen O'Hara, George Sanders, "This Land Is Mine." Selected short subjects.

Sat. "The Dark Command," John Wayne, Claire Trevor and Walter Pidgeon.

Sun. and Mon. "The Human Comedy," Mickey Rooney.

THEATER No. 3

Today and Wednesday: Jon Hall, Maria Montez in "White Savage;" the March of Time and selected short subjects.

Thursday: Charles Laughton, Maureen O'Hara, "This Land Is Mine." Selected short subjects.

Friday and Saturday: Gen. Montgomery's 8th Army, "Desert Victory;" also Allan Jones, Jane Frazee, "Rhythm of the Islands."

Sun. "The Dark Command," John Wayne, Claire Trevor and Walter Pidgeon.

Mon. "I Walked With a Zombie," Frances Dee, Tom Conway, also "Follow the Band," Leon Errol and Mary Beth Hughes.

THEATER No. 4

Today: Betty Grable, John Payne, Carmen Miranda, "Springtime in the Rockies" (technicolor;) also cartoon.

Wednesday: Lupe Velez, Lewis Wilson, "Redhead from Manhattan." Also Tom Conway, Harriet Hilliard in "The Falcon Strikes Back."

Thursday and Friday: Jon Hall, Maria Montez and Sabu in "White Savage." Also March of Time and selected shorts.

Sat. "This Land Is Mine," Charles Laughton and Maureen O'Hara.

Sun. and Mon. "Rhythm of the Islands," Allan Jones and Jane Frazee. Also "Desert Victory."

A sampling of what was available at the Camp Haan Theaters.

Source: Camp Haan Tracer, May 4, 1943
Courtesy of Riverside Historical Society

CAMP HAAN
THE HISTORY OF RIVERSIDE'S WORLD WAR II ANTI-AIRCRAFT TRAINING CENTER

Source: Camp Haan Tracer, Mar 30, 1943
Courtesy of Riverside Historical Society

Source: Camp Haan Tracer, March 30, 1943
Courtesy of Riverside Historical Society

CAMP HAAN
THE HISTORY OF RIVERSIDE'S WORLD WAR II ANTI-AIRCRAFT TRAINING CENTER

JUMPIN' JIVE is what Pvt Howard Green gives at the colorful dance last Thursday evening at Service Club No. 2. Green, a member of Lt. Joseph F. Reilly's Company C, Quartermaster Service Battalion, improvises cuffs for his O.D.'s just long enough to give that zoot-suit effect for his fancy gyrations.

Source: Camp Haan Tracer, March 30, 1943
Courtesy of Riverside Historical Society

Source: Camp Haan Tracer, March 30, 1943
Courtesy of Riverside Historical Society

215th Coast Artillery year book cover 1941.
Source: Sharon Anthony Papers, Riverside Library

CAMP HAAN
THE HISTORY OF RIVERSIDE'S WORLD WAR II ANTI-AIRCRAFT TRAINING CENTER

215th Coast Artillery training in the areas surrounding Camp Haan, 1941.
Source: Sharon Anthony Papers, Riverside Library

CAMP HAAN
THE HISTORY OF RIVERSIDE'S WORLD WAR II ANTI-AIRCRAFT TRAINING
CENTER

2ND LT. WARREN W. SHAKE

- Second Lieut. Warren W. Shake, whose home was at New Ulm, Minnesota, died instantly June 18 when the car in which he was riding overturned on a mountain curve near Lake Arrowhead, California. Lieut. Shake was serving as a range officer with B Battery, 215th C.A.(AA).

Camp Haan Officer Killed. San Bernardino, Calif.—(P)—Lieutenant Warren W. Shake, 24, New Ulm, Minn., stationed at the Camp Haan anti-aircraft base, was killed Wednesday when an automobile overturned. Three other officers were injured.

Source: Winona Daily News, June 19, 1941

Source: Sharon Anthony Papers, Riverside Library

National Archives at Washington DC; Washington DC, USA; Applications for Headstones For U.S. Military Veterans, 1925-1941; *NAID:* 596118; *Record Group Number:* 92; *Record Group Title:* Records of the Office of the Quartermaster General

CAMP HAAN
THE HISTORY OF RIVERSIDE'S WORLD WAR II ANTI-AIRCRAFT TRAINING CENTER

Although considered taboo by some, the military in the WWII era did have their share of death by suicide. Private First Class Kruger is just one example. Army suicide rates in 1940 were approximately 25 per 100,000 troops and that figure dropped to around 20 per 100,000 troops.[283]

PFC. LEROY KRUGER

• Private First Class LeRoy Kruger, 19, died June 18. He was born in Iowa, and joined the army from Magnolia, Minnesota. Pfc. Kruger served with E Battery.

Military Rites for Magnolia Private

RIVERSIDE, CALIF. — (U.P.) — Private Leroy G. Kruger, 20, Magnolia, Minn., who hanged himself from the limb of a tree Wednesday, was given military funeral services on the lawn of the Union Pacific station last night.

Rosary was read by the Rev. Peter Lynch in the chapel of a private funeral home. Officers and men of Kruger's Battery E, 215th coast artillery, held military services.

Kruger's body was shipped to his Minnesota home.

Applications for Headstones for U.S. Military Veterans, 1925-1941. Microfilm publication M1916, 134 rolls. ARC ID: 596118. Records of the Office of the Quartermaster General, Record Group 92. National Archives at Washington, D.C

CAMP HAAN
THE HISTORY OF RIVERSIDE'S WORLD WAR II ANTI-AIRCRAFT TRAINING CENTER

Troops in formation at Camp Haan, circa 1941
Source: Yeager Family Library, March Field Air Museum

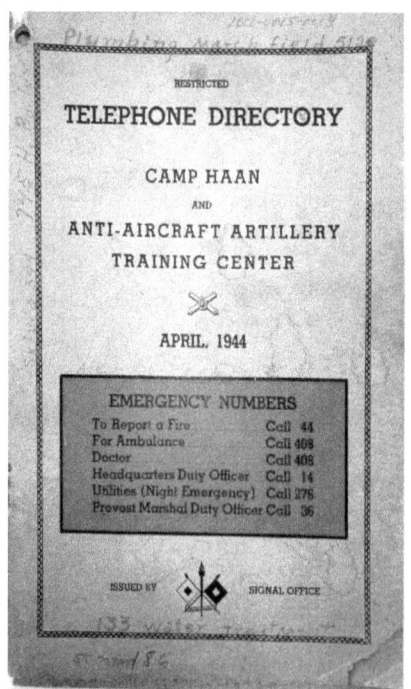

Cover photograph of the 1944 Camp Haan phone directory
Source: Yeager Family Liberary, March Field Air Museum

CAMP HAAN
THE HISTORY OF RIVERSIDE'S WORLD WAR II ANTI-AIRCRAFT TRAINING CENTER

Title: 1944: Dave Brubeck in Army. Camp Haan, Riverside CA
Date: 1944-01-01T07:00:00Z
Collection: Brubeck Collection Medley
Owning Institution: University of the Pacific
Source: Calisphere

CAMP HAAN
THE HISTORY OF RIVERSIDE'S WORLD WAR II ANTI-AIRCRAFT TRAINING CENTER

Worship is over in one of the several Camp Haan chapels.

Postcard of Camp Haan soldiers in front of South Chapel (T-518).
Source: Riverside Historical Society

George Burns and Gracie Allen at Camp Haan, circa 1942
Photo courtesy of Kevin Bash

CAMP HAAN
THE HISTORY OF RIVERSIDE'S WORLD WAR II ANTI-AIRCRAFT TRAINING CENTER

Hutments in the regimental areas. Latrine at the end of the rows, circa 1943. Photo courtesy of Mark Gallagher

Military Jeep in the foreground; mess hall in the background, circa 1943. Photo courtesy of Mark Gallagher

CAMP HAAN
THE HISTORY OF RIVERSIDE'S WORLD WAR II ANTI-AIRCRAFT TRAINING CENTER

Soldiers at ease in a regimental area of Camp Haan, circa 1943. Notice the military vehicles in the background. This picture was taken from the west facing east toward March Air Field. Photo courtesy of Mark Gallagher

An Easter postcard from Camp Haan, circa 1941-1944. Source: personal.

A Coast Artillery Field Manual (FM 4-100). This would have been the same manual that soldiers used at Camp Haan. Source: personal.

Camp Haan Picture Parade, circa 1941. Source: Personal

CAMP HAAN
THE HISTORY OF RIVERSIDE'S WORLD WAR II ANTI-AIRCRAFT TRAINING CENTER

Colonel Charles H. Mason
Commanding Officer—Camp Haan

Source: Picture Parade

Major General Homer R. Oldfield
Commanding General Anti-Aircraft Artillery Training Center

Source: Picture Parade

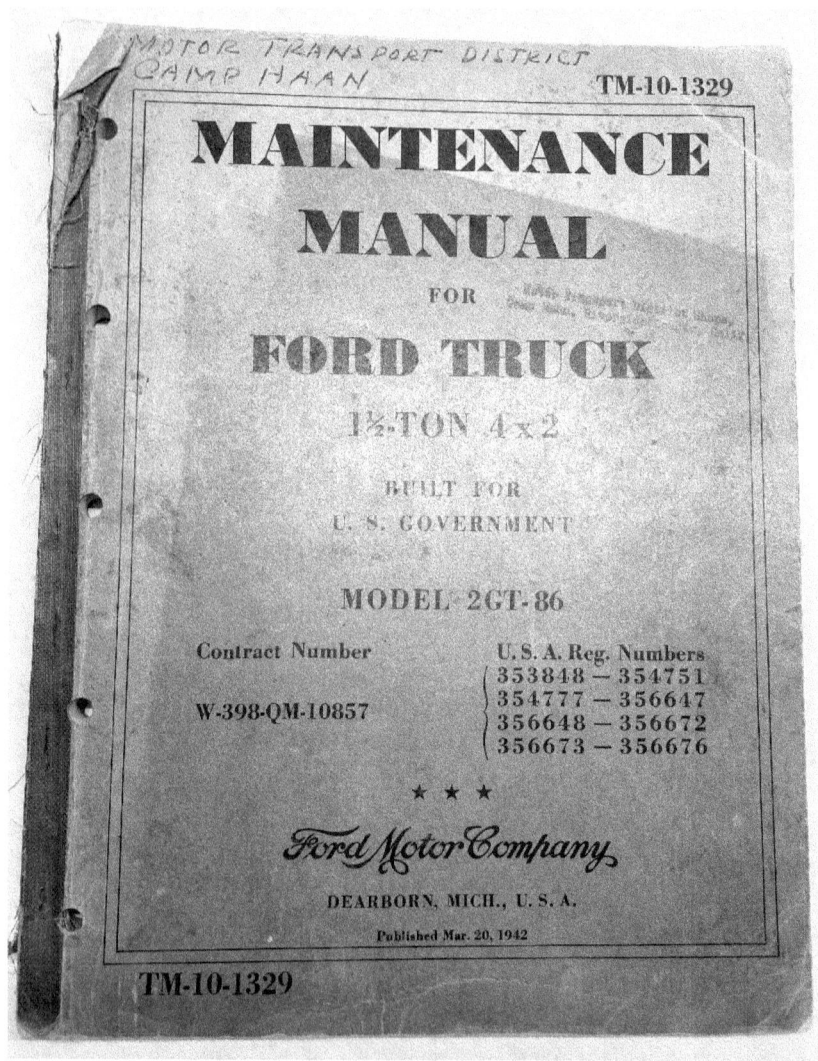

A maintenance manual for a 1.5 ton 4x2 Ford Truck from Camp Haan, circa 1942-1943. Source: Personal

Hanging out at a hutment in Camp Haan. Picture labeled "Andy & Stetson." Source: Personal

CAMP HAAN
THE HISTORY OF RIVERSIDE'S WORLD WAR II ANTI-AIRCRAFT TRAINING CENTER

Source: personal

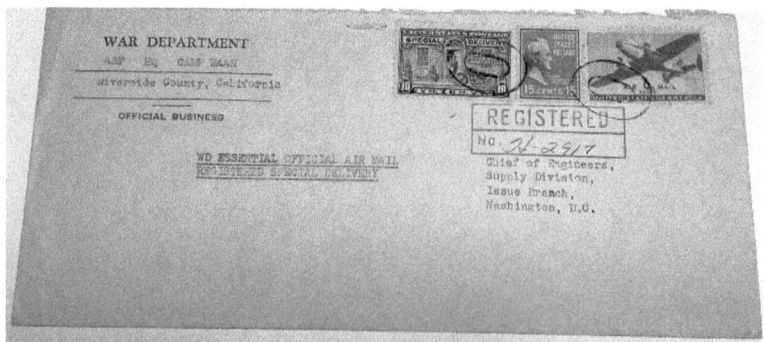

Airmail envelope from Camp Haan to Washington, D.C.. Source: Personal

CAMP HAAN
THE HISTORY OF RIVERSIDE'S WORLD WAR II ANTI-AIRCRAFT TRAINING CENTER

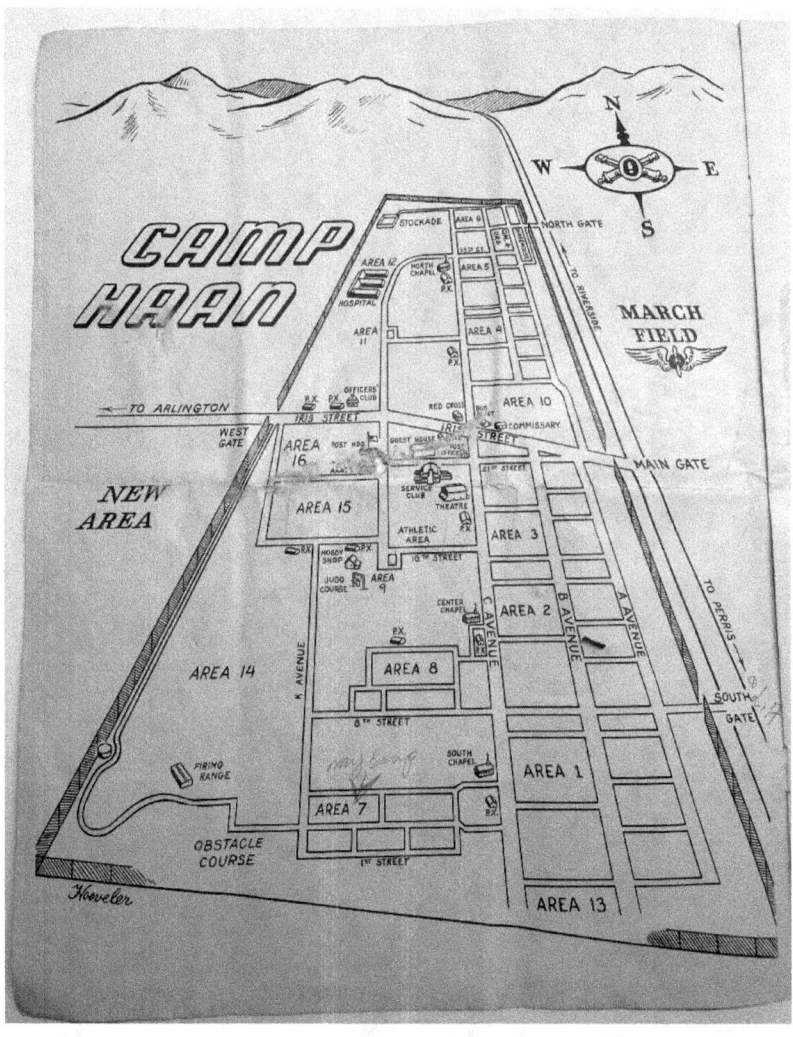

Map of Camp Haan from a welcome booklet given to soldiers. Notice this is before the addition of the "Topside." Circa 1941. Source: Personal

A typical pamphlet that was given to soldiers demobilizing/disembarking the military. Source: personal

African-American soldiers relaxing in a day room at Camp Haan. Circa 1942. Source: Picture Parade.

CAMP HAAN
THE HISTORY OF RIVERSIDE'S WORLD WAR II ANTI-AIRCRAFT TRAINING CENTER

Finance office . . . and no overtime is computed.

Camp Haan finance (T-59) Source: Picture Parade

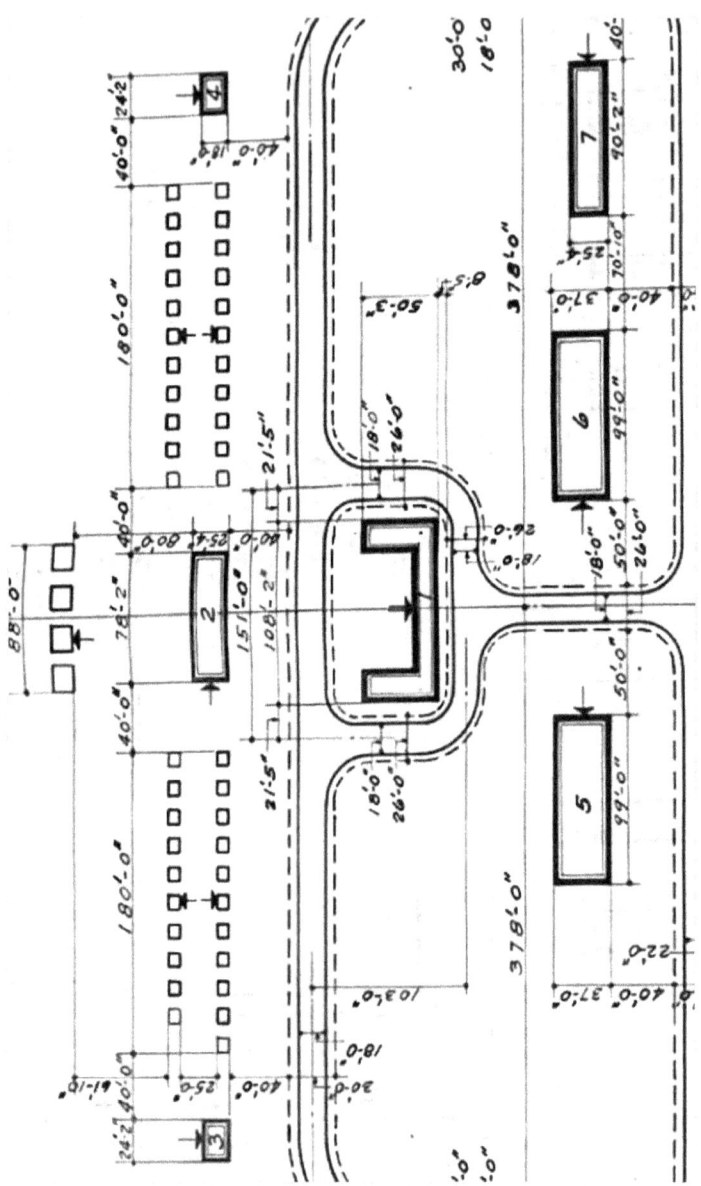

Regimental area. "u" shaped building (labeled 1) is the regiment headquarters. The rectangle building above (labeled 2) was the officers mess. Flanking each side of the officers mess were officers tents. The square buildings (labeled 3 & 4) were officers lavatories. The rectangel building (labeled 5) was the regiment recreation hall, rectangle building (labeled 6) was the exchange, and rectangular building (labeled 7) was the regimental infirmary.

CAMP HAAN
THE HISTORY OF RIVERSIDE'S WORLD WAR II ANTI-AIRCRAFT TRAINING CENTER

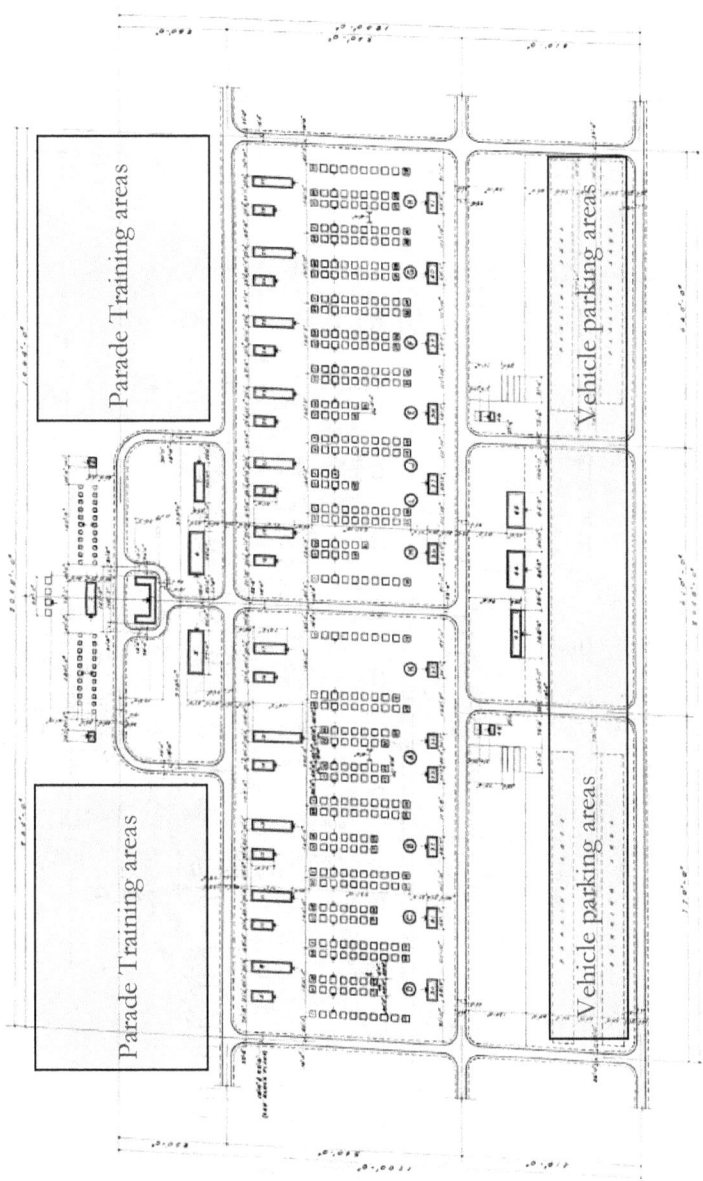

Regimental area. The small squares arranged in rows represented a 16x16 tent for the enlisted men. Just below the tents were the lavatories. Just above the tents were the mess halls (the longer buildings), and the battery office and supply (shorter buildings).

CAMP HAAN
THE HISTORY OF RIVERSIDE'S WORLD WAR II ANTI-AIRCRAFT TRAINING CENTER

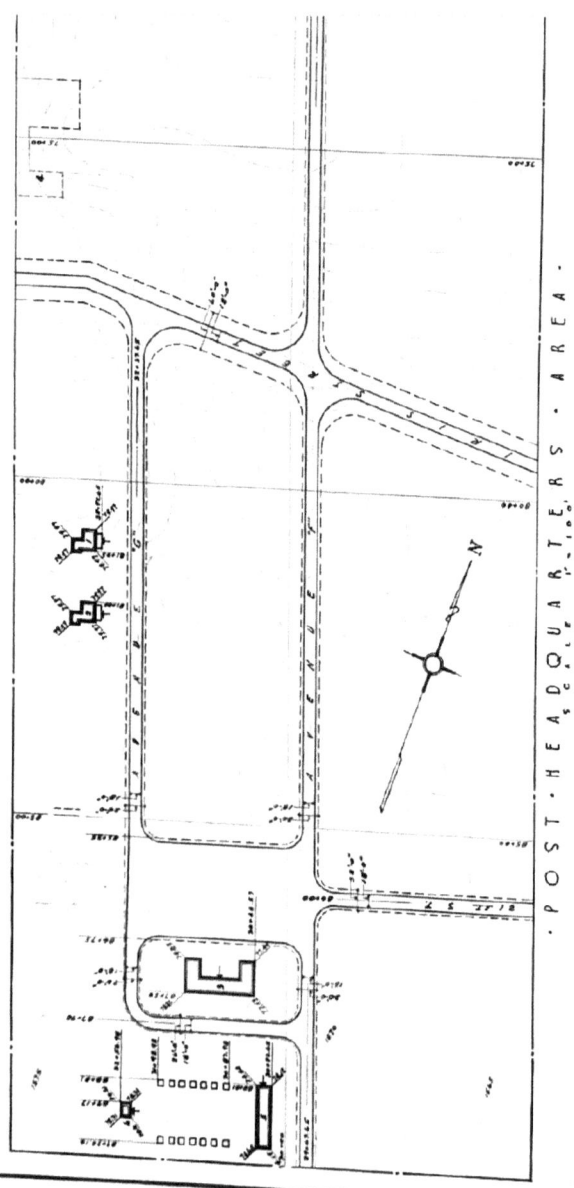

Post Headquarters area. The "c" shaped building was Camp Haan Headquarters. This would have been the very first area to have been built after the railroad infrastructure. Note that Iris Street on this diagram is now present day Van Buren Blvd. Camp Haan post headquarters would have sat very close to the present day administrative building for the Riverside National Cemetery.

CAMP HAAN
THE HISTORY OF RIVERSIDE'S WORLD WAR II ANTI-AIRCRAFT TRAINING CENTER

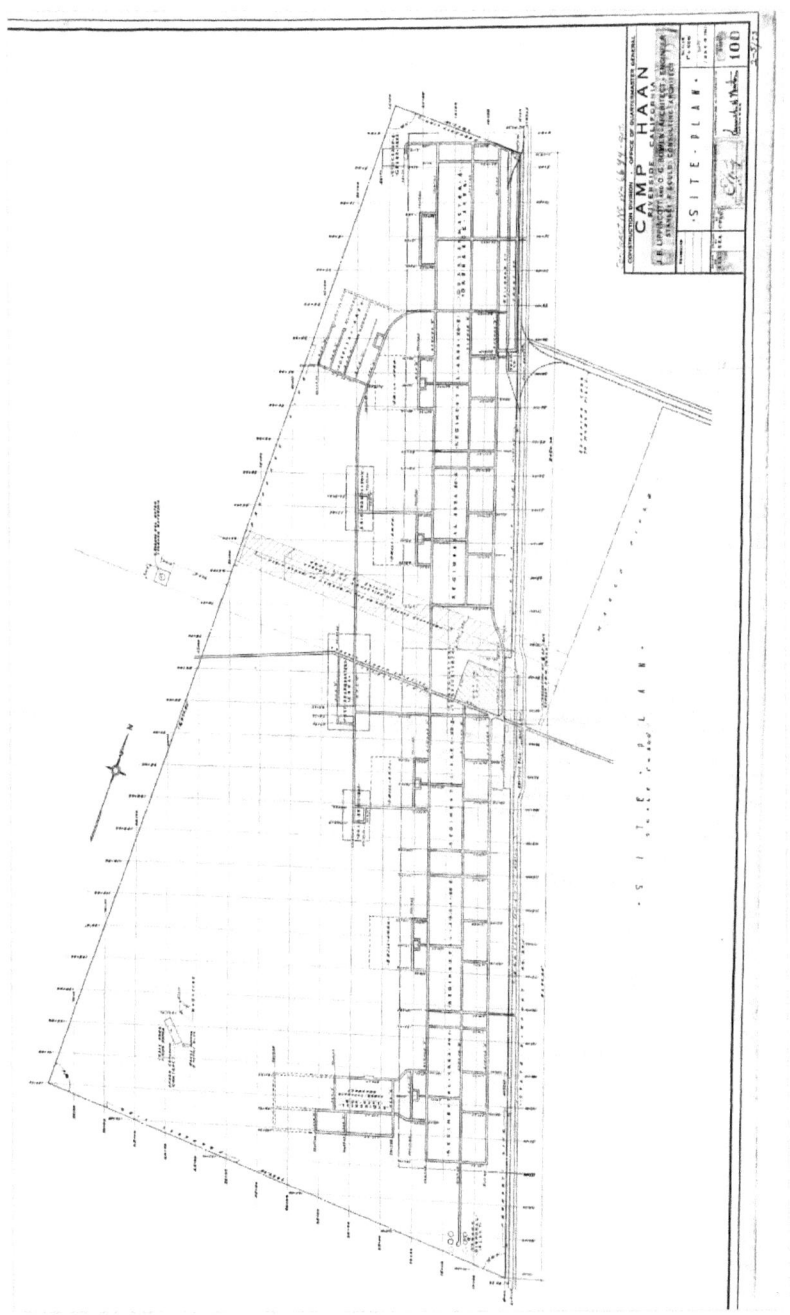

Copy of the original site plan drawing from Lippincott & Bowen. June 1941

CAMP HAAN
THE HISTORY OF RIVERSIDE'S WORLD WAR II ANTI-AIRCRAFT TRAINING CENTER

Complete Camp Haan layout including Topside area. September 1947

CAMP HAAN
THE HISTORY OF RIVERSIDE'S WORLD WAR II ANTI-AIRCRAFT TRAINING CENTER

The preceeding maps were courtesy of the National Archives and Records Administration. The National Archives at Riverside.

Record Group 269, Records of the General Services Administration

Series Southern California Real Property Disposal Case Files, 1946-1962

Box 58

APPENDICES

KEITH A. BEAULIEU

APPENDIX 1
LAND ACQUISITION

Initial Purchase

Tract No.	Grantor/Owner	Acreage	Acquired by
1	Caroline M. Trautwein	1,777.06	Fee
2	Caroline M. Trautwein	1.01	Fee
2A	Caroline M. Trautwein	0.22	Easement
3	Caroline M. Trautwein	20.37	Fee
5	Steve Rachke, et ux	9.39	Fee
6	AT&SF Railroad Company	1.34	Lease

Note: et ux means "and wife"

Expansion

Tract No.	Grantor/Owner	Acreage	Acquired by
1	Mary R. & Caroline R. Trautwein, Heirs	536.45	Fee
1A	Mary R. & Caroline R. Trautwein, Heirs	562.07	Fee
2	Michael Buchko, et ux	80.0	Fee
3	John M. Flowers	20.0	Fee
4	Hazel P. McWiff	10.0	Fee
5	Clarence S. and Hattie R. Smith	5.0	Fee
6	S. A. Blair	5.0	Fee
7	Henry Upton	20.0	Fee
8	Cortland Holden, et ux	20.0	Fee
9	Emily Rita Tibacek	1.85	Fee
10	Marion L. Weddle	1.00	Fee
11	Roy Timmerman	3.00	Fee
12	Lloyd Zimmerman	2.01	Fee
13	Ulysses B. Kelsey, et ux	2.01	Fee
14	Robert M. Flynn	10.39	Fee
15	Ida Watters	1.12	Fee

CAMP HAAN
THE HISTORY OF RIVERSIDE'S WORLD WAR II ANTI-AIRCRAFT TRAINING CENTER

16	Albert Wm De Sart, et ux	0.88	Fee
17	Vern W. Kenison, et ux	2.00	Fee
18	Ernest E. Peer, et ux	2.00	Fee
19	Leo Hilliard, et ux	2.97	Fee
20	Oliver J. Breeding	3.54	Fee
21	Marion L. Kemp, et ux	3.93	Fee
22	Millie Beauchamp	4.10	Fee
23	Nick C. English, et ux	2.04	Fee

Expansion Cont'd

Tract No.	Grantor/Owner	Acreage	Acquired by
24	Sylvester Smith, et ux	2.04	Fee
25	Henry D. Upton	1.02	Fee
26	Lela R. Taylor	1.02	Fee
27	Howard Herman Hartman	1.02	Fee
28	Stephen Fowles, et ux	1.02	Fee
29	Salvador Mora	1.02	Fee
30	Douglas J. & Betsy P. Everett	1.24	Fee
31	Philip Bomar, et ux	2.22	Fee
32	Henry D. Upton	1.0	Fee
33	Joe Vezzetti, et ux	1.0	Fee
34	Joe L. Sheridan	1.0	Fee
35	Walter L. Deardorff	1.0	Fee
36	Stephen Fowles, et ux	2.0	Fee
37	John Corbell	2.0	Fee
38	W.H. Bowser	4.0	Fee
39	F. Orman Schum, et ux	4.63	Fee

40	B.F. Flake, et ux	3.18	Fee
41	Louis Godat	2.0	Fee
42	Mabel B. Bull	2.27	Fee
43	Henry O. Anderson, et ux	4.0	Fee
44	W. L. Green	6.0	Fee
45	Charley C. Curtis, et ux	2.0	Fee
46	G. Edgar Ramsey, et ux	2.22	Fee
47	Henry D. Upton	2.21	Fee
48	Addie R. Aylsworth, et ux	4.0	Fee
49	Robert F. Slater, et ux	4.0	Fee
50	Henry D. Upton	2.0	Fee
51	Ella E. Campbell	2.75	Fee

Note: et ux means "and wife"

Expansion Cont'd

Tract No.	Grantor/Owner	Acreage	Acquired by
52	Helen L. Williams	2.24	Fee
53	Henry D. Upton	1.0	Fee
54	Helen L. Williams	1.39	Fee
55	Emmett S. Jones, et ux	0.61	Fee
56	Emmett Jones, et ux	1.11	Fee
57	Edward Winebrenner	0.86	Fee
58	Foster F. Stuart, et ux	4.0	Fee
59	Walter W. Taylor	2.35	Fee
60	C.O. Davidson & W.H. Vaden	1.05	Fee
61	Henry Upton	2.0	Fee
62	Henry Upton	2.0	Fee
63	Henry D. Upton	1.0	Fee
64	John A. Orser	2.0	Fee
65	Eleanora L. Merrill	2.0	Fee
66	Ida L. Woods	2.0	Fee
67	Lee Osmonson, et ux	6.40	Fee
68	Archie E. Collingham	3.0	Fee
69	Theodore N. Strand, et ux	2.0	Fee
70	S.A. and Paul Lopp	2.31	Fee
71	Merle S. Lopp	3.53	Fee
72	Archie L. McIntosh, et ux	2.0	Fee
73	Michael Buchko, et ux	170.15	Fee
74	Mary H. Trautwein	1533.58	Lease

CAMP HAAN
THE HISTORY OF RIVERSIDE'S WORLD WAR II ANTI-AIRCRAFT TRAINING CENTER

74A	Jansen Woods	80.0	Fee
75	Henry Upton	517.153	Lease
75A	Margaret K. Price	80.0	Fee
76	H.M. Dunn, et al	40.0	Lease
76A	Caroline H. Trautwein, et al	80.0	Fee
77	Bengt G. Lofstedt, et ux	25.00	Lease
78	Sim M. Williams, et ux	30.00	Lease
79	John A. Tindall, et ux	15.87	Lease
80	Joe Peacock	8.18	Lease
81	Dorothy Tankersley, et al	3.14	Lease

Note: et ux means "and wife"

Expansion Cont'd

Tract No.	Grantor/Owner	Acreage	Acquired by
82	Helen M. Winstanley	1.05	Lease
83	State of California	4.10	Lease
84	Elmer L. Smith	2.00	Lease
85	Dora L. Wiley	2.00	Lease
87	Robert H. Smith	2.00	Lease
88	Clara Anna Olivas	2.00	Lease
89	Myrtle Small Marker	2.00	Lease
90	State of California	3.98	Lease
93	Frank E Garrould, et ux	1.00	Lease
95	Lola C. Griswold	3.00	Lease
96	Edward Peterson, et ux	2.00	Lease
97	Robert P. Slaton, et ux	1.00	Lease
98	Albert S. McMillan	2.00	Lease

99	State of California	2.00	Lease
100	Stephen C. Brown, et ux	4.00	Lease
101	K.R. Belvin	4.00	Lease
102	State of California	2.00	Lease
103	Elma Roberts Gault	2.00	Lease
104	Reta Shilling Alexander	2.00	Lease
105	William H. Murphy	2.00	Lease
106	State of California	2.10	Lease
107	Alfred Ivey, et ux	4.21	Lease
108	Samuel Kessler, et ux	2.11	Lease
109	L.E. Carscallen, et ux	6.41	Lease
110	Fred Ischinger	2.00	Lease
111	Clarence S. Hansen	1.00	Lease
112	Donald L. Allison	1.00	Lease
113	Henry Upton	1.61	Lease
114	The Arkwright Holding Co.	3.00	Lease
115	Charles E. Sullivan, et ux	1.00	Lease
116	State of California	31.45	Lease
117	Robert Luker, et ux	3.12	Lease
118	Elmer P. Snyder, et ux	2.14	Lease
120	C.A. Curtis, et ux	0.50	Lease

Note: et ux means "and wife"

Expansion Cont'd

Tract No.	Grantor/Owner	Acreage	Acquired by
123	Lincoln C. Ausmus, et ux	2.00	Lease
124	State of California	4.00	Lease
125	Oliver W. Pullman, et ux	0.50	Lease
127	Ivan Eicher, et ux	1.17	Lease
128	Elliot Wm Bowles, et ux	0.97	Lease
129	Mathew Shelter, et ux	1.00	Lease
131	Gertrude Henry	1.00	Lease
132	Estate of Susie E. Dorse	1.00	Lease
133	Reginald E. Garrould, et ux	2.00	Lease
137	Olin R. Burch, et ux	4.00	Lease
138	Steve J. Albert	2.02	Lease
139	Eva Belle Turner	232.60	Lease
140	Mary H. Trautwein, et al	179.00	Lease
141	Enrico Zega	0.25	Lease
142	Mabel A. Baier	80.00	Lease
143	John A. Wood, et ux	50.32	Lease
144	John A. Wood, et ux	20.15	Lease
145	John A. Wood, et ux	5.01	Lease
146	Eda May Lane	5.04	Lease
147	Ira D. Odell, attorney in fact for John F. Odell	5.04	Lease
148	Sam Elder, et ux	10.08	Lease
149	Cecile Patterson McAllister	10.07	Lease
151	Gus F. Selin, et ux	10.06	Lease

152	William Scot, et ux	4.99	Lease
153	Helen E. Holder	5.00	Lease
154	Edgar H. Slaughter	2.50	Lease
155	Frank H. Slaughter	2.50	Lease
156	Peter Paul Stachowiak, et ux	5.01	Lease
157	Arthur J. Dearborn, et ux	2.51	Lease
158	Eva Anberg Ross	2.50	Lease
159	Mary Hallert	10.06	Lease
160	Louise von der Kuhlen	198.00	Lease
161	Ward H. Price, et ux	80.00	Lease

Note: et ux means "and wife"

Expansion Cont'd

Tract No.	Grantor/Owner	Acreage	Acquired by
162	Masonic Homes of California	120.00	Lease
165	Hilda Sawyer	10.00	Lease
166	J.L. Hughes	10.00	Lease
167	Ward H. Price, et ux	20.00	Lease
168	Mark L. Herron, et ux	40.00	Lease

Note: et ux means "and wife"

Source: Report of Disposition Board Covering Camp Haan (1947) Courtesy of the National Archives Riverside.

Source: Camp Haan Map, Withdrawal from W.A.A. (1947) Southern California Real Property Disposal Case Files, 1946-1962. RG 269 Records of the General Services Administration. Box 58; National Archives and Records Administration, Riverside, CA. December 27, 2019.

Source: Office of the Chief Engineers, Real Estate Division (1950) 3101 Tract Register, Project Camp Haan. Southern California Real Property

CAMP HAAN
THE HISTORY OF RIVERSIDE'S WORLD WAR II ANTI-AIRCRAFT TRAINING CENTER
Disposal Case Files, 1946-1962. RG 269 Records of the General Services Administration. Box 58; National Archives and Records Administration, Riverside, CA. January 9, 2020.

APPENDIX 2
BUILDINGS

CAMP HAAN
THE HISTORY OF RIVERSIDE'S WORLD WAR II ANTI-AIRCRAFT TRAINING CENTER

This is a partial list of the building of Camp Haan. I collated this list from disposition records, inspection records, and other paperwork. Since the camp was only open for five or so years and had many transitions, some of the building were converted to other uses. If I had information of other uses I tried to put them in notes section.

You will notice large gaps in building numbers throughout this list; I removed the building numbers if I did not have any information about the building.

Building Number	Building	Notes
T-1	Headquarters (AATC)	
T-2	Officers Club	Original building destroyed by fire, rebuilt
T-3	Mess Hall	
T-4	Latrine	
T-5	Officer's Quarters	Chief of Staff quarters
T-6	Office Building	Commanding Officer, XO, Adjutant, Control officer, food and mess supervisor, Mimeograph Section, Headquarters Duty Officer, Orders section
T-7	Camp Headquarters	Dir. Personnel Div, Director of Supply Div, Mail and Recordds Section, Morale Srvc Branch, Orientation Section, Commercial Accounts, Contracting Section, Safety Officer, Storage Branch and Supply Group

CAMP HAAN
THE HISTORY OF RIVERSIDE'S WORLD WAR II ANTI-AIRCRAFT TRAINING CENTER

T-8	Office Building	Army General Classification Section, Officers' Candidate Board, Oficers' Identification Card Section
T-9	Office Building	Chemical warfare officer, Army Emergency Relief Office, Insurance Office, Machine Records, Personnel Adjutant
T-10	Officer's Quarters	
T-11	Officer's Quarters	
T-12	Officer's Quarters	Commanding General quarters
T-13	Officer's Quarters	Transient Officer Quarter - 1946
T-14	Officer's Quarters	
T-15	Officer's Quarters	SCU 1967
T-16	Officer's Quarters	
T-17	Officer's Quarters	
T-18	Latrine	
T-19	Administration and Supply	Director of Centralized Officers' School
T-20	Recreation Building	
T-21	Mess Hall	
T-22	Hutment	
T-23	Hutment	
T-24	Hutment	
T-25	Hutment	
T-26	Hutment	
T-27	Hutment	
T-28	Hutment	
T-29	Hutment	
T-30	Hutment	

CAMP HAAN
THE HISTORY OF RIVERSIDE'S WORLD WAR II ANTI-AIRCRAFT TRAINING CENTER

T-31	Hutment	
T-32	Hutment	
T-33	Latrine	
T-34	Aircraft Identification Building	
T-35	Headquarters Annex	Adjutant General, IG, JA, PAO, Special Service Officer, Surgeon
T-36	Latrine	
T-37	Officer's Quarters	
T-38	Officer's Quarters	
T-39	Officer's Quarters	
T-40	Officer's Quarters	
T-41	Officer's Quarters	
T-42	Latrine	
T-43	Latrine	
T-44	//WAS NOT BUILT	
T-45	//WAS NOT BUILT	
T-46	//WAS NOT BUILT	
T-47	//WAS NOT BUILT	
T-48	Post Office	Postal Officer, Locator Files Section
T-49	Civilian Personnel Office	Classification and Wage Administration, Employees relations and training, Payroll
T-50	Fire Station	Fire Chief, headqrts station Remote radio rtransmitter/receiver located in this building
T-51	Service Club	#1 Athletic and Recreation Officer, librarian
T-52	Guest House	
T-53	Guest House	
T-54	Signal School	2-story

CAMP HAAN
THE HISTORY OF RIVERSIDE'S WORLD WAR II ANTI-AIRCRAFT TRAINING CENTER

T-55	Radio NCO Club	2-story
T-56	Signal School	2-story
T-57	Dental Clinic	
T-58	Post Office	Chief operator (telegraph and teletype), cryptographic section, Western Union Bank of 10 telephone stations for calling externally
T-59	Finance Building	Auditor, Dir Fiscal Div, Disbursing Officer, War bond sectin, Commercial Accounting Officer, Enlisted Pay, Officer Pay
T-60	Bank, Citizens National	Converted from the original contractor's building Listed as Red Cross Building on electrical report 1943
T-61	Bakers and Cooks Schools	
T-62	Public Relations Building	Camp Haan Tracer Newspaper, property auditor
T-63	Administration Building	Survey officer, Chief of Military Training Branch, Billeting Section, claims officer, Area Engineer, Report of Survey Section
T-64	PX Gas Station incl. car shed	
T-65	Red Cross Garage	Also listed as a bus station - 1942
T-66	Red Cross Office	Field Director
T-67	Bus Depot	

T-68	Commissary	
T-69	//WAS NOT BUILT	
T-70	//WAS NOT BUILT	
T-71	Telephone and Telegraph Building	Chief operator (telephone), cryptographc officer AKA Signal Communication Office
T-72	Photo Lab	
T-73	Air Horn Tower	
T-74	Theater	Theater Officer, Theater #1
T-79	Main Post Exchange, Office and Warehouse	Exchange Oficer, Asst. Exchange Officer, Gen. Mgr., Personnel, Purchasing, Warehouse
T-82	Theater	13,080 sq. ft., Series 700-1212.1
T-86	Day Room	
T-87	Mess Hall	
T-88	Administration and Supply	
T-89	Latrine	
T-90	Latrine	Identification Bureau
T-91	Military Police Office	Visitor pass section Military Policy Office
T-92	Intelligence Office	Military Police Headquarters, Dir of Security and Intel Div, Intel Officer Radio transmitter/receiver located in this building, antennae was located at 34.17W/117.53N (northwest of the 210 and 15 junction)
T-93	Sentry House (camp entrances)	

CAMP HAAN
THE HISTORY OF RIVERSIDE'S WORLD WAR II ANTI-AIRCRAFT TRAINING CENTER

T-99	Flag Pole	
T-100	Tent	
T-101	Tent	
T-102	Tent	
T-103	Tent	
T-104	Tent	
T-105	Tent	
T-106	Tent	
T-107	Tent	
T-108	Tent	
T-109	Tent	
T-110	Tent	
T-111	Tent	
T-112	Tent	
T-113	Tent	
T-114	Tent	
T-115	Tent	
T-116	Tent	
T-117	Tent	
T-118	Tent	
T-119	Tent	
T-120	Tent	
T-121	Tent	
T-122	Tent	
T-123	Tent	
T-124	Tent	
T-125	Tent	
T-126	Tent	
T-127	Tent	
T-128	Tent	
T-129	Tent	
T-130	Tent	
T-131	Tent	
T-132	Tent	

CAMP HAAN
THE HISTORY OF RIVERSIDE'S WORLD WAR II ANTI-AIRCRAFT TRAINING CENTER

T-133	Tent	
T-134	Tent	
T-135	Tent	
T-136	Tent	
T-137	Tent	
T-138	Tent	
T-139	Tent	
T-140	Tent	
T-141	Tent	
T-142	Tent	
T-143	Tent	
T-144	Tent	
T-145	Tent	
T-146	Tent	
T-147	Tent	
T-148	Tent	
T-149	Tent	
T-150	Tent	
T-151	Tent	
T-152	Tent	
T-153	Tent	
T-201	Brigade Headquarters	
T-202	Latrine	
T-203	Mess Hall	
T-204	Administration and Supply	
T-205	Day Room	
T-206	Latrine	
T-207	Tent	
T-208	Tent	
T-209	Tent	
T-210	Tent	
T-211	Tent	
T-212	Tent	
T-213	Tent	

CAMP HAAN
THE HISTORY OF RIVERSIDE'S WORLD WAR II ANTI-AIRCRAFT TRAINING CENTER

T-214	Tent	
T-215	Tent	
T-216	Tent	
T-217	Tent	
T-218	Tent	
T-219	Tent	
T-220	Tent	
T-221	Tent	
T-222	Tent	
T-223	Tent	
T-224	Tent	
T-225	Tent	
T-226	Tent	
T-227	Tent	
T-228	Tent	
T-229	Tent	
T-230	Tent	
T-231	Tent	
T-232	Tent	
T-233	Tent	
T-234	Tent	
T-235	Tent	
T-236	Tent	
T-239	Officer's Quarters	
T-247	Gasoline Station	10340 gallons
T-248	2nd Eschelon	
T-249	Motor Repair Shop	
T-250	Motor Repair Shop	
T-251	Motor Repair Shop	
T-253	Motor Repair Shop	
T-254	Motor Repair Shop	
T-255	Quartermaster Utility Shop	
T-257	Gasoline Station	
T-258	Oil House	

T-262	Motor Repair Shop	
T-271	Warehouse	#11
T-272	Warehouse	#12
T-273	Warehouse	#9
T-274	Warehouse	
T-275	Warehouse	#7
T-276	Warehouse	#8
T-277	Warehouse	#5
T-278	Warehouse	#16
T-280	Warehouse	
T-281	Warehouse	
T-282	Transformer Vault	Supplied north and center buildings
T-286	Butane Plant	
T-299	Raw Sewage Pump	#2
T-300	Lumber Shed and Carpenter Shop	
T-301	Brigade Headquarters	
T-302	Latrine	
T-303	Administration and Supply	
T-304	Mess Hall	
T-305	Day Room	
T-309	Tent	
T-310	Tent	
T-311	Tent	
T-312	Tent	
T-313	Tent	
T-314	Tent	
T-315	Tent	
T-316	Tent	
T-317	Tent	
T-318	Tent	
T-319	Tent	
T-320	Tent	
T-321	Tent	

T-322	Tent	
T-323	Tent	
T-324	Tent	
T-325	Tent	
T-326	Tent	
T-327	Tent	
T-328	Tent	
T-329	Tent	
T-330	Tent	
T-331	Tent	
T-332	Tent	
T-333	Tent	
T-334	Tent	
T-335	Tent	
T-336	Latrine	
T-337	Paint Shop	
T-338	Officer's Quarters	
T-339	Officer's Quarters	
T-342	Hunt Miniature Range	
T-501	Regimental Headquarters	
T-502	Latrine	
T-503	Mess Hall and Recreation, Officer	
T-504	Latrine	
T-510	Infirmary	Also dispensary
T-511	Post Exchange	
T-512	Recreation Building	
T-517	Mess Hall	
T-518	Chapel	South chapel
T-521	Mess Hall	
T-522	Administration and Supply	
T-523	Day Room	
T-524	Mess Hall	
T-525	Administration and Supply	
T-526	Day Room	

CAMP HAAN
THE HISTORY OF RIVERSIDE'S WORLD WAR II ANTI-AIRCRAFT TRAINING CENTER

T-527	Mess Hall	
T-528	Administration and Supply	
T-529	Day Room	
T-530	Mess Hall	
T-531	Administration and Supply	
T-532	Day Room	
T-533	Mess Hall	
T-534	Administration and Supply	
T-535	Day Room	
T-536	Mess Hall	
T-537	Administration and Supply	
T-538	Day Room	
T-541	Mess Hall	
T-542	Administration and Supply	
T-543	Day Room	
T-544	Mess Hall	
T-545	Administration and Supply	
T-546	Day Room	
T-547	Mess Hall	
T-548	Administration and Supply	
T-549	Day Room	
T-550	Mess Hall	
T-551	Administration and Supply	
T-552	Day Room	
T-553	Mess Hall	
T-554	Administration and Supply	
T-555	Day Room	
T-560	Latrine	
T-561	Latrine	
T-562	Latrine	
T-563	Latrine	
T-564	Latrine	
T-565	Latrine	
T-568	Latrine	

CAMP HAAN
THE HISTORY OF RIVERSIDE'S WORLD WAR II ANTI-AIRCRAFT TRAINING CENTER

T-569	Latrine	
T-570	Latrine	
T-571	Latrine	
T-572	Latrine	
T-573	Latrine	
T-576	Wash Rack	
T-577	Gas Station	
T-578	Grease Rack	
T-580	Physical Examination and Lecture Hall	
T-582	Storehouse	Partitioned for clothing and issue warehouse
T-584	Gas Station	
T-585	Vehicle Shed	
T-586	Grease Rack	
T-587	Wash Rack	
T-588	Officer's Quarters	
T-589	Officer's Quarters	
T-590	Latrine	
T-591	Officer's Quarters	
T-592	Officer's Quarters	
T-593	Latrine	
T-594	Officer's Quarters	
T-595	Officer's Quarters	
T-600	Tent	
T-601	Tent	
T-602	Tent	
T-603	Tent	
T-604	Tent	
T-605	Tent	
T-606	Tent	
T-607	Tent	
T-608	Tent	
T-609	Tent	

T-610	Tent	
T-611	Tent	
T-612	Tent	
T-613	Tent	
T-614	Tent	
T-615	Tent	
T-616	Tent	
T-617	Tent	
T-618	Tent	
T-619	Tent	
T-620	Tent	
T-621	Tent	
T-622	Tent	
T-623	Tent	
T-624	Tent	
T-625	Tent	
T-626	Tent	
T-627	Tent	
T-628	Tent	
T-630	Tent	
T-631	Tent	
T-632	Tent	
T-633	Tent	
T-634	Tent	
T-635	Tent	
T-636	Tent	
T-637	Tent	
T-638	Tent	
T-639	Tent	
T-640	Tent	
T-641	Tent	
T-642	Tent	
T-643	Tent	
T-644	Tent	

CAMP HAAN
THE HISTORY OF RIVERSIDE'S WORLD WAR II ANTI-AIRCRAFT TRAINING CENTER

T-645	Tent	
T-646	Tent	
T-647	Tent	
T-648	Tent	
T-649	Tent	
T-651	Tent	
T-652	Tent	
T-653	Tent	
T-654	Tent	
T-655	Tent	
T-656	Tent	
T-657	Tent	
T-658	Tent	
T-659	Tent	
T-660	Tent	
T-661	Tent	
T-662	Tent	
T-663	Tent	
T-664	Tent	
T-665	Tent	
T-666	Tent	
T-667	Tent	
T-668	Tent	
T-670	Tent	
T-671	Tent	
T-672	Tent	
T-673	Tent	
T-674	Tent	
T-675	Tent	
T-676	Tent	
T-677	Tent	
T-678	Tent	
T-679	Tent	
T-680	Tent	

CAMP HAAN
THE HISTORY OF RIVERSIDE'S WORLD WAR II ANTI-AIRCRAFT TRAINING CENTER

T-681	Tent	
T-682	Tent	
T-683	Tent	
T-684	Tent	
T-685	Tent	
T-686	Tent	
T-687	Tent	
T-688	Tent	
T-689	Tent	
T-691	Tent	
T-692	Tent	
T-693	Tent	
T-694	Tent	
T-695	Tent	
T-696	Tent	
T-697	Tent	
T-698	Tent	
T-699	Tent	
T-700	Tent	
T-701	Tent	
T-702	Tent	
T-703	Tent	
T-704	Tent	
T-705	Tent	
T-706	Tent	
T-707	Tent	
T-708	Tent	
T-710	Tent	
T-711	Tent	
T-712	Tent	
T-713	Tent	
T-714	Tent	
T-715	Tent	
T-716	Tent	

CAMP HAAN
THE HISTORY OF RIVERSIDE'S WORLD WAR II ANTI-AIRCRAFT TRAINING CENTER

T-717	Tent	
T-718	Tent	
T-719	Tent	
T-720	Tent	
T-721	Tent	
T-722	Tent	
T-723	Tent	
T-724	Tent	
T-725	Tent	
T-726	Tent	
T-727	Tent	
T-728	Tent	
T-729	Tent	
T-734	Tent	
T-735	Tent	
T-736	Tent	
T-737	Tent	
T-738	Tent	
T-739	Tent	
T-740	Tent	
T-741	Tent	
T-742	Tent	
T-743	Tent	
T-744	Tent	
T-750	Tent	
T-751	Tent	
T-752	Tent	
T-753	Tent	
T-754	Tent	
T-755	Tent	
T-756	Tent	
T-757	Tent	
T-758	Tent	
T-759	Tent	

CAMP HAAN
THE HISTORY OF RIVERSIDE'S WORLD WAR II ANTI-AIRCRAFT TRAINING CENTER

T-760	Tent	
T-761	Tent	
T-762	Tent	
T-763	Tent	
T-764	Tent	
T-765	Tent	
T-766	Tent	
T-767	Tent	
T-768	Tent	
T-769	Tent	
T-777	Tent	
T-778	Tent	
T-779	Tent	
T-780	Tent	
T-781	Tent	
T-782	Tent	
T-783	Tent	
T-784	Tent	
T-790	Tent	
T-791	Tent	
T-792	Tent	
T-793	Tent	
T-794	Tent	
T-795	Tent	
T-796	Tent	
T-797	Tent	
T-798	Tent	
T-799	Tent	
T-800	Tent	
T-801	Tent	
T-802	Tent	
T-803	Tent	
T-804	Tent	
T-805	Tent	

CAMP HAAN
THE HISTORY OF RIVERSIDE'S WORLD WAR II ANTI-AIRCRAFT TRAINING CENTER

T-807	Tent	
T-808	Tent	
T-809	Tent	
T-814	Tent	
T-815	Tent	
T-816	Tent	
T-817	Tent	
T-818	Tent	
T-819	Tent	
T-820	Tent	
T-821	Tent	
T-822	Tent	
T-823	Tent	
T-824	Tent	
T-830	Tent	
T-831	Tent	
T-832	Tent	
T-833	Tent	
T-834	Tent	
T-835	Tent	
T-836	Tent	
T-837	Tent	
T-838	Tent	
T-839	Tent	
T-840	Tent	
T-841	Tent	
T-842	Tent	
T-843	Tent	
T-844	Tent	
T-845	Tent	
T-846	Tent	
T-847	Tent	
T-848	Tent	
T-849	Tent	

T-871	Tent	
T-872	Tent	
T-873	Tent	
T-874	Tent	
T-875	Tent	
T-876	Tent	
T-877	Tent	
T-878	Tent	
T-879	Tent	
T-880	Tent	
T-881	Tent	
T-882	Tent	
T-883	Tent	
T-884	Tent	
T-885	Tent	
T-886	Tent	
T-887	Tent	
T-888	Tent	
T-889	Tent	
T-890	Tent	
T-891	Tent	
T-892	Tent	
T-893	Tent	
T-894	Tent	
T-895	Tent	
T-896	Tent	
T-897	Tent	
T-898	Tent	
T-901	Tent	
T-902	Tent	
T-903	Tent	
T-904	Tent	
T-905	Tent	
T-906	Tent	

CAMP HAAN
THE HISTORY OF RIVERSIDE'S WORLD WAR II ANTI-AIRCRAFT TRAINING CENTER

T-907	Tent	
T-912	Tent	
T-913	Tent	
T-914	Tent	
T-915	Tent	
T-916	Tent	
T-917	Tent	
T-918	Tent	
T-921	Tent	
T-922	Tent	
T-923	Tent	
T-924	Tent	
T-925	Tent	
T-926	Tent	
T-927	Tent	
T-930	Tent	
T-931	Tent	
T-932	Tent	
T-933	Tent	
T-934	Tent	
T-935	Tent	
T-936	Tent	
T-937	Tent	
T-938	Tent	
T-939	Tent	
T-940	Tent	
T-941	Tent	
T-942	Tent	
T-943	Tent	
T-944	Tent	
T-945	Tent	
T-946	Tent	
T-947	Tent	
T-948	Tent	

T-949	Tent	
T-953	Tent	
T-954	Tent	
T-955	Tent	
T-956	Tent	
T-957	Tent	
T-958	Tent	
T-959	Tent	
T-960	Tent	
T-961	Tent	
T-962	Tent	
T-963	Tent	
T-964	Tent	
T-965	Tent	
T-966	Tent	
T-970	Tent	
T-971	Tent	
T-972	Tent	
T-973	Tent	
T-974	Tent	
T-975	Tent	
T-976	Tent	
T-977	Tent	
T-978	Tent	
T-979	Tent	
T-980	Tent	
T-981	Tent	
T-982	Tent	
T-983	Tent	
T-984	Tent	
T-985	Tent	
T-986	Tent	
T-987	Tent	
T-988	Tent	

CAMP HAAN
THE HISTORY OF RIVERSIDE'S WORLD WAR II ANTI-AIRCRAFT TRAINING CENTER

T-989	Tent	
T-993	Tent	
T-994	Tent	
T-995	Tent	
T-996	Tent	
T-997	Tent	
T-998	Tent	
T-999	Tent	
T-1000	Tent	
T-1001	Tent	
T-1002	Tent	
T-1003	Tent	
T-1004	Tent	
T-1005	Tent	
T-1006	Tent	
T-1010	Tent	
T-1011	Tent	
T-1012	Tent	
T-1013	Tent	
T-1014	Tent	
T-1015	Tent	
T-1016	Tent	
T-1017	Tent	
T-1018	Tent	
T-1019	Tent	
T-1020	Tent	
T-1021	Tent	
T-1022	Tent	
T-1023	Tent	
T-1024	Tent	
T-1025	Tent	
T-1026	Tent	
T-1027	Tent	
T-1028	Tent	

CAMP HAAN
THE HISTORY OF RIVERSIDE'S WORLD WAR II ANTI-AIRCRAFT TRAINING CENTER

T-1033	Tent	
T-1034	Tent	
T-1035	Tent	
T-1036	Tent	
T-1037	Tent	
T-1038	Tent	
T-1039	Tent	
T-1040	Tent	
T-1041	Tent	
T-1042	Tent	
T-1043	Tent	
T-1044	Tent	
T-1045	Tent	
T-1046	Tent	
T-1050	Tent	
T-1051	Tent	
T-1052	Tent	
T-1053	Tent	
T-1054	Tent	
T-1055	Tent	
T-1056	Tent	
T-1057	Tent	
T-1058	Tent	
T-1059	Tent	
T-1101	Regimental Headquarters	
T-1102	Latrine	
T-1103	Mess Hall and Recreation, Officer	
T-1104	Latrine	
T-1105	Officer's Quarters	
T-1106	Latrine	
T-1107	Officer's Quarters	
T-1108	Officer's Quarters	
T-1109	Officer's Quarters	
T-1110	Infirmary	Also dispensary

CAMP HAAN
THE HISTORY OF RIVERSIDE'S WORLD WAR II ANTI-AIRCRAFT TRAINING CENTER

T-1111	Post Exchange	
T-1112	Recreation Building	
T-1113	Latrine	
T-1114	Officer's Quarters	
T-1115	Officer's Quarters	
T-1118	Chapel	Central Chapel
T-1119	Fire Station	Station #2
T-1122	Administration and Supply	
T-1123	Day Room	
T-1125	Administration and Supply	
T-1126	Day Room	
T-1128	Administration and Supply	
T-1129	Day Room	
T-1131	Administration and Supply	
T-1132	Day Room	
T-1133	Mess Hall	
T-1134	Administration and Supply	
T-1135	Day Room	
T-1136	Mess Hall	
T-1137	Administration and Supply	
T-1138	Day Room	
T-1141	Mess Hall	
T-1142	Administration and Supply	
T-1143	Day Room	
T-1144	Mess Hall	
T-1145	Administration and Supply	
T-1146	Day Room	
T-1147	Mess Hall	
T-1148	Administration and Supply	
T-1149	Day Room	
T-1150	Mess Hall	
T-1151	Administration and Supply	
T-1152	Day Room	
T-1153	Mess Hall	

CAMP HAAN
THE HISTORY OF RIVERSIDE'S WORLD WAR II ANTI-AIRCRAFT TRAINING CENTER

T-1154	Administration and Supply	
T-1155	Day Room	
T-1160	Latrine	
T-1161	Latrine	
T-1162	Latrine	
T-1163	Latrine	
T-1164	Latrine	
T-1165	Latrine	
T-1168	Latrine	
T-1169	Latrine	
T-1170	Latrine	
T-1171	Latrine	
T-1172	Latrine	
T-1173	Latrine	
T-1176	Wash Rack	
T-1177	Gas Station	
T-1178	Grease Rack	
T-1179	Radio Shelter and Baggage Room	
T-1180	Motor Repair Shop	
T-1181	Motor Repair Shop	
T-1182	Storehouse	
T-1183	*NOT BUILT*	
T-1184	Gas Station	
T-1185	Vehicle Shed	
T-1186	Grease Rack	
T-1187	Wash Rack	
T-1199	Sentry House (camp entrances)	
T-1200	Tent	
T-1201	Tent	
T-1202	Tent	
T-1203	Tent	
T-1204	Tent	
T-1205	Tent	
T-1206	Tent	

CAMP HAAN
THE HISTORY OF RIVERSIDE'S WORLD WAR II ANTI-AIRCRAFT TRAINING CENTER

T-1207	Tent	
T-1208	Tent	
T-1209	Tent	
T-1211	Tent	
T-1212	Tent	
T-1213	Tent	
T-1214	Tent	
T-1215	Tent	
T-1216	Tent	
T-1217	Tent	
T-1218	Tent	
T-1219	Tent	
T-1220	Tent	
T-1221	Tent	
T-1222	Tent	
T-1223	Tent	
T-1224	Tent	
T-1225	Tent	
T-1226	Tent	
T-1227	Tent	
T-1228	Tent	
T-1230	Tent	
T-1231	Tent	
T-1232	Tent	
T-1233	Tent	
T-1234	Tent	
T-1235	Tent	
T-1236	Tent	
T-1237	Tent	
T-1238	Tent	
T-1239	Tent	
T-1240	Tent	
T-1241	Tent	
T-1242	Tent	

CAMP HAAN
THE HISTORY OF RIVERSIDE'S WORLD WAR II ANTI-AIRCRAFT TRAINING CENTER

T-1243	Tent	
T-1244	Tent	
T-1245	Tent	
T-1246	Tent	
T-1247	Tent	
T-1248	Tent	
T-1249	Tent	
T-1251	Tent	
T-1252	Tent	
T-1253	Tent	
T-1254	Tent	
T-1255	Tent	
T-1256	Tent	
T-1257	Tent	
T-1258	Tent	
T-1259	Tent	
T-1260	Tent	
T-1261	Tent	
T-1262	Tent	
T-1263	Tent	
T-1264	Tent	
T-1265	Tent	
T-1266	Tent	
T-1267	Tent	
T-1268	Tent	
T-1270	Tent	
T-1271	Tent	
T-1272	Tent	
T-1273	Tent	
T-1274	Tent	
T-1275	Tent	
T-1276	Tent	
T-1277	Tent	
T-1278	Tent	

CAMP HAAN
THE HISTORY OF RIVERSIDE'S WORLD WAR II ANTI-AIRCRAFT TRAINING CENTER

T-1279	Tent	
T-1280	Tent	
T-1281	Tent	
T-1282	Tent	
T-1283	Tent	
T-1284	Tent	
T-1285	Tent	
T-1286	Tent	
T-1287	Tent	
T-1288	Tent	
T-1289	Tent	
T-1291	Tent	
T-1292	Tent	
T-1293	Tent	
T-1294	Tent	
T-1295	Tent	
T-1296	Tent	
T-1297	Tent	
T-1298	Tent	
T-1299	Tent	
T-1300	Tent	
T-1301	Tent	
T-1302	Tent	
T-1303	Tent	
T-1304	Tent	
T-1305	Tent	
T-1306	Tent	
T-1307	Tent	
T-1308	Tent	
T-1310	Tent	
T-1311	Tent	
T-1312	Tent	
T-1313	Tent	
T-1314	Tent	

CAMP HAAN
THE HISTORY OF RIVERSIDE'S WORLD WAR II ANTI-AIRCRAFT TRAINING CENTER

T-1315	Tent	
T-1316	Tent	
T-1317	Tent	
T-1318	Tent	
T-1319	Tent	
T-1320	Tent	
T-1321	Tent	
T-1322	Tent	
T-1323	Tent	
T-1324	Tent	
T-1325	Tent	
T-1326	Tent	
T-1327	Tent	
T-1328	Tent	
T-1329	Tent	
T-1334	Tent	
T-1335	Tent	
T-1336	Tent	
T-1337	Tent	
T-1338	Tent	
T-1339	Tent	
T-1340	Tent	
T-1341	Tent	
T-1342	Tent	
T-1343	Tent	
T-1344	Tent	
T-1350	Tent	
T-1351	Tent	
T-1352	Tent	
T-1353	Tent	
T-1354	Tent	
T-1355	Tent	
T-1356	Tent	
T-1357	Tent	

CAMP HAAN
THE HISTORY OF RIVERSIDE'S WORLD WAR II ANTI-AIRCRAFT TRAINING CENTER

T-1358	Tent	
T-1359	Tent	
T-1360	Tent	
T-1361	Tent	
T-1362	Tent	
T-1363	Tent	
T-1364	Tent	
T-1365	Tent	
T-1366	Tent	
T-1367	Tent	
T-1368	Tent	
T-1369	Tent	
T-1377	Tent	
T-1378	Tent	
T-1379	Tent	
T-1380	Tent	
T-1381	Tent	
T-1382	Tent	
T-1383	Tent	
T-1384	Tent	
T-1390	Tent	
T-1391	Tent	
T-1392	Tent	
T-1393	Tent	
T-1394	Tent	
T-1395	Tent	
T-1396	Tent	
T-1397	Tent	
T-1398	Tent	
T-1399	Tent	
T-1400	Tent	
T-1401	Tent	
T-1402	Tent	
T-1403	Tent	

CAMP HAAN
THE HISTORY OF RIVERSIDE'S WORLD WAR II ANTI-AIRCRAFT TRAINING CENTER

T-1404	Tent	
T-1405	Tent	
T-1406	Tent	
T-1407	Tent	
T-1408	Tent	
T-1409	Tent	
T-1414	Tent	
T-1415	Tent	
T-1416	Tent	
T-1417	Tent	
T-1418	Tent	
T-1419	Tent	
T-1420	Tent	
T-1421	Tent	
T-1422	Tent	
T-1423	Tent	
T-1424	Tent	
T-1430	Tent	
T-1431	Tent	
T-1432	Tent	
T-1433	Tent	
T-1434	Tent	
T-1435	Tent	
T-1436	Tent	
T-1437	Tent	
T-1438	Tent	
T-1439	Tent	
T-1440	Tent	
T-1441	Tent	
T-1442	Tent	
T-1443	Tent	
T-1444	Tent	
T-1445	Tent	
T-1446	Tent	

CAMP HAAN
THE HISTORY OF RIVERSIDE'S WORLD WAR II ANTI-AIRCRAFT TRAINING CENTER

T-1447	Tent	
T-1448	Tent	
T-1449	Tent	
T-1471	Tent	
T-1472	Tent	
T-1473	Tent	
T-1474	Tent	
T-1475	Tent	
T-1476	Tent	
T-1477	Tent	
T-1478	Tent	
T-1479	Tent	
T-1480	Tent	
T-1481	Tent	
T-1482	Tent	
T-1483	Tent	
T-1484	Tent	
T-1485	Tent	
T-1486	Tent	
T-1487	Tent	
T-1488	Tent	
T-1489	Tent	
T-1491	Tent	
T-1492	Tent	
T-1493	Tent	
T-1494	Tent	
T-1495	Tent	
T-1496	Tent	
T-1497	Tent	
T-1498	Tent	
T-1501	Tent	
T-1502	Tent	
T-1503	Tent	
T-1504	Tent	

CAMP HAAN
THE HISTORY OF RIVERSIDE'S WORLD WAR II ANTI-AIRCRAFT TRAINING CENTER

T-1505	Tent	
T-1506	Tent	
T-1507	Tent	
T-1512	Tent	
T-1513	Tent	
T-1514	Tent	
T-1515	Tent	
T-1516	Tent	
T-1517	Tent	
T-1518	Tent	
T-1521	Tent	
T-1522	Tent	
T-1523	Tent	
T-1524	Tent	
T-1525	Tent	
T-1526	Tent	
T-1527	Tent	
T-1530	Tent	
T-1531	Tent	
T-1532	Tent	
T-1533	Tent	
T-1534	Tent	
T-1535	Tent	
T-1536	Tent	
T-1537	Tent	
T-1538	Tent	
T-1539	Tent	
T-1540	Tent	
T-1541	Tent	
T-1542	Tent	
T-1543	Tent	
T-1544	Tent	
T-1545	Tent	
T-1546	Tent	

CAMP HAAN
THE HISTORY OF RIVERSIDE'S WORLD WAR II ANTI-AIRCRAFT TRAINING CENTER

T-1547	Tent	
T-1548	Tent	
T-1553	Tent	
T-1554	Tent	
T-1555	Tent	
T-1556	Tent	
T-1557	Tent	
T-1558	Tent	
T-1559	Tent	
T-1560	Tent	
T-1561	Tent	
T-1562	Tent	
T-1563	Tent	
T-1564	Tent	
T-1565	Tent	
T-1566	Tent	
T-1570	Tent	
T-1571	Tent	
T-1572	Tent	
T-1573	Tent	
T-1574	Tent	
T-1575	Tent	
T-1576	Tent	
T-1577	Tent	
T-1578	Tent	
T-1579	Tent	
T-1580	Tent	
T-1581	Tent	
T-1582	Tent	
T-1583	Tent	
T-1584	Tent	
T-1585	Tent	
T-1587	Tent	
T-1588	Tent	

CAMP HAAN
THE HISTORY OF RIVERSIDE'S WORLD WAR II ANTI-AIRCRAFT TRAINING CENTER

T-1589	Tent	
T-1593	Tent	
T-1594	Tent	
T-1595	Tent	
T-1596	Tent	
T-1597	Tent	
T-1598	Tent	
T-1599	Tent	
T-1600	Tent	
T-1601	Tent	
T-1602	Tent	
T-1603	Tent	
T-1604	Tent	
T-1605	Tent	
T-1606	Tent	
T-1610	Tent	
T-1611	Tent	
T-1612	Tent	
T-1613	Tent	
T-1614	Tent	
T-1615	Tent	
T-1616	Tent	
T-1617	Tent	
T-1618	Tent	
T-1619	Tent	
T-1620	Tent	
T-1621	Tent	
T-1622	Tent	
T-1623	Tent	
T-1624	Tent	
T-1625	Tent	
T-1626	Tent	
T-1627	Tent	
T-1628	Tent	

CAMP HAAN
THE HISTORY OF RIVERSIDE'S WORLD WAR II ANTI-AIRCRAFT TRAINING CENTER

T-1629	Tent	
T-1633	Tent	
T-1634	Tent	
T-1635	Tent	
T-1636	Tent	
T-1637	Tent	
T-1638	Tent	
T-1639	Tent	
T-1640	Tent	
T-1641	Tent	
T-1642	Tent	
T-1643	Tent	
T-1644	Tent	
T-1645	Tent	
T-1646	Tent	
T-1650	Tent	
T-1651	Tent	
T-1652	Tent	
T-1653	Tent	
T-1654	Tent	
T-1655	Tent	
T-1656	Tent	
T-1657	Tent	
T-1658	Tent	
T-1659	Tent	
T-1701	Regimental Headquarters	
T-1702	Latrine	
T-1703	Mess Hall and Recreation, Officer	
T-1704	Latrine	
T-1710	Infirmary	Also dispensary
T-1711	Post Exchange	
T-1712	Recreation Building	
T-1722	Administration and Supply	
T-1723	Day Room	

T-1725	Administration and Supply	
T-1726	Day Room	
T-1728	Administration and Supply	
T-1729	Day Room	
T-1731	Administration and Supply	
T-1732	Day Room	
T-1734	Administration and Supply	
T-1735	Day Room	
T-1737	Administration and Supply	
T-1738	Day Room	
T-1741	Mess Hall	
T-1742	Administration and Supply	
T-1743	Day Room	
T-1744	Mess Hall	
T-1745	Administration and Supply	
T-1746	Day Room	
T-1748	Administration and Supply	
T-1749	Day Room	
T-1751	Administration and Supply	
T-1752	Day Room	
T-1754	Administration and Supply	
T-1755	Day Room	
T-1760	Latrine	
T-1761	Latrine	
T-1762	Latrine	
T-1763	Latrine	
T-1764	Latrine	
T-1765	Latrine	
T-1777	Gas Station	
T-1778	Grease Rack	
T-1780	Motor Repair Shop	
T-1781	Motor Repair Shop	
T-1782	Storehhouse	
T-1783	Wash Rack	

CAMP HAAN
THE HISTORY OF RIVERSIDE'S WORLD WAR II ANTI-AIRCRAFT TRAINING CENTER

T-1784	Gas Station	
T-1785	Vehicle Shed	
T-1786	Grease Rack	
T-1787	Wash Rack	
T-1788	Officer's Quarters	
T-1789	Officer's Quarters	
T-1790	Latrine	
T-1791	Officer's Quarters	
T-1792	Officer's Quarters	
T-1793	Latrine	
T-1794	Officer's Quarters	
T-1795	Officer's Quarters	
T-1799	Bus Station	
T-1800	Tent	
T-1801	Tent	
T-1802	Tent	
T-1803	Tent	
T-1804	Tent	
T-1805	Tent	
T-1806	Tent	
T-1807	Tent	
T-1808	Tent	
T-1809	Tent	
T-1811	Tent	
T-1812	Tent	
T-1813	Tent	
T-1814	Tent	
T-1815	Tent	
T-1816	Tent	
T-1817	Tent	
T-1818	Tent	
T-1819	Tent	
T-1820	Tent	
T-1821	Tent	

CAMP HAAN
THE HISTORY OF RIVERSIDE'S WORLD WAR II ANTI-AIRCRAFT TRAINING CENTER

T-1822	Tent	
T-1823	Tent	
T-1824	Tent	
T-1825	Tent	
T-1826	Tent	
T-1827	Tent	
T-1828	Tent	
T-1830	Tent	
T-1831	Tent	
T-1832	Tent	
T-1833	Tent	
T-1834	Tent	
T-1835	Tent	
T-1836	Tent	
T-1837	Tent	
T-1838	Tent	
T-1839	Tent	
T-1840	Tent	
T-1841	Tent	
T-1842	Tent	
T-1843	Tent	
T-1844	Tent	
T-1845	Tent	
T-1846	Tent	
T-1847	Tent	
T-1848	Tent	
T-1849	Tent	
T-1851	Tent	
T-1852	Tent	
T-1853	Tent	
T-1854	Tent	
T-1855	Tent	
T-1856	Tent	
T-1857	Tent	

CAMP HAAN
THE HISTORY OF RIVERSIDE'S WORLD WAR II ANTI-AIRCRAFT TRAINING CENTER

T-1858	Tent	
T-1859	Tent	
T-1860	Tent	
T-1861	Tent	
T-1862	Tent	
T-1863	Tent	
T-1864	Tent	
T-1865	Tent	
T-1866	Tent	
T-1867	Tent	
T-1868	Tent	
T-1870	Tent	
T-1871	Tent	
T-1872	Tent	
T-1873	Tent	
T-1874	Tent	
T-1875	Tent	
T-1876	Tent	
T-1877	Tent	
T-1878	Tent	
T-1879	Tent	
T-1880	Tent	
T-1881	Tent	
T-1882	Tent	
T-1883	Tent	
T-1884	Tent	
T-1885	Tent	
T-1886	Tent	
T-1887	Tent	
T-1888	Tent	
T-1889	Tent	
T-1891	Tent	
T-1892	Tent	
T-1893	Tent	

CAMP HAAN
THE HISTORY OF RIVERSIDE'S WORLD WAR II ANTI-AIRCRAFT TRAINING CENTER

T-1894	Tent	
T-1895	Tent	
T-1896	Tent	
T-1897	Tent	
T-1898	Tent	
T-1899	Tent	
T-1900	Tent	
T-1901	Tent	
T-1902	Tent	
T-1903	Tent	
T-1904	Tent	
T-1905	Tent	
T-1906	Tent	
T-1907	Tent	
T-1908	Tent	
T-1910	Tent	
T-1911	Tent	
T-1912	Tent	
T-1913	Tent	
T-1914	Tent	
T-1915	Tent	
T-1916	Tent	
T-1917	Tent	
T-1918	Tent	
T-1919	Tent	
T-1920	Tent	
T-1921	Tent	
T-1922	Tent	
T-1923	Tent	
T-1924	Tent	
T-1925	Tent	
T-1926	Tent	
T-1927	Tent	
T-1928	Tent	

CAMP HAAN
THE HISTORY OF RIVERSIDE'S WORLD WAR II ANTI-AIRCRAFT TRAINING CENTER

T-1929	Tent	
T-1934	Tent	
T-1935	Tent	
T-1936	Tent	
T-1937	Tent	
T-1938	Tent	
T-1939	Tent	
T-1940	Tent	
T-1941	Tent	
T-1942	Tent	
T-1943	Tent	
T-1944	Tent	
T-1950	Tent	
T-1951	Tent	
T-1952	Tent	
T-1953	Tent	
T-1954	Tent	
T-1955	Tent	
T-1956	Tent	
T-1957	Tent	
T-1958	Tent	
T-1959	Tent	
T-1960	Tent	
T-1961	Tent	
T-1962	Tent	
T-1963	Tent	
T-1964	Tent	
T-1965	Tent	
T-1966	Tent	
T-1967	Tent	
T-1968	Tent	
T-1969	Tent	
T-1977	Tent	
T-1978	Tent	

CAMP HAAN
THE HISTORY OF RIVERSIDE'S WORLD WAR II ANTI-AIRCRAFT TRAINING CENTER

T-1979	Tent	
T-1980	Tent	
T-1981	Tent	
T-1982	Tent	
T-1983	Tent	
T-1984	Tent	
T-1990	Tent	
T-1991	Tent	
T-1992	Tent	
T-1993	Tent	
T-1994	Tent	
T-1995	Tent	
T-1996	Tent	
T-1997	Tent	
T-1998	Tent	
T-1999	Tent	
T-2000	Tent	
T-2001	Tent	
T-2002	Tent	
T-2003	Tent	
T-2004	Tent	
T-2005	Tent	
T-2006	Tent	
T-2007	Tent	
T-2008	Tent	
T-2009	Tent	
T-2014	Tent	
T-2015	Tent	
T-2016	Tent	
T-2017	Tent	
T-2018	Tent	
T-2019	Tent	
T-2020	Tent	
T-2021	Tent	

T-2022	Tent	
T-2023	Tent	
T-2024	Tent	
T-2030	Tent	
T-2031	Tent	
T-2032	Tent	
T-2033	Tent	
T-2034	Tent	
T-2035	Tent	
T-2036	Tent	
T-2037	Tent	
T-2038	Tent	
T-2039	Tent	
T-2040	Tent	
T-2041	Tent	
T-2042	Tent	
T-2043	Tent	
T-2044	Tent	
T-2045	Tent	
T-2046	Tent	
T-2047	Tent	
T-2048	Tent	
T-2049	Tent	
T-2071	Tent	
T-2072	Tent	
T-2073	Tent	
T-2074	Tent	
T-2075	Tent	
T-2076	Tent	
T-2077	Tent	
T-2078	Tent	
T-2079	Tent	
T-2080	Tent	
T-2081	Tent	

CAMP HAAN
THE HISTORY OF RIVERSIDE'S WORLD WAR II ANTI-AIRCRAFT TRAINING CENTER

T-2082	Tent	
T-2083	Tent	
T-2084	Tent	
T-2085	Tent	
T-2086	Tent	
T-2087	Tent	
T-2088	Tent	
T-2089	Tent	
T-2101	Tent	
T-2102	Tent	
T-2103	Tent	
T-2104	Tent	
T-2105	Tent	
T-2106	Tent	
T-2107	Tent	
T-2112	Tent	
T-2113	Tent	
T-2114	Tent	
T-2115	Tent	
T-2116	Tent	
T-2117	Tent	
T-2118	Tent	
T-2121	Tent	
T-2122	Tent	
T-2123	Tent	
T-2124	Tent	
T-2125	Tent	
T-2126	Tent	
T-2127	Tent	
T-2130	Tent	
T-2131	Tent	
T-2132	Tent	
T-2133	Tent	
T-2134	Tent	

CAMP HAAN
THE HISTORY OF RIVERSIDE'S WORLD WAR II ANTI-AIRCRAFT TRAINING CENTER

T-2135	Tent	
T-2136	Tent	
T-2137	Tent	
T-2138	Tent	
T-2139	Tent	
T-2140	Tent	
T-2141	Tent	
T-2142	Tent	
T-2143	Tent	
T-2144	Tent	
T-2145	Tent	
T-2146	Tent	
T-2147	Tent	
T-2148	Tent	
T-2149	Tent	
T-2153	Tent	
T-2154	Tent	
T-2155	Tent	
T-2156	Tent	
T-2157	Tent	
T-2158	Tent	
T-2159	Tent	
T-2160	Tent	
T-2161	Tent	
T-2162	Tent	
T-2163	Tent	
T-2164	Tent	
T-2165	Tent	
T-2166	Tent	
T-2170	Tent	
T-2171	Tent	
T-2172	Latrine	
T-2173	Latrine	
T-2174	Tent	

T-2175	Tent	
T-2176	Tent	
T-2177	Tent	
T-2178	Tent	
T-2179	Tent	
T-2180	Tent	
T-2181	Tent	
T-2182	Tent	
T-2183	Tent	
T-2184	Tent	
T-2185	Tent	
T-2186	Tent	
T-2187	Tent	
T-2188	Tent	
T-2189	Tent	
T-2193	Tent	
T-2194	Tent	
T-2195	Tent	
T-2196	Tent	
T-2197	Tent	
T-2198	Tent	
T-2199	Tent	
T-2200	Tent	
T-2201	Tent	
T-2202	Tent	
T-2203	Tent	
T-2204	Tent	
T-2205	Tent	
T-2206	Tent	
T-2210	Tent	
T-2211	Tent	
T-2212	Tent	
T-2213	Tent	
T-2214	Tent	

CAMP HAAN
THE HISTORY OF RIVERSIDE'S WORLD WAR II ANTI-AIRCRAFT TRAINING CENTER

T-2215	Tent	
T-2216	Tent	
T-2217	Tent	
T-2218	Tent	
T-2219	Tent	
T-2221	Tent	
T-2222	Tent	
T-2223	Tent	
T-2224	Tent	
T-2225	Tent	
T-2226	Tent	
T-2227	Tent	
T-2228	Tent	
T-2229	Tent	
T-2233	Tent	
T-2234	Tent	
T-2235	Tent	
T-2236	Tent	
T-2237	Tent	
T-2238	Tent	
T-2239	Tent	
T-2240	Tent	
T-2241	Tent	
T-2242	Tent	
T-2243	Tent	
T-2244	Tent	
T-2245	Tent	
T-2246	Tent	
T-2250	Tent	
T-2251	Tent	
T-2252	Tent	
T-2253	Tent	
T-2254	Tent	
T-2255	Tent	

T-2256	Tent	
T-2257	Tent	
T-2258	Tent	
T-2259	Tent	
T-2301	Regimental Headquarters	
T-2302	Latrine	
T-2303	Mess Hall and Recreation, Officer	
T-2304	Latrine	
T-2310	Infirmary	Also dispensary
T-2311	Post Exchange	
T-2312	Recreation Building	
T-2321	Mess Hall	
T-2322	Administration and Supply	
T-2323	Day Room	
T-2324	Mess Hall	
T-2325	Administration and Supply	
T-2326	Day Room	
T-2327	Mess Hall	
T-2328	Administration and Supply	
T-2329	Day Room	
T-2330	Mess Hall	
T-2331	Administration and Supply	
T-2332	Day Room	
T-2333	Mess Hall	
T-2334	Administration and Supply	
T-2335	Day Room	
T-2336	Mess Hall	
T-2337	Administration and Supply	
T-2338	Day Room	
T-2341	Mess Hall	
T-2342	Administration and Supply	
T-2343	Day Room	
T-2344	Mess Hall	
T-2345	Administration and Supply	

CAMP HAAN
THE HISTORY OF RIVERSIDE'S WORLD WAR II ANTI-AIRCRAFT TRAINING CENTER

T-2346	Day Room	
T-2347	Mess Hall	
T-2348	Administration and Supply	
T-2349	Day Room	
T-2350	Mess Hall	
T-2351	Administration and Supply	
T-2352	Day Room	
T-2353	Mess Hall	
T-2354	Administration and Supply	
T-2355	Day Room	
T-2360	Latrine	
T-2361	Latrine	
T-2362	Latrine	
T-2363	Latrine	
T-2364	Latrine	
T-2368	Latrine	
T-2369	Latrine	
T-2370	Latrine	
T-2371	Latrine	
T-2372	Latrine	
T-2373	Latrine	
T-2377	Gas Station	
T-2378	Radio Shelter	
T-2379	Grease Rack	
T-2380	Motor Repair Shop	
T-2381	Motor Repair Shop	
T-2382	Storehhouse	
T-2383	*NOT BUILT*	
T-2384	Gas Station	
T-2385	Vehicle Shed	
T-2386	Repair Shop	
T-2387	Latrine	
T-2388	Officer's Quarters	
T-2389	Officer's Quarters	

T-2390	Latrine	
T-2391	Officer's Quarters	
T-2392	Officer's Quarters	
T-2393	Latrine	
T-2394	Officer's Quarters	
T-2395	Officer's Quarters	
T-2396	Wash Rack	
T-2397	Wash Rack	
T-2398	Sewage Pump House	
T-2400	Tent	
T-2401	Tent	
T-2402	Tent	
T-2403	Tent	
T-2404	Tent	
T-2405	Tent	
T-2406	Tent	
T-2407	Tent	
T-2408	Tent	
T-2409	Tent	
T-2411	Tent	
T-2412	Tent	
T-2413	Tent	
T-2414	Tent	
T-2415	Tent	
T-2416	Tent	
T-2417	Tent	
T-2418	Tent	
T-2419	Tent	
T-2420	Tent	
T-2421	Tent	
T-2422	Tent	
T-2423	Tent	
T-2424	Tent	
T-2425	Tent	

CAMP HAAN
THE HISTORY OF RIVERSIDE'S WORLD WAR II ANTI-AIRCRAFT TRAINING CENTER

T-2426	Tent	
T-2427	Tent	
T-2428	Tent	
T-2430	Tent	
T-2431	Tent	
T-2432	Tent	
T-2433	Tent	
T-2434	Tent	
T-2435	Tent	
T-2436	Tent	
T-2437	Tent	
T-2438	Tent	
T-2439	Tent	
T-2440	Tent	
T-2441	Tent	
T-2442	Tent	
T-2443	Tent	
T-2444	Tent	
T-2445	Tent	
T-2446	Tent	
T-2447	Tent	
T-2448	Tent	
T-2449	Tent	
T-2451	Tent	
T-2452	Tent	
T-2453	Tent	
T-2454	Tent	
T-2455	Tent	
T-2456	Tent	
T-2457	Tent	
T-2458	Tent	
T-2459	Tent	
T-2460	Tent	
T-2461	Tent	

CAMP HAAN
THE HISTORY OF RIVERSIDE'S WORLD WAR II ANTI-AIRCRAFT TRAINING CENTER

T-2462	Tent	
T-2463	Tent	
T-2464	Tent	
T-2465	Tent	
T-2466	Tent	
T-2467	Tent	
T-2468	Tent	
T-2470	Tent	
T-2471	Tent	
T-2472	Tent	
T-2473	Tent	
T-2474	Tent	
T-2475	Tent	
T-2476	Tent	
T-2477	Tent	
T-2478	Tent	
T-2479	Tent	
T-2480	Tent	
T-2481	Tent	
T-2482	Tent	
T-2483	Tent	
T-2484	Tent	
T-2485	Tent	
T-2486	Tent	
T-2487	Tent	
T-2488	Tent	
T-2489	Tent	
T-2491	Tent	
T-2492	Tent	
T-2493	Tent	
T-2494	Tent	
T-2495	Tent	
T-2496	Tent	
T-2497	Tent	

CAMP HAAN
THE HISTORY OF RIVERSIDE'S WORLD WAR II ANTI-AIRCRAFT TRAINING CENTER

T-2498	Tent	
T-2499	Tent	
T-2500	Tent	
T-2501	Tent	
T-2502	Tent	
T-2503	Tent	
T-2504	Tent	
T-2505	Tent	
T-2506	Tent	
T-2507	Tent	
T-2508	Tent	
T-2510	Tent	
T-2511	Tent	
T-2512	Tent	
T-2513	Tent	
T-2514	Tent	
T-2515	Tent	
T-2516	Tent	
T-2517	Tent	
T-2518	Tent	
T-2519	Tent	
T-2520	Tent	
T-2521	Tent	
T-2522	Tent	
T-2523	Tent	
T-2524	Tent	
T-2525	Tent	
T-2526	Tent	
T-2527	Tent	
T-2528	Tent	
T-2529	Tent	
T-2534	Tent	
T-2535	Tent	
T-2536	Tent	

CAMP HAAN
THE HISTORY OF RIVERSIDE'S WORLD WAR II ANTI-AIRCRAFT TRAINING CENTER

T-2537	Tent	
T-2538	Tent	
T-2539	Tent	
T-2540	Tent	
T-2541	Tent	
T-2542	Tent	
T-2543	Tent	
T-2544	Tent	
T-2550	Tent	
T-2551	Tent	
T-2552	Tent	
T-2553	Tent	
T-2554	Tent	
T-2555	Tent	
T-2556	Tent	
T-2557	Tent	
T-2558	Tent	
T-2559	Tent	
T-2560	Tent	
T-2561	Tent	
T-2562	Tent	
T-2563	Tent	
T-2564	Tent	
T-2565	Tent	
T-2566	Tent	
T-2567	Tent	
T-2568	Tent	
T-2569	Tent	
T-2577	Tent	
T-2578	Tent	
T-2579	Tent	
T-2580	Tent	
T-2581	Tent	
T-2582	Tent	

CAMP HAAN
THE HISTORY OF RIVERSIDE'S WORLD WAR II ANTI-AIRCRAFT TRAINING CENTER

T-2583	Tent	
T-2584	Tent	
T-2590	Tent	
T-2591	Tent	
T-2592	Tent	
T-2593	Tent	
T-2594	Tent	
T-2595	Tent	
T-2596	Tent	
T-2597	Tent	
T-2598	Tent	
T-2599	Tent	
T-2600	Tent	
T-2601	Tent	
T-2602	Tent	
T-2603	Tent	
T-2604	Tent	
T-2605	Tent	
T-2606	Tent	
T-2607	Tent	
T-2608	Tent	
T-2609	Tent	
T-2614	Tent	
T-2615	Tent	
T-2616	Tent	
T-2617	Tent	
T-2618	Tent	
T-2619	Tent	
T-2620	Tent	
T-2621	Tent	
T-2622	Tent	
T-2623	Tent	
T-2624	Tent	
T-2630	Tent	

T-2631	Tent	
T-2632	Tent	
T-2633	Tent	
T-2634	Tent	
T-2635	Tent	
T-2636	Tent	
T-2637	Tent	
T-2638	Tent	
T-2639	Tent	
T-2640	Tent	
T-2641	Tent	
T-2642	Tent	
T-2671	Tent	
T-2672	Tent	
T-2673	Tent	
T-2674	Tent	
T-2675	Tent	
T-2676	Tent	
T-2677	Tent	
T-2678	Tent	
T-2679	Tent	
T-2680	Tent	
T-2681	Tent	
T-2682	Tent	
T-2683	Tent	
T-2684	Tent	
T-2685	Tent	
T-2686	Tent	
T-2687	Tent	
T-2688	Tent	
T-2689	Tent	
T-2691	Tent	
T-2692	Tent	
T-2693	Tent	

CAMP HAAN
THE HISTORY OF RIVERSIDE'S WORLD WAR II ANTI-AIRCRAFT TRAINING CENTER

T-2694	Tent	
T-2695	Tent	
T-2696	Tent	
T-2697	Tent	
T-2698	Tent	
T-2701	Tent	
T-2702	Tent	
T-2703	Tent	
T-2704	Tent	
T-2705	Tent	
T-2706	Tent	
T-2707	Tent	
T-2712	Tent	
T-2713	Tent	
T-2714	Tent	
T-2715	Tent	
T-2716	Tent	
T-2717	Tent	
T-2718	Tent	
T-2721	Tent	
T-2722	Tent	
T-2723	Tent	
T-2724	Tent	
T-2725	Tent	
T-2726	Tent	
T-2727	Tent	
T-2730	Tent	
T-2731	Tent	
T-2732	Tent	
T-2733	Tent	
T-2734	Tent	
T-2735	Tent	
T-2736	Tent	
T-2737	Tent	

T-2738	Tent	
T-2739	Tent	
T-2740	Tent	
T-2741	Tent	
T-2742	Tent	
T-2743	Tent	
T-2744	Tent	
T-2745	Tent	
T-2746	Tent	
T-2747	Tent	
T-2748	Tent	
T-2749	Tent	
T-2753	Tent	
T-2754	Tent	
T-2755	Tent	
T-2756	Tent	
T-2757	Tent	
T-2758	Tent	
T-2759	Tent	
T-2760	Tent	
T-2761	Tent	
T-2762	Tent	
T-2763	Tent	
T-2764	Tent	
T-2765	Tent	
T-2766	Tent	
T-2770	Tent	
T-2771	Tent	
T-2772	Tent	
T-2773	Tent	
T-2774	Tent	
T-2775	Tent	
T-2776	Tent	
T-2777	Tent	

CAMP HAAN
THE HISTORY OF RIVERSIDE'S WORLD WAR II ANTI-AIRCRAFT TRAINING CENTER

T-2778	Tent	
T-2779	Tent	
T-2780	Tent	
T-2781	Tent	
T-2782	Tent	
T-2783	Tent	
T-2784	Tent	
T-2785	Tent	
T-2786	Tent	
T-2787	Tent	
T-2788	Tent	
T-2789	Tent	
T-2793	Tent	
T-2794	Tent	
T-2795	Tent	
T-2796	Tent	
T-2797	Tent	
T-2798	Tent	
T-2799	Tent	
T-2800	Tent	
T-2801	Tent	
T-2802	Tent	
T-2803	Tent	
T-2804	Tent	
T-2805	Tent	
T-2806	Tent	
T-2810	Tent	
T-2811	Tent	
T-2812	Tent	
T-2813	Tent	
T-2814	Tent	
T-2815	Tent	
T-2816	Tent	
T-2817	Tent	

T-2818	Tent	
T-2819	Tent	
T-2820	Tent	
T-2821	Tent	
T-2822	Tent	
T-2823	Tent	
T-2824	Tent	
T-2825	Tent	
T-2826	Tent	
T-2827	Tent	
T-2828	Tent	
T-2829	Tent	
T-2833	Tent	
T-2834	Tent	
T-2835	Tent	
T-2836	Tent	
T-2837	Tent	
T-2838	Tent	
T-2839	Tent	
T-2840	Tent	
T-2841	Tent	
T-2842	Tent	
T-2843	Tent	
T-2844	Tent	
T-2845	Tent	
T-2846	Tent	
T-2850	Tent	
T-2851	Tent	
T-2852	Tent	
T-2853	Tent	
T-2854	Tent	
T-2855	Tent	
T-2856	Tent	
T-2857	Tent	

CAMP HAAN
THE HISTORY OF RIVERSIDE'S WORLD WAR II ANTI-AIRCRAFT TRAINING CENTER

T-2858	Tent	
T-2859	Tent	
T-2901	Regimental Headquarters	
T-2902	Latrine	
T-2903	Mess Hall and Recreation, Officer	
T-2904	Latrine	
T-2910	Infirmary	Also dispensary
T-2911	Post Exchange	
T-2912	Service Club Colored Troops	
T-2918	Chapel	North Chapel, Chaplain
T-2919	Fire Station	Station #1
T-2922	Administration and Supply	
T-2923	Day Room	
T-2925	Administration and Supply	
T-2926	Day Room	
T-2928	Administration and Supply	
T-2929	Day Room	
T-2931	Administration and Supply	
T-2932	Day Room	
T-2934	Administration and Supply	
T-2935	Day Room	
T-2937	Administration and Supply	
T-2938	Day Room	
T-2941	Mess Hall	
T-2942	Administration and Supply	
T-2943	Day Room	
T-2944	Mess Hall	
T-2945	Administration and Supply	
T-2946	Day Room	
T-2948	Administration and Supply	
T-2949	Day Room	
T-2951	Administration and Supply	
T-2952	Day Room	
T-2954	Administration and Supply	

T-2955	Day Room
T-2977	Gas Station
T-2978	Grease Rack
T-2980	Motor Repair Shop
T-2981	Motor Repair Shop
T-2982	Storehhouse
T-2984	Gas Station
T-2985	Vehicle Shed
T-2986	Sewage Pump House/Lift station
T-2987	Grease Rack
T-2988	Officer's Quarters
T-2989	Officer's Quarters
T-2990	Latrine
T-2991	Officer's Quarters
T-2992	Officer's Quarters
T-2993	Latrine
T-2994	Officer's Quarters
T-2995	Officer's Quarters
T-2996	Wash Rack
T-2997	Wash Rack
T-2998	Road Dept. Office
T-3000	Tent
T-3001	Tent
T-3002	Tent
T-3003	Tent
T-3004	Tent
T-3005	Tent
T-3006	Tent
T-3007	Tent
T-3008	Tent
T-3009	Tent
T-3011	Tent
T-3012	Tent
T-3013	Tent

CAMP HAAN
THE HISTORY OF RIVERSIDE'S WORLD WAR II ANTI-AIRCRAFT TRAINING CENTER

T-3014	Tent	
T-3015	Tent	
T-3016	Tent	
T-3017	Tent	
T-3018	Tent	
T-3019	Tent	
T-3020	Tent	
T-3021	Tent	
T-3022	Tent	
T-3023	Tent	
T-3024	Tent	
T-3025	Tent	
T-3026	Tent	
T-3027	Tent	
T-3028	Tent	
T-3030	Tent	
T-3031	Tent	
T-3032	Tent	
T-3033	Tent	
T-3034	Tent	
T-3035	Tent	
T-3036	Tent	
T-3037	Tent	
T-3038	Tent	
T-3039	Tent	
T-3040	Tent	
T-3041	Tent	
T-3042	Tent	
T-3043	Tent	
T-3044	Tent	
T-3045	Tent	
T-3046	Tent	
T-3047	Tent	
T-3048	Tent	

T-3049	Tent	
T-3051	Tent	
T-3052	Tent	
T-3053	Tent	
T-3054	Tent	
T-3055	Tent	
T-3056	Tent	
T-3057	Tent	
T-3058	Tent	
T-3059	Tent	
T-3060	Tent	
T-3061	Tent	
T-3062	Tent	
T-3063	Tent	
T-3064	Tent	
T-3065	Tent	
T-3066	Tent	
T-3067	Tent	
T-3068	Tent	
T-3070	Tent	
T-3071	Tent	
T-3072	Tent	
T-3073	Tent	
T-3074	Tent	
T-3075	Tent	
T-3076	Tent	
T-3077	Tent	
T-3078	Tent	
T-3079	Tent	
T-3080	Tent	
T-3081	Tent	
T-3082	Tent	
T-3083	Tent	
T-3084	Tent	

CAMP HAAN
THE HISTORY OF RIVERSIDE'S WORLD WAR II ANTI-AIRCRAFT TRAINING CENTER

T-3085	Tent	
T-3086	Tent	
T-3087	Tent	
T-3088	Tent	
T-3089	Tent	
T-3091	Tent	
T-3092	Tent	
T-3093	Tent	
T-3094	Tent	
T-3095	Tent	
T-3096	Tent	
T-3097	Tent	
T-3098	Tent	
T-3099	Tent	
T-3100	Tent	
T-3101	Tent	
T-3102	Tent	
T-3103	Tent	
T-3104	Tent	
T-3105	Tent	
T-3106	Tent	
T-3107	Tent	
T-3108	Tent	
T-3110	Tent	
T-3111	Tent	
T-3112	Tent	
T-3113	Tent	
T-3114	Tent	
T-3115	Tent	
T-3116	Tent	
T-3117	Tent	
T-3118	Tent	
T-3119	Tent	
T-3120	Tent	

CAMP HAAN
THE HISTORY OF RIVERSIDE'S WORLD WAR II ANTI-AIRCRAFT TRAINING CENTER

T-3121	Tent	
T-3122	Tent	
T-3123	Tent	
T-3124	Tent	
T-3125	Tent	
T-3126	Tent	
T-3127	Tent	
T-3128	Tent	
T-3129	Tent	
T-3134	Tent	
T-3135	Tent	
T-3136	Tent	
T-3137	Tent	
T-3138	Tent	
T-3139	Tent	
T-3140	Tent	
T-3141	Tent	
T-3142	Tent	
T-3143	Tent	
T-3144	Tent	
T-3150	Tent	
T-3151	Tent	
T-3152	Tent	
T-3153	Tent	
T-3154	Tent	
T-3155	Tent	
T-3156	Tent	
T-3157	Tent	
T-3158	Tent	
T-3159	Tent	
T-3160	Tent	
T-3161	Tent	
T-3162	Tent	
T-3163	Tent	

CAMP HAAN
THE HISTORY OF RIVERSIDE'S WORLD WAR II ANTI-AIRCRAFT TRAINING CENTER

T-3164	Tent	
T-3165	Tent	
T-3166	Tent	
T-3167	Tent	
T-3168	Tent	
T-3169	Tent	
T-3177	Tent	
T-3178	Tent	
T-3179	Tent	
T-3180	Tent	
T-3181	Tent	
T-3182	Tent	
T-3183	Tent	
T-3184	Tent	
T-3190	Tent	
T-3191	Tent	
T-3192	Tent	
T-3193	Tent	
T-3194	Tent	
T-3195	Tent	
T-3196	Tent	
T-3197	Tent	
T-3198	Tent	
T-3199	Tent	
T-3200	Tent	
T-3201	Tent	
T-3202	Tent	
T-3203	Tent	
T-3204	Tent	
T-3205	Tent	
T-3206	Tent	
T-3207	Tent	
T-3208	Tent	
T-3209	Tent	

T-3214	Tent	
T-3215	Tent	
T-3216	Tent	
T-3217	Tent	
T-3218	Tent	
T-3219	Tent	
T-3220	Tent	
T-3221	Tent	
T-3222	Tent	
T-3223	Tent	
T-3224	Tent	
T-3230	Tent	
T-3231	Tent	
T-3232	Tent	
T-3233	Tent	
T-3234	Tent	
T-3235	Tent	
T-3236	Tent	
T-3237	Tent	
T-3238	Tent	
T-3239	Tent	
T-3240	Tent	
T-3241	Tent	
T-3242	Tent	
T-3243	Tent	
T-3244	Tent	
T-3245	Tent	
T-3246	Tent	
T-3247	Tent	
T-3248	Tent	
T-3249	Tent	
T-3271	Tent	
T-3272	Tent	
T-3273	Tent	

CAMP HAAN
THE HISTORY OF RIVERSIDE'S WORLD WAR II ANTI-AIRCRAFT TRAINING CENTER

T-3274	Tent	
T-3275	Tent	
T-3276	Tent	
T-3277	Tent	
T-3278	Tent	
T-3279	Tent	
T-3280	Tent	
T-3281	Tent	
T-3282	Tent	
T-3283	Tent	
T-3284	Tent	
T-3285	Tent	
T-3286	Tent	
T-3287	Tent	
T-3288	Tent	
T-3289	Tent	
T-3291	Tent	
T-3292	Tent	
T-3293	Tent	
T-3294	Tent	
T-3295	Tent	
T-3296	Tent	
T-3297	Tent	
T-3298	Tent	
T-3301	Tent	
T-3302	Tent	
T-3303	Tent	
T-3304	Tent	
T-3305	Tent	
T-3306	Tent	
T-3307	Tent	
T-3312	Tent	
T-3313	Tent	
T-3314	Tent	

CAMP HAAN
THE HISTORY OF RIVERSIDE'S WORLD WAR II ANTI-AIRCRAFT TRAINING CENTER

T-3315	Tent	
T-3316	Tent	
T-3317	Tent	
T-3318	Tent	
T-3321	Tent	
T-3322	Tent	
T-3323	Tent	
T-3324	Tent	
T-3325	Tent	
T-3326	Tent	
T-3327	Tent	
T-3330	Tent	
T-3331	Tent	
T-3332	Tent	
T-3333	Tent	
T-3334	Tent	
T-3335	Tent	
T-3336	Tent	
T-3337	Tent	
T-3338	Tent	
T-3339	Tent	
T-3340	Tent	
T-3341	Tent	
T-3342	Tent	
T-3343	Tent	
T-3344	Tent	
T-3345	Tent	
T-3346	Tent	
T-3347	Tent	
T-3348	Tent	
T-3349	Tent	
T-3353	Tent	
T-3354	Tent	
T-3355	Tent	

CAMP HAAN
THE HISTORY OF RIVERSIDE'S WORLD WAR II ANTI-AIRCRAFT TRAINING CENTER

T-3356	Tent	
T-3357	Tent	
T-3358	Tent	
T-3359	Tent	
T-3360	Tent	
T-3361	Tent	
T-3362	Tent	
T-3363	Tent	
T-3364	Tent	
T-3365	Tent	
T-3366	Tent	
T-3370	Tent	
T-3371	Tent	
T-3372	Tent	
T-3373	Tent	
T-3374	Tent	
T-3375	Tent	
T-3376	Tent	
T-3377	Tent	
T-3378	Tent	
T-3379	Tent	
T-3380	Tent	
T-3381	Tent	
T-3382	Tent	
T-3383	Tent	
T-3384	Tent	
T-3385	Tent	
T-3386	Tent	
T-3387	Tent	
T-3388	Tent	
T-3389	Tent	
T-3393	Tent	
T-3394	Tent	
T-3395	Tent	

CAMP HAAN
THE HISTORY OF RIVERSIDE'S WORLD WAR II ANTI-AIRCRAFT TRAINING CENTER

T-3396	Tent	
T-3397	Tent	
T-3398	Tent	
T-3399	Tent	
T-3400	Tent	
T-3401	Tent	
T-3402	Tent	
T-3403	Tent	
T-3404	Tent	
T-3405	Tent	
T-3406	Tent	
T-3410	Tent	
T-3411	Tent	
T-3412	Tent	
T-3413	Tent	
T-3414	Tent	
T-3415	Tent	
T-3416	Tent	
T-3417	Tent	
T-3418	Tent	
T-3419	Tent	
T-3420	Tent	
T-3421	Tent	
T-3422	Tent	
T-3423	Tent	
T-3424	Tent	
T-3425	Tent	
T-3426	Tent	
T-3427	Tent	
T-3428	Tent	
T-3429	Tent	
T-3433	Tent	
T-3434	Tent	
T-3435	Tent	

CAMP HAAN
THE HISTORY OF RIVERSIDE'S WORLD WAR II ANTI-AIRCRAFT TRAINING CENTER

T-3436	Tent	
T-3437	Tent	
T-3438	Tent	
T-3439	Tent	
T-3440	Tent	
T-3441	Tent	
T-3442	Tent	
T-3443	Tent	
T-3444	Tent	
T-3445	Tent	
T-3446	Tent	
T-3450	Tent	
T-3451	Tent	
T-3452	Tent	
T-3453	Tent	
T-3454	Tent	
T-3455	Tent	
T-3456	Tent	
T-3457	Tent	
T-3458	Tent	
T-3459	Tent	
T-3501	Latrine	
T-3502	Tent	
T-3503	Tent	
T-3504	Tent	
T-3505	Tent	
T-3506	Theater #2	
T-3507	Civilian Club	#2
T-3508	Post Exchange	
T-3509	Tent	
T-3510	Tent	
T-3511	Tent	
T-3512	Tent	
T-3513	Tent	

CAMP HAAN
THE HISTORY OF RIVERSIDE'S WORLD WAR II ANTI-AIRCRAFT TRAINING CENTER

T-3514	Tent	
T-3515	Tent	
T-3516	Tent	
T-3517	Tent	
T-3518	Tent	
T-3519	Tent	
T-3520	Tent	
T-3521	Tent	
T-3522	Tent	
T-3523	Tent	
T-3525	Latrine	
T-3526	Day Room	
T-3527	Service Club Colored Troops	
T-3528	Service Club Colored Troops	
T-3529	Post Exchange Colored Troops	
T-3530	Latrine	
T-3531	Hutment	
T-3532	Hutment	
T-3533	Hutment	
T-3534	Hutment	
T-3535	Hutment	
T-3536	Hutment	
T-3537	Hutment	
T-3538	Hutment	
T-3539	Hutment	
T-3540	Hutment	
T-3541	Mess Hall	
T-3542	Day Room	
T-3543	Administration and Supply	
T-3544	Infirmary	
T-3545	Post Exchange	
T-3546	Recreation Building	
T-3548	Training Auditorium	
T-3549	Fire Station	

CAMP HAAN
THE HISTORY OF RIVERSIDE'S WORLD WAR II ANTI-AIRCRAFT TRAINING CENTER

T-3550	Mess Hall	
T-3551	Tent	
T-3552	Tent	
T-3553	Tent	
T-3554	Tent	
T-3555	Tent	
T-3556	Tent	
T-3557	Tent	
T-3558	Tent	
T-3559	Tent	
T-3560	Tent	
T-3561	Tent	
T-3562	Tent	
T-3563	Tent	
T-3564	Latrine	
T-3565	Tent	
T-3566	Tent	
T-3567	Tent	
T-3568	Tent	
T-3569	Tent	
T-3570	Tent	
T-3571	Tent	
T-3572	Tent	
T-3573	Tent	
T-3574	Tent	
T-3575	Tent	
T-3576	Tent	
T-3577	Tent	
T-3578	Administration and Supply	
T-3579	Guard Tower	
T-3580	Mess Hall	
T-3591	Guard Tower	
T-3592	Latrine	
T-3613	Administration and Supply	

CAMP HAAN
THE HISTORY OF RIVERSIDE'S WORLD WAR II ANTI-AIRCRAFT TRAINING CENTER

T-3622	Latrine	
T-3630	Mess Hall	
T-3636	Tent	
T-3637	Tent	
T-3638	Latrine	
T-3639	Tent	
T-3640	Tent	
T-3641	Tent	
T-3642	Tent	
T-3643	Tent	
T-3644	Tent	
T-3645	Tent	
T-3646	Tent	
T-3647	Mess Hall	
T-3648	Hutment	
T-3649	Hutment	
T-3650	Hutment	
T-3651	Hutment	
T-3652	Hutment	
T-3653	Hutment	
T-3654	Latrine	
T-3656	Latrine	
T-3657	Hutment	
T-3658	Hutment	
T-3659	Hutment	
T-3660	Hutment	
T-3661	Hutment	
T-3662	Hutment	
T-3663	Hutment	
T-3664	Hutment	
T-3665	Administration and Supply	
T-3667	Mess Hall	
T-3668	Tent	
T-3669	Tent	

CAMP HAAN
THE HISTORY OF RIVERSIDE'S WORLD WAR II ANTI-AIRCRAFT TRAINING CENTER

T-3670	Tent	
T-3671	Tent	
T-3672	Tent	
T-3674	Latrine	
T-3675	Hutment	
T-3676	Hutment	
T-3677	Hutment	
T-3678	Hutment	
T-3679	Hutment	
T-3680	Hutment	
T-3681	Hutment	
T-3682	Hutment	
T-3683	Hutment	
T-3684	Administration and Supply	
T-3701	Latrine	
T-3702	Tent	
T-3703	Tent	
T-3704	Tent	
T-3705	Tent	
T-3706	Tent	
T-3707	Tent	
T-3708	Tent	
T-3709	Tent	
T-3710	Tent	
T-3711	Tent	
T-3712	Tent	
T-3713	Mess Hall	
T-3714	Tent	
T-3715	Tent	
T-3716	Tent	
T-3717	Tent	
T-3718	Tent	
T-3719	Tent	
T-3720	Tent	

T-3721	Tent	
T-3722	Tent	
T-3723	Tent	
T-3724	Tent	
T-3725	Latrine	
T-3726	Tent	
T-3727	Tent	
T-3728	Tent	
T-3729	Tent	
T-3730	Tent	
T-3731	Tent	
T-3732	Tent	
T-3733	Tent	
T-3734	Tent	
T-3735	Tent	
T-3736	Tent	
T-3737	Administration and Supply	
T-3738	Day Room	
T-3739	Tent	
T-3740	Tent	
T-3741	Tent	
T-3742	Tent	
T-3743	Tent	
T-3744	Tent	
T-3745	Tent	
T-3746	Tent	
T-3747	Tent	
T-3748	Tent	
T-3749	Tent	
T-3750	Guard Tower	
T-3751	Tent	
T-3752	Tent	
T-3753	Tent	
T-3754	Tent	

CAMP HAAN
THE HISTORY OF RIVERSIDE'S WORLD WAR II ANTI-AIRCRAFT TRAINING CENTER

T-3755	Tent	
T-3756	Tent	
T-3757	Tent	
T-3758	Tent	
T-3759	Tent	
T-3760	Tent	
T-3761	Tent	
T-3762	Guard Tower	
T-3763	Tent	
T-3764	Tent	
T-3765	Tent	
T-3766	Tent	
T-3767	Tent	
T-3768	Tent	
T-3769	Tent	
T-3770	Tent	
T-3771	Tent	
T-3772	Tent	
T-3773	Tent	
T-3774	Tent	
T-3775	Tent	
T-3776	Tent	
T-3777	Tent	
T-3778	Tent	
T-3779	Tent	
T-3780	Tent	
T-3781	Tent	
T-3782	Tent	
T-3783	Tent	
T-3784	Tent	
T-3785	Tent	
T-3786	Tent	
T-3788	Tent	
T-3789	Tent	

CAMP HAAN
THE HISTORY OF RIVERSIDE'S WORLD WAR II ANTI-AIRCRAFT TRAINING CENTER

T-3790	Tent	
T-3791	Tent	
T-3792	Tent	
T-3793	Tent	
T-3794	Tent	
T-3795	Tent	
T-3796	Tent	
T-3797	Tent	
T-3798	Mess Hall	
T-3799	Administration and Supply	
T-3800	Day Room	
T-3801	Tent	
T-3802	Tent	
T-3803	Tent	
T-3804	Tent	
T-3805	Tent	
T-3806	Tent	
T-3807	Tent	
T-3808	Tent	
T-3809	Tent	
T-3810	Tent	
T-3811	Tent	
T-3812	Tent	
T-3813	Tent	
T-3814	Tent	
T-3815	Tent	
T-3816	Tent	
T-3817	Tent	
T-3818	Tent	
T-3819	Tent	
T-3820	Tent	
T-3821	Tent	
T-3822	Tent	
T-3823	Tent	

CAMP HAAN
THE HISTORY OF RIVERSIDE'S WORLD WAR II ANTI-AIRCRAFT TRAINING CENTER

T-3824	Tent	
T-3825	Tent	
T-3826	Tent	
T-3827	Tent	
T-3828	Tent	
T-3829	Tent	
T-3830	Tent	
T-3831	Latrine	
T-3832	Tent	
T-3833	Tent	
T-3834	Tent	
T-3835	Tent	
T-3836	Tent	
T-3837	Tent	
T-3838	Tent	
T-3839	Tent	
T-3840	Tent	
T-3841	Tent	
T-3842	Mess Hall	
T-3843	Tent	
T-3844	Tent	
T-3845	Tent	
T-3846	Tent	
T-3847	Tent	
T-3848	Tent	
T-3849	Tent	
T-3850	Tent	
T-3851	Tent	
T-3852	Tent	
T-3853	Tent	
T-3854	Tent	
T-3855	Tent	
T-3856	Tent	
T-3857	Tent	

CAMP HAAN
THE HISTORY OF RIVERSIDE'S WORLD WAR II ANTI-AIRCRAFT TRAINING CENTER

T-3858	Tent	
T-3859	Tent	
T-3860	Tent	
T-3861	Tent	
T-3862	Tent	
T-3863	Administration and Supply	
T-3864	Day Room	
T-3865	Tent	
T-3866	Tent	
T-3867	Tent	
T-3868	Tent	
T-3869	Tent	
T-3870	Tent	
T-3871	Tent	
T-3872	Tent	
T-3873	Tent	
T-3874	Tent	
T-3875	Latrine	
T-3876	Tent	
T-3877	Tent	
T-3878	Tent	
T-3879	Tent	
T-3880	Tent	
T-3881	Tent	
T-3882	Tent	
T-3883	Tent	
T-3884	Tent	
T-3885	Tent	
T-3886	Mess Hall	
T-3887	Tent	
T-3888	Tent	
T-3889	Tent	
T-3890	Tent	
T-3891	Tent	

CAMP HAAN
THE HISTORY OF RIVERSIDE'S WORLD WAR II ANTI-AIRCRAFT TRAINING CENTER

T-3892	Tent	
T-3893	Tent	
T-3894	Tent	
T-3895	Tent	
T-3896	Tent	
T-3897	Latrine	
T-3898	Tent	
T-3899	Tent	
T-3900	Tent	
T-3901	Tent	
T-3902	Tent	
T-3903	Tent	
T-3904	Tent	
T-3905	Tent	
T-3906	Tent	
T-3907	Tent	
T-3908	Administration and Supply	
T-3909	Day Room	
T-3910	Tent	
T-3911	Tent	
T-3912	Tent	
T-3913	Tent	
T-3914	Tent	
T-3915	Tent	
T-3916	Tent	
T-3917	Tent	
T-3918	Tent	
T-3919	Tent	
T-3920	Tent	
T-3921	Tent	
T-3922	Tent	
T-3923	Tent	
T-3924	Tent	
T-3925	Tent	

T-3926	Tent	
T-3927	Tent	
T-3928	Tent	
T-3929	Tent	
T-3930	Mess Hall	
T-3931	Tent	
T-3932	Tent	
T-3933	Tent	
T-3934	Tent	
T-3935	Tent	
T-3936	Tent	
T-3937	Tent	
T-3941	Latrine	
T-3944	Tent	
T-3945	Tent	
T-3946	Tent	
T-3947	Tent	
T-3948	Tent	
T-3949	Tent	
T-3950	Tent	
T-3951	Tent	
T-3952	Administration and Supply	
T-3953	Day Room	
T-3954	Tent	
T-3955	Tent	
T-3956	Tent	
T-3957	Tent	
T-3958	Tent	
T-3959	Tent	
T-3960	Tent	
T-3961	Tent	
T-3962	Transporation	Transportation Officer, assistant, administration, civilian passenger clerk,

CAMP HAAN
THE HISTORY OF RIVERSIDE'S WORLD WAR II ANTI-AIRCRAFT TRAINING CENTER

		Incoming/outgoing freight section
T-3963	Tent	
T-3964	Storage Shed	
T-3965	Automotive Shop	
T-3970	Wash Rack	
T-3971	Oil Storage House	
T-3972	Grease Rack	
T-3973	Motor Repair Shop	
T-3975	Salvage Shed	
T-3976	Warehouse	
T-3977	Warehouse	
T-3978	Salvage Shed	
T-3979	Administration	
T-3980	Post Ordinance Office	
T-3982	Salvage Shed	
T-3983	*NOT BUILT*	
T-3985	Inspection Shed	
T-3986	Lubrication Rack w/ Shelters	
T-3988	Administration	
T-3989	Automotive Shop	
T-3990	Pump house for Wash Rack	
T-3991	Wash Rack incl. 2 pump houses	
T-3992	Pump house for Wash Rack	
T-3993	Automotive Shop	
T-3994	Automotive Shop	
T-4000	Gas Station	
T-4001	Oil Storage House	
T-4002	Grease Rack	
T-4003	Lubrication Rack w/ Shelters	
T-4004	Motor Repair	
T-4005	Motor Repair	
T-4006	Motor Repair Shop	
T-4007	Motor Repair	
T-4008	Motor Repair	

T-4009	Motor Repair	
T-4010	Motor Repair	
T-4011	Wash Rack	
T-4012	Wash Rack	
T-4013	Paint Storage Shed	
T-4014	Paint Shop	
T-4015	Post Engineer Utility Shop	
T-4016	Blacksmith Shop	
T-4017	Plumbing and Metal Shop	
T-4018	Grease Rack	
T-4019	Typewriter Shop	
T-4020	Gas Station	
T-4021	Lumber Shed	
T-4022	Lumber Shed	
T-4023	Post Engineer Yard Checking Office	
T-4024	Supply Shed	Warehouse 15
T-4025	Small Arms Repair	
T-4026	Elevated Gravel Hopper	
T-4027	Gun Repair Shop	
T-4028	Ordnance Repair Shop	
T-4029	Warehouse	#4 Storage Branch Chief
T-4030	Warehouse	
T-4031	Ordnance Warehouse	
T-4032	Ordnance Warehouse	
T-4033	Loading Ramp	
T-4034	Loading Ramp	
T-4035	Sentry House (camp entrances)	On leased land outside camp perimeter
T-4038	Quartermaster Warehouse	#2 Ordinance Inventory Crew Chief Fire control and small arms Commercial Truck Dispatcher

T-4040	Quartermaster Warehouse	
T-4041	Quartermaster Warehouse	
T-4042	Quartermaster Warehouse	
T-4043	Quartermaster Warehouse	#13, Property Turn-in
T-4044	Quartermaster Warehouse	
T-4045	Quartermaster Warehouse	
T-4046	Quartermaster Warehouse	#10 Commissary Warehouse, dry storage
T-4047	Quartermaster Warehouse	#9 Office of QM Warehouses Incoming Property
T-4048	Quartermaster Warehouse	Veterinarian (listed in the 1944 telephone book)
T-4049	Quartermaster Warehouse	
T-4050	Cold Storage Plant	
T-4051	Quartermaster Warehouse	
T-4052	Cold Storage Plant	#6
T-4053	Cold Storage Plant	
T-4054	Butane Plant	
T-4055	Ice Storage Building	
T-4056	Yardmaster	
T-4058	Post Utility Storage Shed	
T-4059	Post Utility Storage Shed	
T-4060	Post Utility Storage Shed	
T-4061	Post Utility Storage Shed	
T-4062	Locomotive Shelter	Warehouse #17
T-4063	Quartermaster Warehouse	#3 Ordinance, armament parts Post Quartermaster Clothing Retail Store
T-4064	Laundry	
T-4065	Boiler Shed	
T-4066	Sewage Pumping Plant	

CAMP HAAN
THE HISTORY OF RIVERSIDE'S WORLD WAR II ANTI-AIRCRAFT TRAINING CENTER

T-4067	*NOT BUILT*	
T-4068	Bakery	
T-4069	Warehouse	
T-4070	Warehouse	
T-4071	Quartermaster Salvage Yard Checking Office	
T-4072	Quartermaster Salvage Office	
T-4073	Clothing Equipment Repair	
T-4074	Quartemaster Warehouse	
T-4075	Clothing Equipment Repair	
T-4076	Quartermaster Salvage Shed	
T-4077	Salvage Shed	
T-4078	Storage Shed	
T-4501	Stockade Office	
T-4502	Latrine	
T-4503	Latrine	
T-4504	Mess Hall	
T-4505	Guard Tower	
T-4506	Isolation Cell	
T-4507	Tent	
T-4508	Tent	
T-4509	Tent	
T-4510	Tent	
T-4511	Tent	
T-4512	Tent	
T-4513	Tent	
T-4514	Tent	
T-4515	Tent	
T-4516	Tent	
T-4517	Guard Tower	
T-4518	Latrine	
T-4519	Tent	
T-4520	Tent	
T-4521	Tent	

CAMP HAAN
THE HISTORY OF RIVERSIDE'S WORLD WAR II ANTI-AIRCRAFT TRAINING CENTER

T-4522	Tent	
T-4523	Tent	
T-4524	Tent	
T-4525	Tent	
T-4526	Tent	
T-4527	Tent	
T-4528	Tent	
T-4529	Tent	
T-4530	Tent	
T-4531	Tent	
T-4532	Tent	
T-4533	Tent	
T-4534	Tent	
T-4535	Tent	
T-4536	Tent	
T-4537	Tent	
T-4538	Tent	
T-4540	Tent	
T-4541	Tent	
T-4542	Tent	
T-4543	Tent	
T-4544	Tent	
T-4545	Tent	
T-4546	Tent	
T-4547	Tent	
T-4548	Tent	
T-4549	Tent	
T-4550	Tent	
T-4551	Tent	
T-4552	Guard Tower	
T-4553	Guard Tower	
T-4554	Carpenter Shop	
T-4555	Guard Barracks	
T-4556	Stockade Headquarters	

T-4557	Guard Tower	
T-4558	Guard House	Was listed as a tool shed on the seller deed
T-4559	Prisoner Mess Hall	
T-4560	Tent	
T-4561	Tent	
T-4562	Tent	
T-4563	Tent	
T-4564	Tent	
T-4565	Tent	
T-4566	Tent	
T-4567	Tent	
T-4568	Tent	
T-4569	Tent	
T-4570	Tent	
T-4571	Tent	
T-4572	Tent	Listed as a dayroom on the sellers deed
T-4573	Tent	
T-4574	Tent	
T-4575	Tent	
T-4576	Tent	
T-4577	Tent	
T-4578	Tent	
T-4579	Tent	
T-4580	Tent	
T-4581	Tent	
T-4582	Tent	
T-4583	Tent	
T-4584	Tent	
T-4585	Tent	
T-4586	Tent	
T-4587	Tent	
T-4588	Tent	
T-4589	Tent	

CAMP HAAN
THE HISTORY OF RIVERSIDE'S WORLD WAR II ANTI-AIRCRAFT TRAINING CENTER

T-4595	Latrine (Prisoner)	
T-4600	Tent	
T-4601	Tent	
T-4602	Tent	
T-4603	Tent	
T-4604	Tent	
T-4605	Tent	
T-4606	Tent	
T-4607	Tent	
T-4608	Tent	
T-4609	Tent	
T-4610	Tent	
T-4611	Tent	
T-4612	Tent	
T-4613	Tent	
T-4614	Tent	
T-4615	Tent	
T-4616	Tent	
T-4617	Tent	
T-4628	Tent	
T-4629	Tent	
T-4630	Guard Tower	
T-4631	Guard Tower	
T-4632	Isolation Cell	
T-4633	Isolation Cell	
T-4634	Isolation Cell	
T-4635	Isolation Cell	
T-4636	Isolation Cell	
T-4637	Isolation Cell	
T-4638	Guard Tower	
T-4701	Administration Building	
T-4702	Latrine	
T-4703	Mess Hall and Recreation, Officer	
T-4704	Recreation Building	

CAMP HAAN
THE HISTORY OF RIVERSIDE'S WORLD WAR II ANTI-AIRCRAFT TRAINING CENTER

T-4705	Post Exchange	
T-4706	Infirmary	Also dispensary
T-4707	Tent	
T-4708	Tent	
T-4709	Tent	
T-4710	Tent	
T-4711	Tent	
T-4712	Tent	
T-4713	Tent	
T-4714	Tent	
T-4715	Tent	
T-4716	Tent	
T-4717	Tent	
T-4718	Tent	
T-4719	Tent	
T-4720	Tent	
T-4721	Tent	
T-4722	*NOT BUILT*	
T-4723	*NOT BUILT*	
T-4724	*NOT BUILT*	
T-4725	Officer's Quarters	
T-4726	Latrine	
T-4727	Officer's Quarters	
T-4728	Officer's Quarters	
T-4729	Administration	
T-4730	Post Exchange	
T-4731	Storehouse	
T-4732	Infirmary	Also dispensary
T-4733	Officer's Quarters	
T-4734	Latrine	
T-4735	Officer's Quarters	
T-4736	*NOT BUILT*	
T-4737	*NOT BUILT*	
T-4738	*NOT BUILT*	

CAMP HAAN
THE HISTORY OF RIVERSIDE'S WORLD WAR II ANTI-AIRCRAFT TRAINING CENTER

T-4739	*NOT BUILT*	
T-4740	*NOT BUILT*	
T-4741	Mess Hall	
T-4742	Administration and Supply	
T-4743	Day Room	
T-4744	Mess Hall	
T-4745	Administration and Supply	
T-4746	Day Room	
T-4747	Mess Hall	
T-4748	Administration and Supply	
T-4749	Day Room	
T-4750	Mess Hall	
T-4751	Administration and Supply	
T-4752	Day Room	
T-4753	Mess Hall	
T-4754	Administration and Supply	
T-4755	Day Room	
T-4758	Administration and Supply	
T-4759	Recreation Building	
T-4760	Mess Hall	
T-4761	Administration and Supply	
T-4762	Recreation Building	
T-4763	Mess Hall	
T-4764	Administration and Supply	
T-4765	Recreation Building	
T-4766	Mess Hall	
T-4767	Administration and Supply	
T-4768	Recreation Building	
T-4769	Mess Hall	
T-4770	Administration and Supply	
T-4771	Recreation Building	
T-4772	Mess Hall	
T-4780	Latrine	
T-4781	Latrine	

T-4782	Latrine
T-4783	Latrine
T-4784	Latrine
T-4787	Latrine
T-4788	Latrine
T-4789	Latrine
T-4790	Latrine
T-4791	Latrine
T-4798	Grease Rack
T-4800	Gas Station
T-4801	Motor Repair Shop
T-4802	Motor Repair Shop
T-4803	Battalion Supply
T-4804	Oil Storage House
T-4805	Grease Rack
T-4806	Wash Rack
T-4900	Tent
T-4901	Tent
T-4902	Tent
T-4903	Tent
T-4904	Tent
T-4905	Tent
T-4906	Tent
T-4907	Tent
T-4908	Tent
T-4909	Tent
T-4910	Tent
T-4911	Tent
T-4912	Tent
T-4913	Tent
T-4914	Tent
T-4915	Tent
T-4923	Tent
T-4924	Tent

CAMP HAAN
THE HISTORY OF RIVERSIDE'S WORLD WAR II ANTI-AIRCRAFT TRAINING CENTER

T-4925	Tent	
T-4926	Tent	
T-4927	Tent	
T-4928	Tent	
T-4929	Tent	
T-4930	Tent	
T-4931	Tent	
T-4932	Tent	
T-4933	Tent	
T-4934	Tent	
T-4935	Tent	
T-4936	Tent	
T-4937	Tent	
T-4938	Tent	
T-4939	Tent	
T-4940	Tent	
T-4941	Tent	
T-4942	Tent	
T-4943	Tent	
T-4944	Tent	
T-4945	Tent	
T-4946	Tent	
T-4947	Tent	
T-4948	Tent	
T-4949	Tent	
T-4950	Tent	
T-4951	Tent	
T-4952	Tent	
T-4953	Tent	
T-4954	Tent	
T-4955	Tent	
T-5000	Tent	
T-5001	Tent	
T-5002	Tent	

CAMP HAAN
THE HISTORY OF RIVERSIDE'S WORLD WAR II ANTI-AIRCRAFT TRAINING CENTER

T-5003	Tent	
T-5004	Tent	
T-5005	Tent	
T-5006	Tent	
T-5007	Tent	
T-5008	Tent	
T-5009	Tent	
T-5010	Tent	
T-5011	Tent	
T-5012	Tent	
T-5013	Tent	
T-5014	Tent	
T-5015	Tent	
T-5016	Tent	
T-5017	Tent	
T-5018	Tent	
T-5019	Tent	
T-5020	Tent	
T-5021	Tent	
T-5022	Tent	
T-5023	Tent	
T-5024	Tent	
T-5025	Tent	
T-5026	Tent	
T-5027	Tent	
T-5028	Tent	
T-5029	Tent	
T-5031	Tent	
T-5032	Tent	
T-5033	Tent	
T-5034	Tent	
T-5035	Tent	
T-5036	Tent	
T-5037	Tent	

CAMP HAAN
THE HISTORY OF RIVERSIDE'S WORLD WAR II ANTI-AIRCRAFT TRAINING CENTER

T-5042	Tent	
T-5043	Tent	
T-5044	Tent	
T-5045	Tent	
T-5046	Tent	
T-5047	Tent	
T-5048	Tent	
T-5049	Tent	
T-5050	Tent	
T-5051	Tent	
T-5052	Tent	
T-5053	Tent	
T-5054	Tent	
T-5055	Tent	
T-5056	Tent	
T-5057	Tent	
T-5058	Tent	
T-5059	Tent	
T-5060	Tent	
T-5061	Tent	
T-5062	Tent	
T-5063	Tent	
T-5064	Tent	
T-5065	Tent	
T-5066	Tent	
T-5067	Tent	
T-5068	Tent	
T-5069	Tent	
T-5070	Tent	
T-5071	Tent	
T-5072	Tent	
T-5073	Tent	
T-5074	Tent	
T-5075	Tent	

CAMP HAAN
THE HISTORY OF RIVERSIDE'S WORLD WAR II ANTI-AIRCRAFT TRAINING CENTER

T-5076	Tent	
T-5077	Tent	
T-5078	Tent	
T-5079	Tent	
T-5080	Tent	
T-5081	Tent	
T-5082	Tent	
T-5083	Tent	
T-5084	Tent	
T-5085	Tent	
T-5086	Tent	
T-5087	Tent	
T-5088	Tent	
T-5089	Tent	
T-5090	Tent	
T-5091	Tent	
T-5092	Tent	
T-5106	Tent	
T-5107	Tent	
T-5108	Tent	
T-5109	Tent	
T-5110	Tent	
T-5111	Tent	
T-5112	Tent	
T-5113	Tent	
T-5114	Tent	
T-5115	Tent	
T-5116	Tent	
T-5117	Tent	
T-5118	Tent	
T-5119	Tent	
T-5120	Hutment	
T-5121	Hutment	
T-5122	Hutment	

CAMP HAAN
THE HISTORY OF RIVERSIDE'S WORLD WAR II ANTI-AIRCRAFT TRAINING CENTER

T-5123	Hutment	
T-5124	Hutment	
T-5125	Hutment	
T-5126	Hutment	
T-5127	Hutment	
T-5128	Hutment	
T-5129	Hutment	
T-5130	Hutment	
T-5131	Hutment	
T-5132	Hutment	
T-5133	Hutment	
T-5134	Hutment	
T-5135	Hutment	
T-5136	Hutment	
T-5137	Hutment	
T-5138	Hutment	
T-5139	Hutment	
T-5140	Hutment	
T-5141	Hutment	
T-5142	Hutment	
T-5143	Hutment	
T-5144	Hutment	
T-5145	Hutment	
T-5146	Hutment	
T-5147	Hutment	
T-5148	Hutment	
T-5149	Hutment	
T-5150	Hutment	
T-5151	Hutment	
T-5152	Hutment	
T-5153	Hutment	
T-5154	Hutment	
T-5155	Hutment	
T-5156	Hutment	

CAMP HAAN
THE HISTORY OF RIVERSIDE'S WORLD WAR II ANTI-AIRCRAFT TRAINING CENTER

T-5157	Hutment	
T-5158	Hutment	
T-5159	Hutment	
T-5160	Hutment	
T-5161	Hutment	
T-5162	Hutment	
T-5163	Hutment	
T-5164	Hutment	
T-5165	Hutment	
T-5166	Hutment	
T-5167	Hutment	
T-5168	Hutment	
T-5169	Hutment	
T-5170	Hutment	
T-5171	Hutment	
T-5172	Hutment	
T-5173	Hutment	
T-5174	Hutment	
T-5175	Hutment	
T-5176	Hutment	
T-5201	Administration	
T-5202	Officer's Quarters	
T-5203	Latrine	
T-5204	Officer's Quarters	
T-5205	Officer's Quarters	
T-5206	Post Exchange	
T-5207	Storehouse	
T-5208	Infirmary	Also dispensary
T-5222	Administration and Supply	
T-5223	Mess Hall	
T-5224	Recreation Building	
T-5225	Administration and Supply	
T-5226	Mess Hall	
T-5227	Recreation Building	

CAMP HAAN
THE HISTORY OF RIVERSIDE'S WORLD WAR II ANTI-AIRCRAFT TRAINING CENTER

T-5228	Administration and Supply	
T-5229	Mess Hall	
T-5230	Recreation Building	
T-5231	Administration and Supply	
T-5232	Mess Hall	
T-5233	Recreation Building	
T-5234	Administration and Supply	
T-5235	Mess Hall	
T-5250	Hutment	
T-5251	Hutment	
T-5252	Hutment	
T-5253	Hutment	
T-5254	Hutment	
T-5255	Hutment	
T-5256	Hutment	
T-5257	Hutment	
T-5258	Hutment	
T-5259	Hutment	
T-5260	Hutment	
T-5261	Hutment	
T-5262	Hutment	
T-5263	Hutment	
T-5264	Hutment	
T-5265	Hutment	
T-5266	Hutment	
T-5267	Hutment	
T-5268	Hutment	
T-5269	Hutment	
T-5270	Hutment	
T-5271	Hutment	
T-5272	Hutment	
T-5273	Hutment	
T-5274	Hutment	
T-5275	Hutment	

CAMP HAAN
THE HISTORY OF RIVERSIDE'S WORLD WAR II ANTI-AIRCRAFT TRAINING CENTER

T-5276	Hutment	
T-5277	Hutment	
T-5278	Hutment	
T-5279	Hutment	
T-5280	Hutment	
T-5281	Hutment	
T-5282	Hutment	
T-5283	Hutment	
T-5284	Hutment	
T-5285	Hutment	
T-5286	Hutment	
T-5287	Hutment	
T-5288	Hutment	
T-5289	Hutment	
T-5290	Hutment	
T-5291	Hutment	
T-5292	Hutment	
T-5293	Hutment	
T-5294	Hutment	
T-5295	Hutment	
T-5296	Hutment	
T-5297	Hutment	
T-5298	Hutment	
T-5299	Hutment	
T-5300	Hutment	
T-5301	Hutment	
T-5302	Hutment	
T-5303	Hutment	
T-5304	Hutment	
T-5305	Hutment	
T-5306	Hutment	
T-5320	Latrine	
T-5321	Latrine	
T-5322	Latrine	

CAMP HAAN
THE HISTORY OF RIVERSIDE'S WORLD WAR II ANTI-AIRCRAFT TRAINING CENTER

T-5323	Latrine	
T-5324	Latrine	
T-5325	Motor Repair Shop	
T-5326	Oil Storage House	
T-5327	Grease Rack	
T-5601	Hospital Administration Building	
T-5602	Nurse's Club	
T-5603	Nurses Quarters	
T-5604	Nurses Quarters	
T-5605	Nurse's Quarters	
T-5606	Nurses Recreation Hall	
T-5607	Nurse's Quarters	
T-5608	Nurse's Mess	
T-5609	Officer's Quarters	
T-5610	Officer's Quarters	
T-5611	Infirmary Ward	Also dispensary
T-5612	Officer's Quarters	
T-5613	Infirmary Ward	
T-5614	Nurse's Quarters	
T-5615	Nurse's Quarters	
T-5616	Nurse's Quarters	
T-5617	Nurse's Quarters	
T-5618	Nurse's Quarters	
T-5619	Infirmary Ward S-8	
T-5620	Officer's Quarters	
T-5621	Dental Clinic	
T-5622	Officer's Quarters and Mess	
T-5623	Infirmary Ward	
T-5624	//WAS NOT BUILT//	
T-5625	//WAS NOT BUILT//	
T-5626	//WAS NOT BUILT//	
T-5627	//WAS NOT BUILT//	
T-5628	//WAS NOT BUILT//	

CAMP HAAN
THE HISTORY OF RIVERSIDE'S WORLD WAR II ANTI-AIRCRAFT TRAINING CENTER

T-5629	//WAS NOT BUILT//	
T-5630	Infirmary Ward S-19	
T-5631	Infirmary Ward S-17	
T-5632	Infirmary Ward S-18	
T-5633	Boiler House	
T-5634	Infirmary Ward S-15	
T-5635	Infirmary Ward S-16	
T-5636	//WAS NOT BUILT//	
T-5637	Infirmary Ward S-14	
T-5638	Infirmary Ward S-13	
T-5639	Infirmary Ward S-12	
T-5640	//WAS NOT BUILT//	
T-5641	Physiotherapy Lab	
T-5642	Infirmary Ward S-11	
T-5643	Medical Lab	Hospital Chaplain Office
T-5644	Surgical Lab	
T-5645	Infirmary Ward S-10	
T-5646	Infirmary Ward S-9	
T-5647	//WAS NOT BUILT//	
T-5648	X-Ray	
T-5649	Infirmary Ward A-8	
T-5650	Infirmary Ward S-7	
T-5651	Infirmary Ward S-6	
T-5652	Boiler House	
T-5653	//WAS NOT BUILT//	
T-5654	Infirmary Ward S-4	
T-5655	Infirmary Ward S-5	
T-5656	//WAS NOT BUILT//	
T-5657	Infirmary Ward S-3	
T-5658	Infirmary Ward S-1	
T-5659	Infirmary Ward S-2	

CAMP HAAN
THE HISTORY OF RIVERSIDE'S WORLD WAR II ANTI-AIRCRAFT TRAINING CENTER

T-5660	//WAS NOT BUILT//	
T-5661	//WAS NOT BUILT//	
T-5662	//WAS NOT BUILT//	
T-5663	//WAS NOT BUILT//	
T-5664	//WAS NOT BUILT//	
T-5665	//WAS NOT BUILT//	
T-5666	//WAS NOT BUILT//	
T-5667	//WAS NOT BUILT//	
T-5668	//WAS NOT BUILT//	
T-5669	//WAS NOT BUILT//	
T-5670	Infirmary Ward M-20	
T-5671	Infirmary Ward M-19	
T-5672	Infirmary Ward M-18	
T-5673	Boiler House	
T-5674	Patient Mess	
T-5675	Infirmary Ward M-17	
T-5676	//WAS NOT BUILT//	
T-5677	Infirmary Ward M-16	
T-5678	Infirmary Ward M-14	
T-5679	Infirmary Ward M-15	
T-5680	//WAS NOT BUILT//	
T-5681	Infirmary Ward M-13	
T-5682	Infirmary Ward M-12	
T-5683	Infirmary Ward M-11	
T-5684	Patient Mess	Addition of 790 sq ft kitchen
T-5685	Infirmary Ward M-10	
T-5686	Infirmary Ward	
T-5687	//WAS NOT BUILT//	
T-5688	Infirmary Ward M-8	
T-5689	Infirmary Ward M-7	
T-5690	Infirmary Ward M-5	
T-5691	Infirmary Ward M-6	

CAMP HAAN
THE HISTORY OF RIVERSIDE'S WORLD WAR II ANTI-AIRCRAFT TRAINING CENTER

T-5692	Patient Mess	
T-5693	//WAS NOT BUILT//	
T-5694	Ward, Detention M-3	
T-5695	Ward, Detention M-4	
T-5696	//WAS NOT BUILT//	
T-5697	Ward, Detention M-1	
T-5698	Ward, Detention M-2	
T-5699	Ward, Detention	
T-5700	//WAS NOT BUILT//	
T-5701	//WAS NOT BUILT//	
T-5702	//WAS NOT BUILT//	
T-5703	//WAS NOT BUILT//	
T-5704	//WAS NOT BUILT//	
T-5705	//WAS NOT BUILT//	
T-5706	//WAS NOT BUILT//	
T-5707	//WAS NOT BUILT//	
T-5708	//WAS NOT BUILT//	
T-5709	//WAS NOT BUILT//	
T-5710	Infirmary Ward D-22	
T-5711	Infirmary Ward D-21	Converted to nurses quarters by 1944
T-5712	Infirmary Ward D-20	
T-5713	//WAS NOT BUILT//	
T-5714	Infirmary Ward D-19	
T-5715	//WAS NOT BUILT//	
T-5716	Infirmary Ward	
T-5717	Infirmary Ward D-18	
T-5718	//WAS NOT BUILT//	
T-5719	Infirmary Ward	
T-5720	Infirmary Ward D-15	
T-5721	Infirmary Ward D-14	
T-5722	//WAS NOT BUILT//	
T-5723	Infirmary Ward D-13	
T-5724	Infirmary Ward	

CAMP HAAN
THE HISTORY OF RIVERSIDE'S WORLD WAR II ANTI-AIRCRAFT TRAINING CENTER

T-5725	Infirmary Ward D-11 & D12	
T-5726	Detachment Mess	Additon of 2795 sq ft
T-5727	Boiler House	
T-5728	Morgue	
T-5729	Red Cross recreation	
T-5730	Infirmary Ward D-1	Converted to office for Utiliies Officer as of 1944
T-5731	Warehouse	
T-5732	Warehouse	
T-5733	Warehouse	
T-5734	//WAS NOT BUILT//	
T-5735	Warehouse	
T-5736	Warehouse	
T-5737	Warehouse	
T-5738	//WAS NOT BUILT//	
T-5739	Warehouse	
T-5740	Warehouse	
T-5741	Warehouse	
T-5742	//WAS NOT BUILT//	
T-5743	//WAS NOT BUILT//	
T-5744	//WAS NOT BUILT//	
T-5745	//WAS NOT BUILT//	
T-5746	//WAS NOT BUILT//	
T-5747	Red Cross recreation	2-story
T-5748	//WAS NOT BUILT//	
T-5749	Gate House	
T-5750	Barracks	
T-5751	Barracks	
T-5752	Barracks	
T-5753	Barracks	
T-5754	Barracks	
T-5755	Barracks	
T-5756	Ambulance Garage	

CAMP HAAN
THE HISTORY OF RIVERSIDE'S WORLD WAR II ANTI-AIRCRAFT TRAINING CENTER

T-5757	Latrine	
T-5758	Unit Supply warehouse	
T-5759	Recreation Hall (day room)	
T-5760	Hospital Detachment Office	
T-5761	Recreation Hall (day room)	
T-5762	Detachment Mess	
T-5763	Post Exchange	
T-5764	Post Exhange Telephone booth	
T-5765	Supply Office	
T-5766	Hospital Shop	
T-5767	Recreation Hall (day room)	
T-5768	Barracks	
T-5769	Latrine	
T-5770	Narcotic Vault	
T-5771	Barracks	
T-5772	Barracks	
T-5773	Barracks	
T-5774	Barracks	
T-5775	Barracks	
T-5776	Barracks	
T-5777	Latrine	
T-5778	Barracks	
T-5779	Barracks	
T-5780	Barracks	
T-5781	Barracks	
T-5782	Barracks	
T-5789	Gas Chamber	
T-5790	WAC Mess	
T-5791	WAC Barracks	
T-5792	WAC Barracks	
T-5793	WAC Detachment Administration	
T-5794	WAC Barracks	

CAMP HAAN
THE HISTORY OF RIVERSIDE'S WORLD WAR II ANTI-AIRCRAFT TRAINING CENTER

T-5795	WAC Barracks	
T-5796	WAC Barracks	
T-5799	Flag Pole	
T-5901	Disposal Plant	
T-5911	Incinerator	
T-6000	Debarkation Towers	
T-6001	Gas Chamber	
T-6002	Gas Chamber	
T-6003	Pistol Range Office	Labeled as Firing Range in 1944 Telephone Directory
T-6004	Latrine	
T-6005	Magazine Igloo	
T-6006	Pistol Range Target Pits	
T-6007	Water Treatment Plant	
T-6008	Water Tank	
T-6010	Pump Station	Supply for the topside area Pump 1 - Worthington centrifugal, 1450 GPM powered by 40 HP GE motor Pump 2 - Worthington centrifugal, 1150 GPM powered by 25 HP GE motor Pump 3 - Worthington centrifugal, 1150 GPM powered by 25 HP GE motor Pump 4 - Worthington centrifugal, 750 GPM, gasoline powered for standby Pump 5 - Worthington centrifugal, 750 GPM, gasoline powered for standby

CAMP HAAN
THE HISTORY OF RIVERSIDE'S WORLD WAR II ANTI-AIRCRAFT TRAINING CENTER

T-6011	Pump Station	Supply for the topside area (installed to provide water to topside in an emergency Pump 1 -Worthington centrifugal, 750 GPM, 48 HP gasoline powered Waukesha motor Pump 2 -Worthington centrifugal, 750 GPM, 48 HP gasoline powered Waukesha motor
T-6101	Infirmary	Also dispensary
T-6102	Storehouse	
T-6103	Post Exchange	
T-6104	Administration	
T-6105	Officer's Quarters	
T-6106	Latrine	
T-6107	Officer's Quarters	
T-6108	Officer's Quarters	
T-6109	Mess Hall	
T-6110	Officer's Quarters	
T-6111	Officer's Quarters	
T-6112	Latrine	
T-6113	Officer's Quarters	
T-6114	Administration	
T-6115	Post Exchange	
T-6116	Storehouse	
T-6117	Infirmary	Also dispensary
T-6118	Mess Hall	
T-6119	Administration and Supply	
T-6120	Recreation Building	
T-6121	Mess Hall	
T-6122	Administration and Supply	
T-6123	Recreation Building	

CAMP HAAN
THE HISTORY OF RIVERSIDE'S WORLD WAR II ANTI-AIRCRAFT TRAINING CENTER

T-6124	Mess Hall	
T-6125	Administration and Supply	
T-6126	Recreation Building	
T-6127	Mess Hall	
T-6128	Administration and Supply	
T-6129	Recreation Building	
T-6130	Mess Hall	
T-6131	Administration and Supply	
T-6132	Recreation Building	
T-6135	Administration and Supply	
T-6136	Mess Hall	
T-6137	Recreation Building	
T-6138	Administration and Supply	
T-6139	Mess Hall	
T-6140	Recreation Building	
T-6141	Administration and Supply	
T-6142	Mess Hall	
T-6143	Recreation Building	
T-6144	Administration and Supply	
T-6145	Mess Hall	
T-6146	Recreation Building	
T-6147	Administration and Supply	
T-6148	Mess Hall	
T-6160	Latrine	
T-6161	Latrine	
T-6162	Latrine	
T-6163	Latrine	
T-6164	Latrine	
T-6165	Latrine	
T-6166	Latrine	
T-6167	Latrine	
T-6168	Latrine	
T-6169	Latrine	
T-6170	Motor Repair Shop	

CAMP HAAN
THE HISTORY OF RIVERSIDE'S WORLD WAR II ANTI-AIRCRAFT TRAINING CENTER

T-6171	Motor Repair Shop	
T-6172	Oil Storage House	
T-6174	Grease Rack	
T-6175	Grease Rack	
T-6180	Hutment	
T-6181	Hutment	
T-6182	Hutment	
T-6183	Hutment	
T-6184	Hutment	
T-6185	Hutment	
T-6186	Hutment	
T-6187	Hutment	
T-6188	Hutment	
T-6189	Hutment	
T-6190	Hutment	
T-6191	Hutment	
T-6192	Hutment	
T-6193	Hutment	
T-6261	Oil Storage House	
T-6301	Infirmary	Also dispensary
T-6302	Storehouse	
T-6303	Post Exchange	
T-6304	Administration	
T-6305	Latrine	
T-6306	Officer's Quarters	
T-6307	Officer's Quarters	
T-6308	Mess Hall	
T-6309	Officer's Quarters	
T-6310	Officer's Quarters	
T-6311	Latrine	
T-6313	Administration	
T-6314	Post Exchange	
T-6315	Storehouse	
T-6316	Infirmary	Also dispensary

CAMP HAAN
THE HISTORY OF RIVERSIDE'S WORLD WAR II ANTI-AIRCRAFT TRAINING CENTER

T-6319	Administration and Supply	
T-6320	Recreation Building	
T-6321	Mess Hall	
T-6322	Administration and Supply	
T-6323	Recreation Building	
T-6324	Mess Hall	
T-6325	Administration and Supply	
T-6326	Recreation Building	
T-6327	Mess Hall	
T-6328	Administration and Supply	
T-6329	Recreation Building	
T-6330	Mess Hall	
T-6331	Administration and Supply	
T-6332	Recreation Building	
T-6335	Administration and Supply	
T-6336	Mess Hall	
T-6337	Recreation Building	
T-6338	Administration and Supply	
T-6339	Mess Hall	
T-6340	Recreation Building	
T-6341	Administration and Supply	
T-6342	Mess Hall	
T-6343	Recreation Building	
T-6344	Administration and Supply	
T-6345	Mess Hall	
T-6346	Recreation Building	
T-6347	Administration and Supply	
T-6360	Latrine	
T-6361	Latrine	
T-6362	Latrine	
T-6363	Latrine	
T-6364	Latrine	
T-6365	Latrine	
T-6366	Latrine	

CAMP HAAN
THE HISTORY OF RIVERSIDE'S WORLD WAR II ANTI-AIRCRAFT TRAINING CENTER

T-6367	Latrine	
T-6368	Latrine	
T-6369	Latrine	
T-6370	Motor Repair Shop	
T-6371	Motor Repair Shop	
T-6372	Oil Storage House	
T-6373	Oil Storage House	
T-6374	Grease Rack	
T-6375	Grease Rack	
T-6379	Sentry House (camp entrances)	
T-6380	Hutment	
T-6381	Hutment	
T-6382	Hutment	
T-6383	Hutment	
T-6384	Hutment	
T-6385	Hutment	
T-6386	Hutment	
T-6387	Hutment	
T-6388	Hutment	
T-6389	Hutment	
T-6390	Hutment	
T-6391	Hutment	
T-6392	Hutment	
T-6393	Hutment	
T-6394	Hutment	
T-6395	Hutment	
T-6396	Hutment	
T-6397	Hutment	
T-6398	Hutment	
T-6399	Hutment	
T-6400	Hutment	
T-6401	Hutment	
T-6402	Hutment	
T-6403	Hutment	

CAMP HAAN
THE HISTORY OF RIVERSIDE'S WORLD WAR II ANTI-AIRCRAFT TRAINING CENTER

T-6404	Hutment	
T-6405	Hutment	
T-6406	Hutment	
T-6407	Hutment	
T-6408	Hutment	
T-6409	Hutment	
T-6410	Hutment	
T-6411	Hutment	
T-6412	Hutment	
T-6413	Hutment	
T-6414	Hutment	
T-6415	Hutment	
T-6416	Hutment	
T-6417	Hutment	
T-6418	Hutment	
T-6419	Hutment	
T-6420	Hutment	
T-6421	Hutment	
T-6422	Hutment	
T-6423	Hutment	
T-6424	Hutment	
T-6425	Hutment	
T-6426	Hutment	
T-6427	Hutment	
T-6428	Hutment	
T-6429	Hutment	
T-6430	Hutment	
T-6431	Hutment	
T-6432	Hutment	
T-6433	Hutment	
T-6434	Hutment	
T-6435	Hutment	
T-6436	Hutment	
T-6437	Hutment	

CAMP HAAN
THE HISTORY OF RIVERSIDE'S WORLD WAR II ANTI-AIRCRAFT TRAINING CENTER

T-6438	Hutment	
T-6439	Hutment	
T-6440	Hutment	
T-6441	Hutment	
T-6442	Hutment	
T-6443	Hutment	
T-6444	Hutment	
T-6445	Hutment	
T-6446	Hutment	
T-6447	Hutment	
T-6448	Hutment	
T-6449	Hutment	
T-6450	Hutment	
T-6451	Hutment	
T-6452	Hutment	
T-6453	Hutment	
T-6454	Hutment	
T-6455	Hutment	
T-6456	Hutment	
T-6457	Hutment	
T-6458	Hutment	
T-6459	Hutment	
T-6460	Hutment	
T-6461	Hutment	
T-6462	Hutment	
T-6463	Hutment	
T-6464	Hutment	
T-6465	Hutment	
T-6466	Hutment	
T-6467	Hutment	
T-6468	Hutment	
T-6469	Hutment	
T-6470	Hutment	
T-6471	Hutment	

CAMP HAAN
THE HISTORY OF RIVERSIDE'S WORLD WAR II ANTI-AIRCRAFT TRAINING CENTER

T-6472	Hutment	
T-6473	Hutment	
T-6474	Hutment	
T-6475	Hutment	
T-6476	Hutment	
T-6477	Hutment	
T-6478	Hutment	
T-6479	Hutment	
T-6480	Hutment	
T-6481	Hutment	
T-6482	Hutment	
T-6483	Hutment	
T-6484	Hutment	
T-6485	Hutment	
T-6486	Hutment	
T-6487	Hutment	
T-6488	Hutment	
T-6489	Hutment	
T-6490	Hutment	
T-6491	Hutment	
T-6492	Hutment	
T-6493	Hutment	
T-6500	Oil Storage Tank	
T-6501	Warehouse	
T-6504	Warehouse	
T-6508	Warehouse	Warehousing and Storage Superintendent
T-6513	Oil Storage Tank	
T-6515	Loading Ramp	
T-6516	Loading Ramp	
T-6523	Motor Repair Shop	
T-6524	Paint Storage Shed	
T-6525	Equipment Shed	

CAMP HAAN
THE HISTORY OF RIVERSIDE'S WORLD WAR II ANTI-AIRCRAFT TRAINING CENTER

T-6601	Water Tank	102' diameter, steel constructed on 1-17-41
T-6700	Debarkation Towers	
T-6800	Water Tank, Elevated	
T-6802	Radio School	
T-6810	Pump House, Water	
T-6811	Pump House, Water	
T-6850	Skeet Range Low House	
T-6851	Skeet Range High House	
T-7001	Administration Building	
T-7002	Latrine	
T-7003	Officers Mess	
T-7004	Officer's Quarters	
T-7005	Officer's Quarters	
T-7006	Officer's Quarters	
T-7010	Infirmary	
T-7012	Recreation Building	
T-7013	Battalion Supply	
T-7020	Barracks	
T-7021	Barracks	
T-7022	Administration and Supply	
T-7023	Barracks	
T-7024	Barracks	
T-7025	Barracks	
T-7026	Barracks	
T-7028	Mess Hall	
T-7029	Mess Hall	
T-7031	Barracks	
T-7032	Barracks	
T-7033	Barracks	
T-7034	Barracks	
T-7035	Administration and Supply	
T-7036	Latrine	
T-7037	Latrine	

CAMP HAAN
THE HISTORY OF RIVERSIDE'S WORLD WAR II ANTI-AIRCRAFT TRAINING CENTER

T-7038	Administration and Supply	
T-7039	Barracks	
T-7040	Barracks	
T-7041	Barracks	
T-7042	Barracks	
T-7044	Mess Hall	
T-7045	Mess Hall	
T-7047	Barracks	
T-7048	Barracks	
T-7049	Barracks	
T-7050	Barracks	
T-7051	Administration and Supply	
T-7052	Administration and Supply	
T-7053	Barracks	
T-7054	Mess Hall	
T-7055	Latrine	
T-7056	Latrine	
T-7057	Latrine	
T-7060	Motor Repair and Grease Inspection	
T-7061	Oil Storage House	
T-7062	Grease and Inspection Rack	
T-7101	Administration Building	
T-7102	Latrine	
T-7103	Officers Mess	
T-7104	Officer's Quarters	
T-7105	Officer's Quarters	
T-7106	Officer's Quarters	
T-7110	Infirmary	
T-7112	Recreation Building	
T-7113	Battalion Supply	
T-7120	Barracks	
T-7121	Barracks	
T-7122	Barracks	

T-7123	Barracks	
T-7124	Barracks	
T-7125	Barracks	
T-7126	Barracks	
T-7128	Mess Hall	
T-7129	Mess Hall	
T-7131	Barracks	
T-7132	Barracks	
T-7133	Barracks	
T-7134	Barracks	
T-7135	Administration and Supply	
T-7136	Latrine	
T-7137	Latrine	
T-7138	Administration and Supply	
T-7139	Barracks	
T-7140	Barracks	
T-7141	Barracks	
T-7142	Barracks	
T-7144	Mess Hall	
T-7145	Mess Hall	
T-7147	Barracks	
T-7148	Barracks	
T-7149	Barracks	
T-7150	Barracks	
T-7151	Administration and Supply	
T-7152	Administration and Supply	
T-7153	Barracks	
T-7154	Mess Hall	
T-7155	Latrine	
T-7156	Latrine	
T-7157	Latrine	
T-7160	Motor Repair and Grease Inspection	
T-7161	Oil Storage House	

CAMP HAAN
THE HISTORY OF RIVERSIDE'S WORLD WAR II ANTI-AIRCRAFT TRAINING CENTER

T-7162	Grease and Inspection Rack	
T-7201	Administration Building	
T-7202	Latrine	
T-7203	Officers Mess	
T-7204	Officer's Quarters	
T-7205	Officer's Quarters	
T-7206	Officer's Quarters	
T-7207		
T-7208	Training Auditorium	
T-7210	Infirmary	
T-7211	Post Exchange	
T-7212	Recreation Building	
T-7213	Battalion Supply	
T-7214	Dental Clinic	Chief Dentist
T-7220	Barracks	
T-7221	Barracks	
T-7222	Barracks	
T-7223	Barracks	
T-7224	Barracks	
T-7225	Barracks	
T-7226	Barracks	
T-7228	Mess Hall	
T-7229	Mess Hall	
T-7231	Barracks	
T-7232	Barracks	
T-7233	Barracks	
T-7234	Barracks	
T-7235	Administration and Supply	
T-7236	Latrine	
T-7237	Latrine	
T-7238	Administration and Supply	
T-7239	Barracks	
T-7240	Barracks	
T-7241	Barracks	

T-7242	Barracks	
T-7244	Mess Hall	
T-7245	Mess Hall	
T-7247	Barracks	
T-7248	Barracks	
T-7249	Barracks	
T-7250	Barracks	
T-7251	Administration and Supply	
T-7252	Administration and Supply	
T-7253	Barracks	
T-7254	Mess Hall	
T-7255	Latrine	
T-7256	Latrine	
T-7257	Latrine	
T-7260	Motor Repair and Grease Inspection	
T-7261	Oil Storage House	
T-7262	Grease and Inspection Rack	
T-7301	Administration Building	
T-7302	Latrine	
T-7303	Officers Mess	
T-7304	Officer's Quarters	
T-7305	Officer's Quarters	
T-7306	Officer's Quarters	
T-7310	Infirmary	
T-7312	Recreation Building	converted to a post office in 1943 (Camp Haan Tracer, 11/16/1943)
T-7313	Battalion Supply	
T-7320	Barracks	
T-7321	Barracks	
T-7322	Barracks	
T-7323	Barracks	
T-7324	Barracks	
T-7325	Barracks	

CAMP HAAN
THE HISTORY OF RIVERSIDE'S WORLD WAR II ANTI-AIRCRAFT TRAINING CENTER

T-7326	Barracks	
T-7328	Mess Hall	
T-7329	Mess Hall	
T-7331	Barracks	
T-7332	Barracks	
T-7333	Barracks	
T-7334	Barracks	
T-7335	Administration and Supply	
T-7336	Latrine	
T-7337	Latrine	
T-7338	Administration and Supply	
T-7339	Barracks	
T-7340	Barracks	
T-7341	Barracks	
T-7342	Barracks	
T-7344	Mess Hall	
T-7345	Mess Hall	
T-7348	Barracks	
T-7349	Barracks	
T-7350	Barracks	
T-7351	Administration and Supply	
T-7352	Administration and Supply	
T-7353	Barracks	
T-7354	Mess Hall	
T-7355	Latrine	
T-7356	Latrine	
T-7357	Latrine	
T-7360	Motor Repair and Grease Inspection	
T-7361	Oil Storage House	
T-7362	Grease and Inspection Rack	
T-7401	Administration Building	
T-7402	Latrine	
T-7403	Officers Mess	

CAMP HAAN
THE HISTORY OF RIVERSIDE'S WORLD WAR II ANTI-AIRCRAFT TRAINING CENTER

T-7404	Officer's Quarters	
T-7405	Officer's Quarters	
T-7406	Officer's Quarters	
T-7410	Infirmary	
T-7412	Recreation Building	
T-7413	Battalion Supply	
T-7420	Barracks	
T-7421	Barracks	
T-7422	Administration and Supply	
T-7423	Barracks	
T-7424	Barracks	
T-7425	Barracks	
T-7426	Barracks	
T-7428	Mess Hall	
T-7429	Mess Hall	
T-7431	Barracks	
T-7432	Barracks	
T-7433	Barracks	
T-7434	Barracks	
T-7435	Administration and Supply	
T-7436	Latrine	
T-7437	Latrine	
T-7438	Administration and Supply	
T-7439	Barracks	
T-7440	Barracks	
T-7441	Barracks	
T-7442	Barracks	
T-7444	Mess Hall	
T-7445	Mess Hall	
T-7447	Barracks	
T-7448	Barracks	
T-7449	Barracks	
T-7450	Barracks	
T-7451	Administration and Supply	

CAMP HAAN
THE HISTORY OF RIVERSIDE'S WORLD WAR II ANTI-AIRCRAFT TRAINING CENTER

T-7452	Administration and Supply	
T-7453	Barracks	
T-7454	Mess Hall	
T-7455	Latrine	
T-7456	Latrine	
T-7457	Latrine	
T-7460	Motor Repair and Grease Inspection	
T-7461	Oil Storage House	
T-7462	Grease and Inspection Rack	
T-7501	Administration Building	
T-7502	Latrine	
T-7503	Officers Mess	
T-7504	Officer's Quarters	
T-7505	Officer's Quarters	
T-7506	Officer's Quarters	
T-7510	Infirmary	
T-7512	Recreation Hall	
T-7513	Battalion Supply	
T-7520	Barracks	
T-7521	Barracks	
T-7522	Administration and Supply	
T-7523	Barracks	
T-7524	Barracks	
T-7525	Barracks	
T-7526	Barracks	
T-7528	Mess Hall	
T-7529	Mess Hall	
T-7531	Barracks	
T-7532	Barracks	
T-7533	Barracks	
T-7534	Barracks	
T-7535	Administration and Supply	
T-7536	Latrine	

CAMP HAAN
THE HISTORY OF RIVERSIDE'S WORLD WAR II ANTI-AIRCRAFT TRAINING CENTER

T-7537	Latrine	
T-7538	Administration and Supply	
T-7539	Barracks	
T-7540	Barracks	
T-7541	Barracks	
T-7542	Barracks	
T-7544	Mess Hall	
T-7545	Mess Hall	
T-7547	Barracks	
T-7548	Barracks	
T-7549	Barracks	
T-7550	Barracks	
T-7551	Administration and Supply	
T-7552	Administration and Supply	
T-7553	Barracks	
T-7554	Mess Hall	
T-7555	Latrine	
T-7556	Latrine	
T-7557	Latrine	
T-7560	Motor Repair and Grease Inspection	
T-7561	Oil Storage House	
T-7562	Grease and Inspection Rack	
T-7613	Telephone and Telegraph Building	
T-7614	Fire Station	
T-7615	Recreation Building	Labeled as Service club in 1944 telephone directory
T-7616	Serivce Club	#3
T-7715	Recreation Auditorium	
T-7716	Service Club	
T-7801	Administration Building	
T-7802	Latrine	
T-7803	Officers Mess	
T-7804	Classroom	Converted from

CAMP HAAN
THE HISTORY OF RIVERSIDE'S WORLD WAR II ANTI-AIRCRAFT TRAINING CENTER

		officer's quarters
T-7805	Classroom	Converted from officer's quarters
T-7806	Prisoner Visitors Room	Converted from Officer's Quarters
T-7810	Infirmary	
T-7812	Administration Building	converted from recreation building
T-7813	Battalion Supply	
T-7814	Sentry House, Stockade	
T-7820	Barracks	
T-7821	Barracks	
T-7822	Administration and Supply	
T-7823	Barracks	
T-7824	Barracks	
T-7825	Barracks	
T-7826	Barracks	
T-7828	Mess Hall	
T-7829	Mess Hall	
T-7831	Barracks	
T-7832	Barracks	
T-7833	Barracks	
T-7834	Barracks	
T-7835	Administration and Supply	
T-7836	Latrine	
T-7837	Latrine	
T-7838	Administration and Supply	
T-7839	Barracks	
T-7840	Barracks	
T-7841	Barracks	
T-7842	Barracks	
T-7844	Mess Hall	
T-7845	Mess Hall	
T-7847	Barracks	
T-7848	Barracks	

CAMP HAAN
THE HISTORY OF RIVERSIDE'S WORLD WAR II ANTI-AIRCRAFT TRAINING CENTER

T-7849	Barracks	
T-7850	Barracks	
T-7851	Administration and Supply	
T-7852	Administration and Supply	
T-7853	Barracks	
T-7854	Mess Hall	
T-7855	Latrine	
T-7856	Latrine	
T-7857	Latrine	
T-7860	Motor Repair and Grease Inspection	
T-7861	Oil Storage House	
T-7862	Grease and Inspection Rack	
T-7901	Administration Building	
T-7902	Latrine	
T-7903	Officers Mess	
T-7904	Officer's Quarters	
T-7905	Officer's Quarters	
T-7906	Officer's Quarters	Converted to Med Supply and ward attendant quarters
T-7910	Infirmary	
T-7911	Post Exchange	
T-7912	Recreation Building	
T-7913	Battalion Supply	
T-7914	Sentry House, Stockade	
T-7920	Barracks	
T-7921	Barracks	
T-7922	Administration and Supply	
T-7923	Barracks	
T-7924	Barracks	
T-7925	Barracks	
T-7926	Barracks	
T-7928	Mess Hall	
T-7929	Mess Hall	

CAMP HAAN
THE HISTORY OF RIVERSIDE'S WORLD WAR II ANTI-AIRCRAFT TRAINING CENTER

T-7931	Barracks	
T-7932	Barracks	
T-7933	Barracks	
T-7934	Barracks	
T-7935	Administration and Supply	
T-7936	Latrine	
T-7937	Latrine	
T-7938	Administration and Supply	
T-7939	Barracks	
T-7940	Barracks	
T-7941	Barracks	
T-7942	Barracks	
T-7944	Mess Hall	
T-7945	Mess Hall	
T-7947	Barracks	
T-7948	Barracks	
T-7949	Barracks	
T-7950	Barracks	
T-7951	Administration and Supply	
T-7952	Administration and Supply	
T-7953	Barracks	
T-7954	Mess Hall	
T-7955	Latrine	
T-7956	Latrine	
T-7957	Latrine	
T-7960	Motor Repair and Grease Inspection	
T-7961	Oil Storage House	
T-7962	Grease and Inspection Rack	
T-7963	Sentry House, Stockade	
T-8008	Training Auditorium	
T-8010	Infirmary	
T-8012	Administration Building	converted from recreation building
T-8013	Battalion Supply	

CAMP HAAN
THE HISTORY OF RIVERSIDE'S WORLD WAR II ANTI-AIRCRAFT TRAINING CENTER

T-8014	Sentry House, Stockade	
T-8019	Sentry House, Stockade	
T-8020	Barracks	
T-8021	Barracks	
T-8022	Administration and Supply	
T-8023	Barracks	
T-8024	Barracks	
T-8025	Barracks	
T-8026	Barracks	
T-8028	Mess Hall	
T-8029	Mess Hall	
T-8031	Barracks	
T-8032	Barracks	
T-8033	Barracks	
T-8034	Barracks	
T-8035	Administration and Supply	
T-8036	Latrine	
T-8037	Latrine	
T-8038	Administration and Supply	
T-8039	Barracks	
T-8040	Barracks	
T-8041	Barracks	
T-8042	Barracks	
T-8044	Mess Hall	
T-8045	Mess Hall	
T-8047	Barracks	
T-8048	Barracks	
T-8049	Barracks	
T-8050	Barracks	
T-8051	Administration and Supply	
T-8052	Administration and Supply	
T-8053	Barracks	
T-8054	Mess Hall	
T-8055	Latrine	

CAMP HAAN
THE HISTORY OF RIVERSIDE'S WORLD WAR II ANTI-AIRCRAFT TRAINING CENTER

T-8056	Latrine	
T-8057	Latrine	
T-8060	Motor Repair and Grease Inspection	
T-8061	Oil Storage House	
T-8062	Sentry House, Stockade	
T-8063	Medium Security Disciplinary Barracks	
T-8064	Medium Security Disciplinary Barracks	
T-8066	Sentry House, Stockade	
T-8101	Administration Building	
T-8102	Latrine	
T-8103	Officers Mess	
T-8104	Officer's Quarters	
T-8105	Officer's Quarters	
T-8106	Officer's Quarters	
T-8110	Infirmary	
T-8111	Administration Building	
T-8112	Administration Building	converted from recreation building
T-8113	Administration Building	Converted from a storehouse
T-8114	Administration Building	
T-8115	Battalion Supply	converted from mess hall
T-8116	Prisoner Visitors Room	Converted from Officer's Quarters
T-8117	Officer's Quarters	
T-8118	Officer's Quarters	
T-8119	Latrine	
T-8120	Barracks	
T-8121	Barracks	
T-8122	Barracks	
T-8123	Barracks	
T-8124	Barracks	
T-8125	Barracks	
T-8126	Barracks	

CAMP HAAN
THE HISTORY OF RIVERSIDE'S WORLD WAR II ANTI-AIRCRAFT TRAINING CENTER

T-8128	Mess Hall	
T-8129	Mess Hall	
T-8131	Barracks	
T-8132	Barracks	
T-8133	Barracks	
T-8134	Barracks	
T-8135	Administration and Supply	
T-8136	Latrine	
T-8137	Latrine	
T-8138	Administration and Supply	
T-8139	Barracks	
T-8140	Barracks	
T-8141	Barracks	
T-8142	Barracks	
T-8144	Mess Hall	
T-8145	Mess Hall	
T-8147	Barracks	
T-8148	Barracks	
T-8149	Barracks	
T-8150	Barracks	
T-8151	Administration and Supply	
T-8152	Administration and Supply	
T-8153	Barracks	
T-8154	Mess Hall	
T-8155	Latrine	
T-8156	Latrine	
T-8157	Latrine	
T-8160	Motor Repair and Grease Inspection	
T-8161	Oil Storage House	
T-8162	Grease and Inspection Rack	
T-8201	Administration Building	
T-8202	Latrine	
T-8203	Officers Mess	

CAMP HAAN
THE HISTORY OF RIVERSIDE'S WORLD WAR II ANTI-AIRCRAFT TRAINING CENTER

T-8204	Officer's Quarters	
T-8205	Officer's Quarters	
T-8206	Officer's Quarters	
T-8210	Infirmary	
T-8211	Post Exchange	
T-8212	Recreation Building	
T-8213	Battalion Supply	
T-8220	Barracks	
T-8221	Barracks	
T-8222	Barracks	
T-8223	Barracks	
T-8224	Barracks	
T-8225	Barracks	
T-8226	Barracks	
T-8228	Mess Hall	
T-8229	Mess Hall	
T-8231	Barracks	
T-8232	Barracks	
T-8233	Barracks	
T-8234	Barracks	
T-8235	Administration and Supply	
T-8236	Latrine	
T-8237	Latrine	
T-8238	Administration and Supply	
T-8239	Barracks	
T-8240	Barracks	
T-8241	Barracks	
T-8242	Barracks	
T-8244	Mess Hall	
T-8245	Mess Hall	
T-8247	Barracks	
T-8248	Barracks	
T-8249	Barracks	
T-8250	Barracks	

T-8251	Administration and Supply	
T-8252	Administration and Supply	
T-8253	Barracks	
T-8254	Mess Hall	
T-8255	Latrine	
T-8256	Latrine	
T-8257	Latrine	
T-8260	Motor Repair and Grease Inspection	
T-8261	Oil Storage House	
T-8262	Grease and Inspection Rack	
T-8301	Administration Building	
T-8302	Latrine	
T-8303	Officers Mess	
T-8304	Officer's Quarters	
T-8305	Officer's Quarters	
T-8306	Officer's Quarters	
T-8308	Training Auditorium	AKA Theater #3
T-8310	Infirmary	
T-8312	Recreation Building	
T-8313	Battalion Supply	
T-8320	Barracks	
T-8321	Barracks	
T-8322	Barracks	
T-8323	Barracks	
T-8324	Barracks	
T-8325	Barracks	
T-8326	Barracks	
T-8328	Mess Hall	
T-8329	Mess Hall	
T-8331	Barracks	
T-8332	Barracks	
T-8333	Barracks	
T-8334	Barracks	

CAMP HAAN
THE HISTORY OF RIVERSIDE'S WORLD WAR II ANTI-AIRCRAFT TRAINING CENTER

T-8335	Administration and Supply	
T-8336	Latrine	
T-8337	Latrine	
T-8338	Administration and Supply	
T-8339	Barracks	
T-8340	Barracks	
T-8341	Barracks	
T-8342	Barracks	
T-8344	Mess Hall	
T-8345	Mess Hall	
T-8347	Barracks	
T-8348	Barracks	
T-8349	Barracks	
T-8350	Barracks	
T-8351	Administration and Supply	
T-8352	Administration and Supply	
T-8353	Barracks	
T-8354	Mess Hall	
T-8355	Latrine	
T-8356	Latrine	
T-8357	Latrine	
T-8360	Motor Repair and Grease Inspection	
T-8361	Oil Storage House	
T-8362	Grease and Inspection Rack	
T-8380	Theater	#4
T-8401	Administration Building	
T-8402	Latrine	
T-8403	Officers Mess	
T-8404	Officer's Quarters	
T-8405	Officer's Quarters	
T-8406	Officer's Quarters	
T-8410	Infirmary	
T-8412	Recreation Building	

CAMP HAAN
THE HISTORY OF RIVERSIDE'S WORLD WAR II ANTI-AIRCRAFT TRAINING CENTER

T-8413	Battalion Supply	
T-8420	Barracks	
T-8421	Barracks	
T-8422	Barracks	
T-8423	Barracks	
T-8424	Barracks	
T-8425	Barracks	
T-8426	Barracks	
T-8428	Mess Hall	
T-8429	Mess Hall	
T-8431	Barracks	
T-8432	Barracks	
T-8433	Barracks	
T-8434	Barracks	
T-8435	Administration and Supply	
T-8436	Latrine	
T-8437	Latrine	
T-8438	Administration and Supply	
T-8439	Barracks	
T-8440	Barracks	
T-8441	Barracks	
T-8442	Barracks	
T-8443		
T-8444	Mess Hall	
T-8445	Mess Hall	
T-8447	Barracks	
T-8448	Barracks	
T-8449	Barracks	
T-8450	Barracks	
T-8451	Administration and Supply	
T-8452	Administration and Supply	
T-8453	Barracks	
T-8454	Mess Hall	
T-8455	Latrine	

CAMP HAAN
THE HISTORY OF RIVERSIDE'S WORLD WAR II ANTI-AIRCRAFT TRAINING CENTER

T-8456	Latrine	
T-8457	Latrine	
T-8460	Motor Repair and Grease Inspection	
T-8461	Oil Storage House	
T-8462	Grease and Inspection Rack	
T-9001	Guard Tower	
T-9002	Guard Tower	
T-9003	Guard Tower	
T-9004	Guard Tower	
T-9005	Guard Tower	
T-9006	Guard Tower	
T-9007	Guard Tower	
T-9008	Guard Tower	
T-9009	Guard Tower	
T-9010	Guard Tower	
T-9011	Guard Tower	
T-9012	Guard Tower	
T-9013	Guard Tower	
T-9014	Guard Tower	
T-9015	Guard Tower	
T-9016	Guard Tower	
T-9017	Guard Tower	
T-9018	Guard Tower	
T-9019	Guard Tower	
T-9200	Debarkation Towers	
T-9203	Loading Platform, Flat Car	
T-9301	Sewage Pump Plant	
T-9302	Chlorinator Building	
T-9303	Imhoff Tank	
T-9304	Imhoff Tank	
T-9305	Dosing Chamber	
T-9306	Filter	

CAMP HAAN
THE HISTORY OF RIVERSIDE'S WORLD WAR II ANTI-AIRCRAFT TRAINING CENTER

T-9307	Final Settling Tank	
T-9308	Digester	
T-15001	Underground Magazine	
T-15002	Underground Magazine	
T-15003	Underground Magazine	
T-15004	Underground Magazine	
T-15005	Underground Magazine	
T-15006	Underground Magazine	
T-15007	Underground Magazine	
T-15008	Underground Magazine	
T-15009	Underground Magazine	On leased land
T-15010	Underground Magazine	On leased land
T-15011	Underground Magazine	On leased land
T-15012	Underground Magazine	
T-15013	Underground Magazine	
T-15014	Underground Magazine	
T-15015	Underground Magazine	
T-15016	Underground Magazine	
T-15017	Ordnance Ammunition Office	
T-15019	Sentry Box for Magazine Area	
T-15020	Sentry Box for Magazine Area	
T-15021	Tent	

APPENDIX 3
SAMPLE WEEKLY CHAPEL ACTIVITIES
CAMP HAAN (1943)

Tuesday		
8:00pm	North Chapel	Organ Recital

Wednesday		
2:15pm	Hospital	
6:30pm	Central Chapel	
7:00pm	South Chapel	Organ Recital
7:00pm	North Chapel	

Thursday		
6:30pm	Central Chapel	Record Concert

Friday		
6:30pm	Central Chapel	
7:00pm	North Chapel	

Saturday		
7:00-8:00pm	North Chapel	Confessions
8:00-9:00pm	South Chapel	Confessions

Sunday - PROTESTANT		
7:30am	Area 16 Recreation Hall	Episcopal Communion
8:30am	Central Chapel	Episcopal Communion
9:30am	South Chapel	
9:30am	Central Chapel	
9:30am	North Chapel	
9:30am	Area 16 Recreation Hall	
10:45am	North Chapel	537th Bn.
11:00am	Stockade	
2:00pm	Hospital	
4:00pm	North Chapel	Organ Recital
6:30pm	South Chapel	
6:30pm	Central Chapel	

6:30pm	North Chapel	
6:30pm	Area 16 Recreation Hall	

Sunday
ROMAN CATHOLIC

6:30am	Hospital	
7:30am	South Chapel	
8:30am	North Chapel	
11:00am	Central Chapel	

Monday

7:00pm	Central Chapel	Organ Recital

KEITH A. BEAULIEU

APPENDIX 4
CAMP HAAN BUILDING DISPOSITION

CAMP HAAN
THE HISTORY OF RIVERSIDE'S WORLD WAR II ANTI-AIRCRAFT TRAINING CENTER

Please note this is not an exhaustive list; this was just the buildings that I could find disposition record for in the archives.

Building Number	Building	Disposition
T-2	Officers Club	Retained by March Field October 1948
T-3	Mess Hall	Sold to Midland School District, Moreno Valley, CA in May 1949 and used as a cafeteria
T-5	Officer's Quarters	Retained by March Field October 1948
T-10	Officer's Quarters	Retained by March Field October 1948
T-11	Officer's Quarters	Retained by March Field October 1948
T-12	Officer's Quarters	Retained by March Field October 1948
T-52	Guest House	Transferred to Federal Public Housing Authority (FPHA) to provide housing for veterans in April 1947
T-53	Guest House	Transferred to Federal Public Housing Authority (FPHA) to provide housing for veterans in April 1947
T-57	Dental Clinic	Sold to Beulah College in Upland, CA in July 1949 and used for a science classroom
T-58	Post Office	Sold to the First Congressional Church, Perris, CA in November 1947
T-60	Bank, Citizens National	Sold to Hugo Reid Elementary, Arcadia School District, Arcadia, CA
T-71	Telephone and Telegraph Building	Sold to Midland School District, Moreno Valley, CA in May 1949 and used as a classroom
T-74	Theater	Sold to Beulah College in Upland, CA in July 1949 and used for a gym
T-86	Day Room	Sold to Midland School District, Moreno Valley in March 1948
T-87	Mess Hall	Sold to Allesandro Valley Community Church, Sunnymead, CA in November 1947
T-99	Flag Pole	Sold to Colton Union High School

CAMP HAAN
THE HISTORY OF RIVERSIDE'S WORLD WAR II ANTI-AIRCRAFT TRAINING CENTER

T-127	Tent	Retained by March Field October 1948
T-130	Tent	Retained by March Field October 1948
T-178		Sold to Colton Union High School
T-302	Latrine	Sold to San Dimas Junior Chamber of Commerce
T-305	Day Room	Sold to the Boy Scouts of America, Troop 93, Edgemont, CA in December 1947
T-518	Chapel	Sold to Woodcrest Church
T-1118	Chapel	Sold to the Roman Catholic Bishop of San Diego, CA in November 1947
T-1149	Day Room	Sold to Seventh Day Adventist Church, Riverside in April 1947
T-1712	Recreation Building	Sold to Elsinore Social and Cultural Center in May 1948
T-1780	Motor Repair Shop	Sold to Beulah College in Upland, CA in July 1949 and used for a classroom for wood shop
T-2310	Infirmary	Sold to Beulah College in Upland, CA in July 1949 and used for science classrooms
T-2312	Recreation Building	Sold to Beulah College in Upland, CA in July 1949 and used for music room, auditorium, and chapel
T-2321	Mess Hall	Sold to Elsinore Progressive League on October 1947
T-2918	Chapel	Sold to Trinity Lutheran Church, Baldwin Park, CA
T-2919	Fire Station	Sold to B'nai Brith Community Center, Fontana
T-2921		Sold to Beulah College in Upland, CA in July 1949 and used for a cafeteria
T-2937	Administration and Supply	Sold to Boy's Town Hall Club, Pomona, CA in November 1947
T-2944	Mess Hall	Sold to Romoland School District, Romoland, CA in December 1947 and used as a classroom
T-2947		Sold to Beulah College in Upland, CA in July 1949 and used for a classroom for home economics

T-2993	Latrine	Sold to Morongo Valley Chamber of Commerce in December 1947
T-3526	Day Room	Sold to Santa Anita Avenue Elementary, Arcadia School District, Arcadia, CA
T-3534	Hutment	Sold to Seventh Day Adventist Church, Riverside in April 1947
T-4558	Guard House	Sold to Seventh Day Adventist Church, Riverside in April 1947
T-4572	Tent	Sold to St. John's Lutheran Church, Hemet, CA
T-4701	Administration Building	Sold to Winchester Elementary School, Winchester, CA in December 1947
T-4704	Recreation Building	Sold to the American Legion Post, Hemet, CA in November 1947
T-4705	Post Exchange	Sold to Woodcrest Community Church in December 1947
T-4732	Infirmary	Sold to Southern California Council of Religious Education, Idyllwild, CA in November 1947
T-4741	Mess Hall	Sold to Southern California Council of Religious Education, Idyllwild, CA in November 1947
T-4744	Mess Hall	Sold to Southern California Council of Religious Education, Idyllwild, CA in November 1947
T-4747	Mess Hall	Sold to the city of La Verne, CA in November 1947
T-4750	Mess Hall	Sold to Riverside Farm Bureau in December 1947
T-4753	Mess Hall	Sold to Riverside Farm Bureau in December 1947
T-4780	Latrine	Sold to Southern California Council of Religious Education, Idyllwild, CA in November 1947
T-5208	Infirmary	Grace Community Church, Riverside, CA in December 1947

T-5601	Hospital Administration Building	Sold to the State of California Dept. of Finance in August 1947
T-5602	Nurse's Club	Sold to the State of California Dept. of Finance in August 1947
T-5603	Nurses Quarters	Sold to the State of California Dept. of Finance in August 1947
T-5604	Nurses Quarters	Sold to the State of California Dept. of Finance in August 1947
T-5605	Nurse's Quarters	Sold to the State of California Dept. of Finance in August 1947
T-5606	Nurses Recreation Hall	Sold to the State of California Dept. of Finance in August 1947
T-5607	Nurse's Quarters	Sold to the State of California Dept. of Finance in August 1947
T-5608	Nurse's Mess	Sold to the State of California Dept. of Finance in August 1947
T-5609	Officer's Quarters	Sold to the State of California Dept. of Finance in August 1947
T-5610	Officer's Quarters	Sold to the State of California Dept. of Finance in August 1947
T-5611	Infirmary Ward	Sold to the State of California Dept. of Finance in August 1947
T-5612	Officer's Quarters	Sold to the State of California Dept. of Finance in August 1947
T-5613	Infirmary Ward	Sold to the State of California Dept. of Finance in August 1947
T-5614	Nurse's Quarters	Sold to the State of California Dept. of Finance in August 1947
T-5615	Nurse's Quarters	Sold to the State of California Dept. of Finance in August 1947
T-5616	Nurse's Quarters	Sold to the State of California Dept. of Finance in August 1947
T-5617	Nurse's Quarters	Sold to the State of California Dept. of Finance in August 1947
T-5618	Nurse's Quarters	Sold to the State of California Dept. of Finance in August 1947

CAMP HAAN
THE HISTORY OF RIVERSIDE'S WORLD WAR II ANTI-AIRCRAFT TRAINING CENTER

T-5619	Infirmary Ward S-8	Sold to the State of California Dept. of Finance in August 1947
T-5620	Officer's Quarters	Sold to the State of California Dept. of Finance in August 1947
T-5621	Dental Clinic	Sold to the State of California Dept. of Finance in August 1947
T-5622	Officer's Quarters and Mess	Sold to the State of California Dept. of Finance in August 1947
T-5623	Infirmary Ward	Sold to the State of California Dept. of Finance in August 1947
T-5630	Infirmary Ward S-19	Sold to the State of California Dept. of Finance in August 1947
T-5631	Infirmary Ward S-17	Sold to the State of California Dept. of Finance in August 1947
T-5632	Infirmary Ward S-18	Sold to the State of California Dept. of Finance in August 1947
T-5633	Boiler House	Sold to the State of California Dept. of Finance in August 1947
T-5634	Infirmary Ward S-15	Sold to the State of California Dept. of Finance in August 1947
T-5635	Infirmary Ward S-16	Sold to the State of California Dept. of Finance in August 1947
T-5637	Infirmary Ward S-14	Sold to the State of California Dept. of Finance in August 1947
T-5638	Infirmary Ward S-13	Sold to the State of California Dept. of Finance in August 1947
T-5639	Infirmary Ward S-12	Sold to the State of California Dept. of Finance in August 1947
T-5641	Physiotherapy Lab	Sold to the State of California Dept. of Finance in August 1947
T-5642	Infirmary Ward S-11	Sold to the State of California Dept. of Finance in August 1947
T-5643	Medical Lab	Sold to the State of California Dept. of Finance in August 1947
T-5644	Surgical Lab	Sold to the State of California Dept. of Finance in August 1947
T-5645	Infirmary Ward S-10	Sold to the State of California Dept. of Finance in August 1947

T-5646	Infirmary Ward S-9	Sold to the State of California Dept. of Finance in August 1947
T-5648	X-Ray	Sold to the State of California Dept. of Finance in August 1947
T-5649	Infirmary Ward A-8	Sold to the State of California Dept. of Finance in August 1947
T-5650	Infirmary Ward S-7	Sold to the State of California Dept. of Finance in August 1947
T-5651	Infirmary Ward S-6	Sold to the State of California Dept. of Finance in August 1947
T-5652	Boiler House	Sold to the State of California Dept. of Finance in August 1947
T-5654	Infirmary Ward S-4	Sold to the State of California Dept. of Finance in August 1947
T-5655	Infirmary Ward S-5	Sold to the State of California Dept. of Finance in August 1947
T-5657	Infirmary Ward S-3	Sold to the State of California Dept. of Finance in August 1947
T-5658	Infirmary Ward S-1	Sold to the State of California Dept. of Finance in August 1947
T-5659	Infirmary Ward S-2	Sold to the State of California Dept. of Finance in August 1947
T-5670	Infirmary Ward M-20	Sold to the State of California Dept. of Finance in August 1947
T-5671	Infirmary Ward M-19	Sold to the State of California Dept. of Finance in August 1947
T-5672	Infirmary Ward M-18	Sold to the State of California Dept. of Finance in August 1947
T-5673	Boiler House	Sold to the State of California Dept. of Finance in August 1947
T-5674	Patient Mess	Sold to the State of California Dept. of Finance in August 1947
T-5675	Infirmary Ward M-17	Sold to the State of California Dept. of Finance in August 1947
T-5677	Infirmary Ward M-16	Sold to the State of California Dept. of Finance in August 1947
T-5678	Infirmary Ward M-14	Sold to the State of California Dept. of Finance in August 1947

CAMP HAAN
THE HISTORY OF RIVERSIDE'S WORLD WAR II ANTI-AIRCRAFT TRAINING CENTER

T-5679	Infirmary Ward M-15	Sold to the State of California Dept. of Finance in August 1947
T-5681	Infirmary Ward M-13	Sold to the State of California Dept. of Finance in August 1947
T-5682	Infirmary Ward M-12	Sold to the State of California Dept. of Finance in August 1947
T-5683	Infirmary Ward M-11	Sold to the State of California Dept. of Finance in August 1947
T-5684	Patient Mess	Sold to the State of California Dept. of Finance in August 1947
T-5685	Infirmary Ward M-10	Sold to the State of California Dept. of Finance in August 1947
T-5686	Infirmary Ward	Sold to the State of California Dept. of Finance in August 1947
T-5688	Infirmary Ward M-8	Sold to the State of California Dept. of Finance in August 1947
T-5689	Infirmary Ward M-7	Sold to the State of California Dept. of Finance in August 1947
T-5690	Infirmary Ward M-5	Sold to the State of California Dept. of Finance in August 1947
T-5691	Infirmary Ward M-6	Sold to the State of California Dept. of Finance in August 1947
T-5692	Patient Mess	Sold to the State of California Dept. of Finance in August 1947
T-5694	Ward, Detention M-3	Sold to the State of California Dept. of Finance in August 1947
T-5695	Ward, Detention M-4	Sold to the State of California Dept. of Finance in August 1947
T-5697	Ward, Detention M-1	Sold to the State of California Dept. of Finance in August 1947
T-5698	Ward, Detention M-2	Sold to the State of California Dept. of Finance in August 1947
T-5699	Ward, Detention	Sold to the State of California Dept. of Finance in August 1947
T-5710	Infirmary Ward D-22	Sold to the State of California Dept. of Finance in August 1947
T-5711	Infirmary Ward D-21	Sold to the State of California Dept. of Finance in August 1947

T-5712	Infirmary Ward D-20	Sold to the State of California Dept. of Finance in August 1947
T-5714	Infirmary Ward D-19	Sold to the State of California Dept. of Finance in August 1947
T-5716	Infirmary Ward	Sold to the State of California Dept. of Finance in August 1947
T-5717	Infirmary Ward D-18	Sold to the State of California Dept. of Finance in August 1947
T-5719	Infirmary Ward	Sold to the State of California Dept. of Finance in August 1947
T-5720	Infirmary Ward D-15	Sold to the State of California Dept. of Finance in August 1947
T-5721	Infirmary Ward D-14	Sold to the State of California Dept. of Finance in August 1947
T-5723	Infirmary Ward D-13	Sold to the State of California Dept. of Finance in August 1947
T-5724	Infirmary Ward	Sold to the State of California Dept. of Finance in August 1947
T-5725	Infirmary Ward D-11 & D12	Sold to the State of California Dept. of Finance in August 1947
T-5726	Detachment Mess	Sold to the State of California Dept. of Finance in August 1947
T-5727	Boiler House	Sold to the State of California Dept. of Finance in August 1947
T-5728	Morgue	Sold to the State of California Dept. of Finance in August 1947
T-5729	Red Cross recreation	Sold to the State of California Dept. of Finance in August 1947
T-5730	Infirmary Ward D-1	Sold to the State of California Dept. of Finance in August 1947
T-5731	Warehouse	Sold to the State of California Dept. of Finance in August 1947
T-5732	Warehouse	Sold to the State of California Dept. of Finance in August 1947
T-5733	Warehouse	Sold to the State of California Dept. of Finance in August 1947
T-5735	Warehouse	Sold to the State of California Dept. of Finance in August 1947

CAMP HAAN
THE HISTORY OF RIVERSIDE'S WORLD WAR II ANTI-AIRCRAFT TRAINING CENTER

T-5736	Warehouse	Sold to the State of California Dept. of Finance in August 1947
T-5737	Warehouse	Sold to the State of California Dept. of Finance in August 1947
T-5739	Warehouse	Sold to the State of California Dept. of Finance in August 1947
T-5740	Warehouse	Sold to the State of California Dept. of Finance in August 1947
T-5741	Warehouse	Sold to the State of California Dept. of Finance in August 1947
T-5747	Red Cross recreation	Sold to the State of California Dept. of Finance in August 1947
T-5749	Gate House	Sold to the State of California Dept. of Finance in August 1947
T-5750	Barracks	Sold to the State of California Dept. of Finance in August 1947
T-5751	Barracks	Sold to the State of California Dept. of Finance in August 1947
T-5752	Barracks	Sold to the State of California Dept. of Finance in August 1947
T-5753	Barracks	Sold to the State of California Dept. of Finance in August 1947
T-5754	Barracks	Sold to the State of California Dept. of Finance in August 1947
T-5755	Barracks	Sold to the State of California Dept. of Finance in August 1947
T-5756	Ambulance Garage	Sold to the State of California Dept. of Finance in August 1947
T-5757	Latrine	Sold to the State of California Dept. of Finance in August 1947
T-5758	Recreation Hall	Sold to the State of California Dept. of Finance in August 1947
T-5759	Recreation Hall (day room)	Sold to the State of California Dept. of Finance in August 1947
T-5760	Hospital Detachment Office	Sold to the State of California Dept. of Finance in August 1947
T-5761	Recreation Hall (day room)	Sold to the State of California Dept. of Finance in August 1947

CAMP HAAN
THE HISTORY OF RIVERSIDE'S WORLD WAR II ANTI-AIRCRAFT TRAINING CENTER

T-5762	Detachment Mess	Sold to the State of California Dept. of Finance in August 1947
T-5763	Post Exchange	Sold to Colton Union High School
T-5765	Supply Office	Sold to the State of California Dept. of Finance in August 1947
T-5766	Hospital Shop	Sold to Colton Union High School
T-5767	Recreation Hall (day room)	Sold to the State of California Dept. of Finance in August 1947
T-5768	Barracks	Sold to the State of California Dept. of Finance in August 1947
T-5769	Latrine	Sold to the State of California Dept. of Finance in August 1947
T-5770	Narcotic Vault	Sold to the State of California Dept. of Finance in August 1947
T-5771	Barracks	Sold to the State of California Dept. of Finance in August 1947
T-5772	Barracks	Sold to the State of California Dept. of Finance in August 1947
T-5773	Barracks	Sold to the State of California Dept. of Finance in August 1947
T-5774	Barracks	Sold to the State of California Dept. of Finance in August 1947
T-5775	Barracks	Sold to the State of California Dept. of Finance in August 1947
T-5776	Barracks	Sold to the State of California Dept. of Finance in August 1947
T-5777	Latrine	Sold to the State of California Dept. of Finance in August 1947
T-5778	Barracks	Sold to the State of California Dept. of Finance in August 1947
T-5779	Barracks	Sold to the State of California Dept. of Finance in August 1947
T-5780	Barracks	Sold to the State of California Dept. of Finance in August 1947
T-5781	Barracks	Sold to the State of California Dept. of Finance in August 1947
T-5782	Barracks	Sold to the State of California Dept. of Finance in August 1947

CAMP HAAN
THE HISTORY OF RIVERSIDE'S WORLD WAR II ANTI-AIRCRAFT TRAINING CENTER

T-6001	Gas Chamber	Sold to San Dimas Junior Chamber of Commerce
T-6003	Pistol Range Office	Sold to Riverside Farm Bureau in December 1947
T-6105	Officer's Quarters	Sold to Pentecostal Church of God, Perris, CA in January 1948
T-6107	Officer's Quarters	Sold to Pentecostal Church of God, Perris, CA in December 1947
T-6110	Officer's Quarters	Sold to Edgemont Union Sunday School, Edgemont, CA in December 1947
T-6113	Officer's Quarters	Sold to San Dimas Junior Chamber of Commerce
T-6117	Infirmary	Sold to Grace Community Church in December 1947
T-6301	Infirmary	Retained by March Field October 1948
T-6463	Hutment	Sold to Juvenille Forestry Camp, Riverside and used as a kithcen in May 1949
T-6464	Hutment	Sold to Juvenille Forestry Camp, Riverside and used as a cafeteria in May 1949
T-6465	Hutment	Sold to Juvenille Forestry Camp, Riverside and used as a classroom in May 1949
T-6466	Hutment	Sold to Juvenille Forestry Camp, Riverside and used as a dorm in May 1949
T-6483	Hutment	Sold to Southeastern California Conference of S.D.A in April 1948
T-6486	Hutment	Sold to Southeastern California Conference of S.D.A in April 1948
T-6488	Hutment	Sold to Southeastern California Conference of S.D.A in April 1948
T-6490	Hutment	Sold to Southeastern California Conference of S.D.A in April 1948
T-6491	Hutment	Sold to Southeastern California Conference of S.D.A in April 1948
T-6492	Hutment	Sold to Southeastern California Conference of S.D.A in April 1948

CAMP HAAN
THE HISTORY OF RIVERSIDE'S WORLD WAR II ANTI-AIRCRAFT TRAINING CENTER

T-7401	Administration Building	Sold to Community Church of Cucamunga in June 1948
T-8452	Administration and Supply	Sold to the Braille Institute of America, Los Angeles
T-8460	Motor Repair and Grease Inspection	Sold to Fallbrook, CA
T-8461	Oil Storage House	Sold to Fallbrook, CA
T-8462	Grease and Inspection Rack	Sold to Fallbrook, CA

KEITH A. BEAULIEU

APPENDIX 5
KNOWN UNITS
CAMP HAAN

CAMP HAAN
THE HISTORY OF RIVERSIDE'S WORLD WAR II ANTI-AIRCRAFT TRAINING CENTER

This list was sourced from the California Military Department, www.militarymusueam.org/cphaan.html.

37th Coast Artillery Brigade (Anti-Aircraft)
    Headquarters and Headquarters Battery
    65th Coast Artillery Regiment (Anti-Aircraft)
    78th Coast Artillery Regiment (Anti-Aircraft)
    205th Coast Artillery Regiment (Anti-Aircraft)
47th Quartermasters Corps
49th Quartermasters Corps
101st Coastal Artillery Brigade (Anti-Aircraft)
    Headquarters and Headquarters Battery
    206th Coast Artillery Regiment (Anti-Aircraft)
    215th Coast Artillery Regiment (Anti-Aircraft)
    216th Coast Artillery Regiment (Anti-Aircraft)
    217th Coast Artillery Regiment (Anti-Aircraft)
121st Coast Artillery Battalion (Anti-Aircraft)
7th Ordnance Company (Medium Maintenace)
18th Ordnance Company (Medium Maintenance)
Corps Area Support Unit 1967 (Station Complement)
Band (Anti-Aircraft Training Center No. 1)
Band (Anti-Aircraft Training Center No. 2)
Band (507th Coast Artillery Regiment
Antiaircraft Training Center
    Headquarters and Headquarters Battery
Post Photogrphic Laboratory
6th Antiaircraft Artillery Group
    Headquarters and Headquarters Battery
7th Antiaircraft Artillery Group
    Headquarters and Headquarters Battery
15th Antiaircraft Artillery Group
    Headquarters and Headquarters Battery
25th Antiaircraft Artillery Group

CAMP HAAN
THE HISTORY OF RIVERSIDE'S WORLD WAR II ANTI-AIRCRAFT TRAINING CENTER

    Headquarters and Headquarters Battery
35th Antiaircraft Artillery Group
    Headquarters and Headquarters Battery
36th Antiaircraft Artillery Group
    Headquarters and Headquarters Battery
37th Antiaircraft Artillery Group
    Headquarters and Headquarters Battery
39th Antiaircraft Artillery Group
    Headquarters and Headquarters Battery
40th Antiaircraft Artillery Group
    Headquarters and Headquarters Battery
41st Antiaircraft Artillery Group
    Headquarters and Headquarters Battery
42nd Antiaircraft Artillery Group
    Headquarters and Headquarters Battery
54th Antiaircraft Artillery Brigade
    Headquarters and Headquarters Battery
57th Antiaircraft Artillery Brigade
    Headquarters and Headquarters Battery
59th Antiaircraft Artillery Brigade
    Headquarters and Headquarters Battery
105th Infantry
109th Antiaircraft Artillery Group
    Headquarters and Headquarters Battery
    161st Coast Artillery Battalion (Anti-Aircraft)
    195th Antiaircraft Artillery Automatic Weapons Battalion
    222nd Antiaircraft Artillery Seachlight Battalion (Semi-Mobile)
113th Antiaircraft Artillery Group
    Headquarters and Headquarters Battery
    165st Coast Artillery Battalion (Anti-Aircraft)
    199th Antiaircraft Artillery Automatic Weapons Battalion
    226th Antiaircraft Artillery Seachlight Battalion (Semi-Mobile)

118th Coast Artillery Battalion (Anti-Aircraft)(Gun)(Semi-Mobile)(Separate)
119th Coast Artillery Battalion (Anti-Aircraft)(Gun)(Semi-Mobile)(Separate)
120th Coast Artillery Battalion (Anti-Aircraft)(Gun)(Semi-Mobile)(Separate)
124th Coast Artillery Battalion (Anti-Aircraft)(Gun)(Mobile)(Separate)
125th Coast Artillery Battalion (Anti-Aircraft)(Gun)(Mobile)(Separate)
126th Coast Artillery Battalion (Anti-Aircraft)(Gun)(Mobile)(Separate)
127th Coast Artillery Battalion (Anti-Aircraft)(Gun)(Mobile)(Separate)
143rd Antiaircraft Artillery Gun Battalion (Mobile) *
144th Antiaircraft Artillery Gun Battalion (Mobile) *
267th Ordnance Maintenance Company, Antiaircraft
282nd Ordnance Maintenance Company, Antiaircraft
283rd Ordnance Maintenance Company, Antiaircraft
307th Ordnance Maintenance Company, Antiaircraft *
311th Ordnance Battalion
    Heaqquarters and Headquarters Detachment
326th Antiaircraft Artillery Searchlight Battalion (Semi-Mobile)
330th Antiaircraft Artillery Searchlight Battalion (Semi-Mobile) *
352nd Ordnance Maintenance Company, Antiaircraft *
353rd Ordnance Maintenance Company, Antiaircraft *
390th Antiaircraft Artillery Automatic Weapons Battalion (Self Propelled)
407th Coast Artillery Battalion (Anti-Aircraft)(Gun)(Semi-Mobile)(Separate)
413th Coast Artillery Battalion (Anti-Aircraft)(Gun)(Mobile)(Separate)
463rd Antiaircraft Artillery Automatic Weapons Battalion (Mobile)
468th Antiaircraft Artillery Automatic Weapons Battalion (Mobile)
487th Antiaircraft Artillery Automatic Weapons Battalion (Semi-

Mobile)

507th Coast Artillery Regiment (Anti-Aircraft)(Mobile) (WDC)

535th Antiaircraft Artillery Automatic Weapons Battalion (Mobile)

546th Antiaircraft Artillery Automatic Weapons Battalion (Mobile)

547th Antiaircraft Artillery Automatic Weapons Battalion (Mobile)

548th Antiaircraft Artillery Automatic Weapons Battalion (Mobile)

557th Antiaircraft Artillery Automatic Weapons Battalion (Mobile)

568th Antiaircraft Artillery Automatic Weapons Battalion (Mobile)

569th Antiaircraft Artillery Automatic Weapons Battalion (Mobile)

778th Antiaircraft Artillery Automatic Weapons Battalion (Self-Propelled)

779th Antiaircraft Artillery Automatic Weapons Battalion (Semi-Mobile)

780th Antiaircraft Artillery Automatic Weapons Battalion (Semi-Mobile)

781st Antiaircraft Artillery Automatic Weapons Battalion (Semi-Mobile)

782nd Antiaircraft Artillery Automatic Weapons Battalion (Semi-Mobile)

783rd Antiaircraft Artillery Automatic Weapons Battalion (Semi-Mobile)

797th Antiaircraft Artillery Automatic Weapons Battalion (Semi-Mobile)

798th Antiaircraft Artillery Automatic Weapons Battalion (Semi-Mobile)

799th Antiaircraft Artillery Automatic Weapons Battalion (Semi-Mobile)

800th Antiaircraft Artillery Automatic Weapons Battalion (Semi-Mobile)

815th Antiaircraft Artillery Automatic Weapons Battalion (Semi-Mobile)

816th Antiaircraft Artillery Automatic Weapons Battalion (Semi-

Mobile)

817th Antiaircraft Artillery Automatic Weapons Battalion (Semi-Mobile)

818th Antiaircraft Artillery Automatic Weapons Battalion (Semi-Mobile)

828nd Antiaircraft Artillery Automatic Weapons Battalion (Semi-Mobile)

823rd Antiaircraft Artillery Automatic Weapons Battalion (Semi-Mobile)

824th Antiaircraft Artillery Automatic Weapons Battalion (Semi-Mobile)

832nd Antiaircraft Artillery Automatic Weapons Battalion (Semi-Mobile)

833rd Antiaircraft Artillery Automatic Weapons Battalion (Semi-Mobile)

834th Antiaircraft Artillery Automatic Weapons Battalion (Semi-Mobile)

835th Antiaircraft Artillery Automatic Weapons Battalion (Semi-Mobile)

1929th Service Command Unit (Branch School for Bakers and Cooks)

1965th Service Command Unit (Ordnance Service Command Shop)

1967th Service Command Unit (Station Complement)

Army Service Forces Regional Hospital

3rd Italian Quartermaster Service Company

66th Ordnance Bomb Disposal Squad

739th Military Police Battalion

1948th Service Command Unit (Dud Searching Detachment

1967th Service Command Unit (Station Complement)
    Area Veterinary Detachment
    Prisoner of War Camp

1990th Service Command Unit (Sub-School for Bakers and Cooks)

Army Service Forces Depot (Classification)
    Salvage Segragation Center
    9198th Quartermaster Corps Technical Service Unit

(Quartermaster Section)

    9313th Ordnance Corps Technical Service Unit (Ordnance Section)

    9516th Signal Corps Technical Service Unit (Signal Section)

    9758th Chemical Warfare Service Technical Service Unit (Chemical Warfare Section)

    9832nd Corps of Engineers Technical Serice Unit (Engineer Section)

    9924th Surgeon General's Office Technical Service Unit (Medical Section)

739th Military Police Battalion

1938th Service Command Unit (Southwestern Branch, US Army Disciplinary Barracks)

1967th Service Command Unit (Station Complement)

    Area Veterinary Detachment

    Film Library

    Los Angeles Port of Embarkation Debarkation Center

    Quartermaster Laundry

    Salvage Segragation Center

    Station Hospital

    Prisoner of War Camp

Quartermaster Depot (Classification)

    Detachment 2 (Classification Sub-Depot), 9193rd Quartermaster Corps Technical Service Unit (Mira Loma Quartermaster Depot)

REFERENCES

Arlington National Cemetery (2007) William George Haan. www.arlintoncemetery.net/wghaan.htm. Accessed 12/20/2019.

Berhow, Mark. (2015) American Seacoast Defense: A Reference Guide. 3rd ed. CDSG Press.

Boyne, W. (1997) Beyond the Wild Blue: A History of the United States Air Force. St. Martin's Griffin, New York.

Camp Haan Map Boundary Data. General Records, 1935-1942. RG 114 Records of the Natural Resources Conservation Service. Box 14; National Archives and Records Administration, Riverside, CA. December 27, 2019.

Camp Haan Map Block Plans Hospital Area. Military Construction Drawings, 1916-. RG 77 Records of the Office of Chief Engineers. Box 162; National Archives and Records Administration, Riverside, CA. December 26, 2019.

Camp Haan Map Block Plans Typical Regimental Area. Military Construction Drawings, 1916-. RG 77 Records of the Office of Chief Engineers. Box 162; National Archives and Records Administration, Riverside, CA. December 26, 2019.

Camp Haan Map Block Plans Regimental Area No. 2. Military Construction Drawings, 1916-. RG 77 Records of the Office of Chief Engineers. Box 165; National Archives and Records Administration, Riverside, CA. December 26, 2019.

Camp Haan Map Block Plans Regimental Area No. 3. Military Construction Drawings, 1916-. RG 77 Records of the Office of Chief Engineers. Box 165; National Archives and Records Administration, Riverside, CA. December 26, 2019

Camp Haan Map Block Plans Regimental Area No. 4. Military Construction Drawings, 1916-. RG 77 Records of the Office of Chief Engineers. Box 165; National Archives and Records Administration, Riverside, CA. December 26, 2019

CAMP HAAN
THE HISTORY OF RIVERSIDE'S WORLD WAR II ANTI-AIRCRAFT TRAINING CENTER

Camp Haan Map Block Plans Regimental Area No. 5. Military Construction Drawings, 1916-. RG 77 Records of the Office of Chief Engineers. Box 165; National Archives and Records Administration, Riverside, CA. December 26, 2019

Camp Haan Map Block Plans Quartermaster Area. Military Construction Drawings, 1916-. RG 77 Records of the Office of Chief Engineers. Box 166; National Archives and Records Administration, Riverside, CA. December 26, 2019

Camp Haan Map Spur Tracks. Military Construction Drawings, 1916-. RG 77 Records of the Office of Chief Engineers. Box 166; National Archives and Records Administration, Riverside, CA. December 26, 2019

Camp Haan Map Miscellaneous Areas. Military Construction Drawings, 1916-. RG 77 Records of the Office of Chief Engineers. Box 166; National Archives and Records Administration, Riverside, CA. December 26, 2019

Camp Haan Map Electrical Distribution Center Foundation and Lighting Details. Military Construction Drawings, 1916-. RG 77 Records of the Office of Chief Engineers. Box 173; National Archives and Records Administration, Riverside, CA. December 26, 2019

Camp Haan Map Electric Distribution System. Military Construction Drawings, 1916-. RG 77 Records of the Office of Chief Engineers. Box 162; National Archives and Records Administration, Riverside, CA. December 26, 2019.

Camp Haan Map Steam Supply Mains Hospital Area. Military Construction Drawings, 1916-. RG 77 Records of the Office of Chief Engineers. Box 162; National Archives and Records Administration, Riverside, CA. December 26, 2019.

Camp Haan Map Gas Distribution System Hospital Area. Military Construction Drawings, 1916-. RG 77 Records of the Office of Chief Engineers. Box 162; National Archives and Records Administration, Riverside, CA. December 26, 2019.

Camp Haan Map Roadway Plans Hospital Area. Military Construction Drawings, 1916-. RG 77 Records of the Office of Chief Engineers. Box 162; National Archives and Records Administration, Riverside, CA. December 26, 2019.

CAMP HAAN
THE HISTORY OF RIVERSIDE'S WORLD WAR II ANTI-AIRCRAFT TRAINING CENTER

Camp Haan Map Utility Ploy Plan-Laundry, Bakery, and Boiler Plant. Military Construction Drawings, 1916-. RG 77 Records of the Office of Chief Engineers. Box 166; National Archives and Records Administration, Riverside, CA. December 26, 2019.

Camp Haan Map Water Distribution System. Military Construction Drawings, 1916-. RG 77 Records of the Office of Chief Engineers. Box 162; National Archives and Records Administration, Riverside, CA. December 26, 2019.

Camp Haan Map Graded-Gun Parking and Drill Areas. Military Construction Drawings, 1916-. RG 77 Records of the Office of Chief Engineers. Box 162; National Archives and Records Administration, Riverside, CA. December 26, 2019.

Camp Haan Map Roads and Streets. Military Construction Drawings, 1916-. RG 77 Records of the Office of Chief Engineers. Box 162; National Archives and Records Administration, Riverside, CA. December 26, 2019.

Camp Haan Map Drainage Map. Military Construction Drawings, 1916-. RG 77 Records of the Office of Chief Engineers. Box 162; National Archives and Records Administration, Riverside, CA. December 26, 2019.

Camp Haan Map Layout Plan. Southern California Real Property Disposal Case Files, 1946-1962. RG 269 Records of the General Services Administration. Box 57; National Archives and Records Administration, Riverside, CA. December 27, 2019.

Camp Haan Map General Layout Plan Building Schedule. Southern California Real Property Disposal Case Files, 1946-1962. RG 269 Records of the General Services Administration. Box 58; National Archives and Records Administration, Riverside, CA. December 27, 2019.

Camp Haan Map Withdrawal from W.A.A. Southern California Real Property Disposal Case Files, 1946-1962. RG 269 Records of the General Services Administration. Box 58; National Archives and Records Administration, Riverside, CA. December 27, 2019.

Camp Haan Map Project Map. Southern California Real Property Disposal Case Files, 1946-1962. RG 269 Records of the General Services

Administration. Box 58; National Archives and Records Administration, Riverside, CA. December 27, 2019.

Conn, S.; Engleman, R.; Fairchild, B. (2000) United States Army in World War II: the Western Hemisphere: Guarding the United States and its Outpost. Center of Military History: Washington D.C.

Churchill, M. (2010) The Riverside National Cemetery Story: A Field of Warriors. Donning Company Publishers. Virginia Beach.

Department of the Army (2001). Field Manual 3-09.22, Tactics, Techniques, and Procedures for the Corps Artillery, Division Artillery, and Field Artillery Brigade Operations. Washington.

Fine, L; Remington, Jesse (1989) The Corps of Engineers: Construction in the United States. Center of Military History: Washington DC.

Gallagher, Mark. (2015) Chapter 3 – Camp Haan, California. A Story by Robert F. Gallaghar. https://gallagherstory.com/ww2/chapter3.html

Garner, John (1993). World War II Temporary Buildings. U.S Army Corps of Engineers.

Kirkpatrick, K. 2012. Prisoner of War Camps Across America. GenTracer, Salt Lake City.

McGibony, J. (1948) Control of Army Patient Traffic in the Zone of Interior. Military Review. Vol. 27:10. Fort Leavenworth, Kansas

National Cemetery Administration. *U.S. Veterans' Gravesites, ca.1775-2006* [database on-line]. Search: William A. Ryan. Provo, UT, USA: Ancestry.com Operations Inc, 2006.

National Park Service (1993) Historic American Buildings Survey. Department of the Interior. Denver.

National Park Service (nd) Historic American Landscapes Survey: Meuse-Argonne American Cemetery and Memorial, Written Historical and Descriptive Data.
http://lcweb2.loc.gov/master/pnp/habshaer/us/us0000/us0005/data/us0005data.pdf

Office of Government Reports (1941) National Defense Program Contracts and Expenditures as Reported, May 16-May 30, 1941.

Risch, E; Kieffer, C (1995) The Quartermaster Corps: Organization, Supply, and Services Vol. II. Center for Military History, CMH Pub 10-13-1. Washington, D.C.

Seelye, D., Frank, D. (2019) The complete Book of World War II USA POW & Internment Camp Chits. The Coin & Currency Institute, Vermont

Smith, C. (1956) The Medical Department: Hospitalization and Evacuation, Zone of Interior. Department of the Army. Washington, D.C.

State Archives of North Carolina. Box 9, Folder 7, WWII5, Military Papers. Camp Haan Tracer

Smith JA, Doidge M, Hanoa R, Frueh BC. A Historical Examination of Military Records of US Army Suicide, 1819 to 2017. JAMA Netw Open. 2019 Dec 2;2(12):e1917448. doi: 10.1001/jamanetworkopen.2019.17448. PMID: 31834395; PMCID: PMC6991201.

United States Air Force (1996) Final Environmental Impact Statement (FEIS): Disposal of Portions of March Air Force Base, California, Volume 1.

United States Congress, Committee on Appropriations (1941). Fourth Supplemental National Defense Appropriation Bill for 1941. Accessed 12/12/2019.

U.S. Army Corps of Engineers (1994) Defense Environmental Restoration Program. Archives Search Report Findings: March Air Force Base and Associated Sites. U.S Army Corps of Engineers, St. Louis District.

United States War Department. (1941). Citadels of Democracy: Camps and Plants for Men and Munitions. U.S. Government Printing Office, Washington.

United States War Department (1941). Completion Report on the Design and Construction of the East Half of the Sixth Regimental Area.

Wasch, D.; Bush, P.; Landreth, K; Glass, J. (nd) World War II and the U.S. Army Mobilization Program: A History of 700 and 800 Series Cantonment Construction. Legacy Resource Management Program, Department of Defense.

Youngs, R. (1983). A History of U.S. Corrections. https://apps.dtic.mil/dtic/tr/fulltext/u2/a128007.pdf

ABOUT THE AUTHOR

Keith A. Beaulieu is a native of Florida who began a successful military career in the U.S. Air Force in 1997. Serving as an Aerospace Medical Technician, he served in many assignments from emergency room technician to a critical care program instructor at the Center for the Sustainment of Trauma and Readiness Skills (C-STARS) in Baltimore, MD.

Using tuition assistance and the GI Bill, Keith has earned an MBA and a Bachelor of Arts degree in Business Administration from Saint Leo University, and a Bachelor of Science degree in Emergency Management from University of Maryland. He also holds an associate degree in Allied Health Science from the Community College of the Air Force. He deployed several times in support of ongoing military operations for both Iraq and Afghanistan, receiving both U.S. Air Force Commendation Medal, U.S. Air Force and U.S. Army Achievement Medals, and a NATO Service Medal. He received the Meritorious Service Medal in 2012 after retiring from the U.S. Air Force.

Keith has an affinity for history, particularly local history, and World War II history.

Keith and his family moved to southern California in 2013 and currently works at the University of California Irvine.

CAMP HAAN
THE HISTORY OF RIVERSIDE'S WORLD WAR II ANTI-AIRCRAFT TRAINING CENTER

NOTES

[1] Leuchtenburg, William (2019) Franklin D. Roosevelt: Foreign Affairs. University of Virginia, Miller Center. Http://millercenter.org. Accessed 12/20/2019.
[2] Department of State, Office of the Historian. Neutrality Acts, 1930s.https://history.state.gov/milestones/1921-1936/neutrality-acts
[3] Center of Military History. (1993) Logistics in World War II: Final Report of the Army Service Forces. United States Army.
[4] The transformation of industry from its peacetime activity to the industrial program necessary to support the national military objectives. It includes the mobilization of materials, labor, capital, production facilities, and contributory items and services essential to the industrial program. Dictionary of Military and Associated Terms. US Department of Defense 2005.
[5] 1940 State of the Union Address
[6] [Wasch, D.; Bush, P.; Landreth, K; Glass, J. (nd) World War II and the U.S. Army Mobilization Program: A History of 700 and 800 Series Cantonment Construction. Legacy Resource Management Program, Department of Defense.
[7] Garner, John (1993). World War II Temporary Buildings. U.S Army Corps of Engineers.
[8] Dr. Stetson Conn of the Office of the Chief of Military History (now US Army Center of Military History) for official. The original is on file in the Historical Manuscripts Collection (HMC) under file number 2-3.7 AF.B
[9] Center of Military History. (1993) Logistics in World War II: Final Report of the Army Service Forces. United States Army.
[10] https://history.army.mil/books/wwii/csppp/ch11.htm
[11] Center of Military History (1993). Logistics in World War II: Final Report of the Army Service Forces. Washington DC
[12] Center of Military History. (1993) Logistics in World War II: Final Report of the Army Service Forces. United States Army.
[13] Center of Military History. (1993) Logistics in World War II: Final Report of the Army Service Forces. United States Army.
[14] Center of Military History. (1993) Logistics in World War II: Final Report of the Army Service Forces. United States Army.
[15] Garner, John (1993). World War II Temporary Buildings. U.S Army Corps of Engineers.
[16] Took place between April 21, 1898 and August 13, 1898.
[17] Annual Reports of the War Department, Volume 1. U.S. Government (1919) U.S. Government Printing Office.
[18] B. June 27, 1882
D. April 9, 1973

[19] Fine, L; Remington, Jesse (1989) The Corps of Engineers: Construction in the United States. Center of Military History: Washington DC.
[20] National Park Service (nd) Historic American Landscapes Survey: Meuse-Argonne American Cemetery and Memorial, Written Historical and Descriptive Data.
[21] Named for Meriweather Lewis of the Lewis and Clark Expedition
[22] A store at a military post that sells food, clothing, and other items.
[23] Enacted through the Federal Unemployment Relief Act of 1933, the Civilian Conservation Corps was a voluntary work relief program that operated from 1933-1942 in the United States for unemployed, unmarried men. It was designed to provide jobs for young men who had difficulty finding jobs after the Great Depression (1929-1941)
[24] Fine, L; Remington, Jesse (1989) The Corps of Engineers: Construction in the United States. Center of Military History: Washington DC.
[25] Fine, L; Remington, Jesse (1989) The Corps of Engineers: Construction in the United States. Center of Military History: Washington DC.
[26] I realize that this is unacceptable terminology; however, this was the generally accepted term for African American soldiers in the segregated U.S. Army of World War II. In writing this booth I endeavor to remain consistant with the terminology used for that time and in historical documents.
[27] Fine, L; Remington, Jesse (1989) The Corps of Engineers: Construction in the United States. Center of Military History: Washington DC.
[28] Fine, L; Remington, Jesse (1989) The Corps of Engineers: Construction in the United States. Center of Military History: Washington DC.
[29] http://old.quartermasterfoundation.org/BG_Charles_Hartman.htm
[30] Wasch, D.; Bush, P.; Landreth, K; Glass, J. (nd) World War II and the U.S. Army Mobilization Program: A History of 700 and 800 Series Cantonment Construction. Legacy Resource Management Program, Department of Defense.
[31] Wasch, D.; Bush, P.; Landreth, K; Glass, J. (nd) World War II and the U.S. Army Mobilization Program: A History of 700 and 800 Series Cantonment Construction. Legacy Resource Management Program, Department of Defense.
[32] Fine, L; Remington, Jesse (1989) The Corps of Engineers: Construction in the United States. Center of Military History: Washington DC.
[33] Fine, L; Remington, Jesse (1989) The Corps of Engineers: Construction in the United States. Center of Military History: Washington DC.
[34] August 24, 1912
AKA - Manchu Law
[35] Fine, L; Remington, Jesse (1989) The Corps of Engineers: Construction in the United States. Center of Military History: Washington DC.
[36] The term "700 series" is derived from the nomenclature of the U.S. Army building plans for cantonment buildings. Each building plan in the series started off with 700 followed by another four-digit number (e.g. 700-1120).
[37] Operations, planning, and training
[38] Fine, L; Remington, Jesse (1989) The Corps of Engineers: Construction in the United States. Center of Military History: Washington DC.

[39] Fine, L; Remington, Jesse (1989) The Corps of Engineers: Construction in the United States. Center of Military History: Washington DC.
[40] Fine, L; Remington, Jesse (1989) The Corps of Engineers: Construction in the United States. Center of Military History: Washington DC.
[41] H Subcomm of the Comm Apprns, 76th Congress, 3rd session, Hearings on the Second Supplemental National Defense Appropriations Bill for 1941, p. 148.
[42] Statement of Gen Hartman, 5 Jul 55, p. 17. Excerpted from Fine, L; Remington, Jesse (1989) the Corps of Engineers: Construction in the United States. Center of Military History: Washington DC.
[43] Stimson Diary, 11 Dec 40. Excerpted from Fine, L; Remington, Jesse (1989) the Corps of Engineers: Construction in the United States. Center of Military History: Washington DC.
[44] His 5th day in office (December 16, 1940)
[45] National Park Service (n.d.). Historical American Buildings Survey. Presidio of San Francisco, World War II Buildings of Area B. San Francisco.
[46] Fine, L; Remington, Jesse (1989) the Corps of Engineers: Construction in the United States. Center of Military History: Washington DC.
[47] Wasch, D.; Bush, P.; Landreth, K; Glass, J. (nd) World War II and the U.S. Army Mobilization Program: A History of 700 and 800 Series Cantonment Construction. Legacy Resource Management Program, Department of Defense.
[48] Wasch, D.; Bush, P.; Landreth, K; Glass, J. (nd) World War II and the U.S. Army Mobilization Program: A History of 700 and 800 Series Cantonment Construction. Legacy Resource Management Program, Department of Defense.
[49] Divisional cantonment layout in 1940 estimated the total length of roads to be 71,290 ft. Divisional cantonments in 1942 estimated the total length of roads to be 40,140 ft. Fine, L; Remington, Jesse (1989) the Corps of Engineers: Construction in the United States. Center of Military History: Washington DC.
[50] Fine, L; Remington, Jesse (1989) the Corps of Engineers: Construction in the United States. Center of Military History: Washington DC.
[51] Fine, L; Remington, Jesse (1989) the Corps of Engineers: Construction in the United States. Center of Military History: Washington DC.
[52] Wasch, D.; Bush, P.; Landreth, K; Glass, J. (nd) World War II and the U.S. Army Mobilization Program: A History of 700 and 800 Series Cantonment Construction. Legacy Resource Management Program, Department of Defense.
[53] Garner, John (1993). World War II Temporary Buildings. U.S Army Corps of Engineers.
[54] Lippincott, J.; Bowen, O. (1941) Completion Report on the Design and Construction of Camp Haan Anti-Aircraft Training Center
[55] Dudley B. Wheelock, President of the Riverside Chamber of Commerce.
[56] Hanford Sentinel (Hanford, CA), August 31, 1940. Downloaded 9 January 2020 from Newspapers.com
[57] Santa Ana Register (Santa Ana, California) Tuesday, October 22, 1940. Downloaded from Newspapers.com on January 10, 2020.
[58] Handled 8% of all embarkations.
[59] The Desert Sun (Palm Springs, CA) Friday, September 27, 1940. Downloaded 9 January 2020 from Newspapers.com

60 San Bernardino Sun April 4, 1941
61 LA Times, April 4, 1941
62 San Bernardino County Sun (San Bernardino, CA. Thur July 24, 1941. Downloaded from Newspapers.com on January 10, 2020.
63 Times-Advocate (esconditio, CA) Tues, Aug 12, 1941. Downloaded from Newspapers.com on January 10, 2020.
64 U.S. Army Corps of Engineers, Office of Chief Engineers Real Estate Division3103 Audit, May 23, 1950
65 San Bernardino County Sun (San Bernardino, CA) Sun June 15, 1941. Downloaded fron Newspapers.com on January 10, 2020.
66 Memorandum (certificate No. 23) dated August 11, 1943 from Secretary of War Henry L. Stimson to Major General Thomas M. Morris, Assistant Chief of Engineers. Courtesy of the National Archives of Riverside, CA.
67 War Department (1943). Report of Survey of Electrical Distribution System. U.S. Engineer Office, San Bernardino, California. Report dated August 13, 1943. Prepared by C.N. Parker
68 Coast Artillery Journal, Vol. 85, May June 1942
69 Water and Power Associates, Inc. https://waterandpower.org/museum/Construction_of_the_LA_Aqueduct.html
70 Lippincott, J.; Bowen, O. (1941) Completion Report on the Design and Construction of Camp Haan Anti-Aircraft Training Center
71 Fine, L; Remington, Jesse (1989) the Corps of Engineers: Construction in the United States. Center of Military History: Washington DC.
72 Lippincott, J.; Bowen, O. (1941) Completion Report on the Design and Construction of Camp Haan Anti-Aircraft Training Center
73 Middle name: Hudson
B. 1910 Hennepin, Minnesota
D. 1988 Hillsbourgh County, FL
74 Lippincott, J.; Bowen, O. (1941) Completion Report on the Design and Construction of Camp Haan Anti-Aircraft Training Center
75 Ibid
76 Sharon Anthony Papers, Riverside Public Library
77 Fine, L; Remington, Jesse (1989) the Corps of Engineers: Construction in the United States. Center of Military History: Washington DC.
78 Lippincott, J.; Bowen, O. (1941) Completion Report on the Design and Construction of Camp Haan Anti-Aircraft Training Center
79 Ibid
80 Fine, L; Remington, Jesse (1989) the Corps of Engineers: Construction in the United States. Center of Military History: Washington DC.
81 Los Angeles Times (Los Angeles, CA) Sat, January, 18, 1941. Downloaded 10 January 2020.
82 Fourth Supplemental National Defense Appropriation Bill for 1941
83 Source – Letter from Colonel William A. Ryan to Sharon Anthony, April 18, 1988
84 Los Angeles Times (Los Angeles, CA) Sat, January, 18, 1941. Downloaded 10 January 2020.

85 Foster, L (2018) U.S. Army Life 1941 – 1945: In the Letters of Theodore Pattengill Foster. Self Published. Permission obtained by L. Foster to use excerpts in publication.
86 Sharon Anthony Papers, Riverside Public Library
87 San Bernardino County Sun Thur May 22, 1941. Downloaded from Newspapers.com on January 10, 2020.
Office of Government Reports (1941) National Defense Program Contracts and Expenditures as Reported, May 16-May 30, 1941.
88 Camp Meade was 21-months behind schedule
89 War Department (1941) Record of Equipment and Condition of Buildings.
90 Gallagher, Robert. World War II Story. Chapter 3 – Camp Haan, California. Retrieved from https://gallagherstory.com/ww2/chapter3.html.
91 War Department (1941). Completion Report on the Design and Construction of the East Half of the Sixth Regimental Area.
92 Wasch, D.; Bush, P.; Landreth, K; Glass, J. (nd) World War II and the U.S. Army Mobilization Program: A History of 700 and 800 Series Cantonment Construction. Legacy Resource Management Program, Department of Defense.
93 Wasch, D.; Bush, P.; Landreth, K; Glass, J. (nd) World War II and the U.S. Army Mobilization Program: A History of 700 and 800 Series Cantonment Construction. Legacy Resource Management Program, Department of Defense.
94 Lippincott, J.; Bowen, O. (1941) Completion Report on the Design and Construction of Camp Haan Anti-Aircraft Training Center
95 Wasch, D.; Bush, P.; Landreth, K; Glass, J. (nd) World War II and the U.S. Army Mobilization Program: A History of 700 and 800 Series Cantonment Construction. Legacy Resource Management Program, Department of Defense.
96 Wasch, D.; Bush, P.; Landreth, K; Glass, J. (nd) World War II and the U.S. Army Mobilization Program: A History of 700 and 800 Series Cantonment Construction. Legacy Resource Management Program, Department of Defense.
97 San Pedro News (San Pedro, CA) Tuesday, October 14, 1941. Downloaded from Newspapers.com on January 10, 2020
98 LA Times (Los Angeles, CA) Tuesday, October 14, 1941. Downloaded from Newspapers.com on January 10, 2020.
99 San Bernardino County Sun (San Bernardino, CA) Sun November 30, 1941. Downloaded from Newspapers.com on January 10, 2020.
100 Lippincott, J.; Bowen, O. (1941) Completion Report on the Design and Construction of Camp Haan Anti-Aircraft Training Center
101 U.S. Army Corps of Engineers (1995) Defense Environmental Restoration Program- Formaly Used Defense Sites Findings and Determination of Eligibility: Camp Haan J09CA027900.
102 Oakland Tribune (Oakland, CA) Friday, November 21, 1941. Downloaded January 10, 2020 from Newspapers.com
103 Sharon Anthony Papers, Riverside Public Library
104 Gallagher, Robert. World War II Story. Chapter 3 – Camp Haan, California. Retrieved from https://gallagherstory.com/ww2/chapter3.html.

[105] Cotton duck, also simply duck, sometimes duck cloth or duck canvas, is a heavy, plain woven cotton fabric. Duck canvas is more tightly woven than plain canvas. There is also linen duck, which is less often used.

[106] https://nvlpubs.nist.gov/nistpubs/nbstechnologic/nbstechnologicpaperT264.pdf

[107] Fine, L; Remington, Jesse (1989) the Corps of Engineers: Construction in the United States. Center of Military History: Washington DC.

[108] Wasch, D.; Bush, P.; Landreth, K; Glass, J. (nd) World War II and the U.S. Army Mobilization Program: A History of 700 and 800 Series Cantonment Construction. Legacy Resource Management Program, Department of Defense.

109 a measure of capacity equal to 64 US pints (equivalent to 35.2 liters), used for dry goods.

[110] Camp Haan Tracer, May 4, 1943

[111] 1944 Camp Haan Phone Directory

112 Camp Haan Tracer, May 4, 1943

[113] Regimental Layout Plan, Camp Haan (1941). Military Construction Drawings 1916-. RG 77 Records of the Office of Chief of Engineers, Box 163. National Archives, Riverside.

[114] Department of the Army (2001). Field Manual 3-09.22, Tactics, Techniques, and Procedures for the Corps Artillery, Division Artillery, and Field Artillery Brigade Operations. Washington.

115 Center of Military History. (1993) Logistics in World War II: Final Report of the Army Service Forces. United States Army.

[116] Camp Haan Tracer. November 9, 1943. Vol 4, no. 6

[117] Ibid

[118] Ibid

[119] Ibid

[120] Camp Haan Tracer. November 16, 1943. Vol 4, no. 7.

[121] Quartermaster records from June 30, 1941. Source: Yeager Family Library, March Airfield Museum.

122 Desert Sun (Palm Springs, CA) July 25, 1941. Downloaded January 10, 2020.

123 Camp Haan Tracer, May 4, 1943

124 Camp Haan Tracer, May 4, 1943

[125] Information excerpted from Trainees' Guidebook, Antiaircraft Replacement Training Center, Camp Callan, CA. Arts and Crafts Press, San Diego. 1940.

[126] The National Archives at Washington, D.C.; Washington, D.C.; Record Group Title: *Records of the Office of the Provost Marshal General, 1920 - 1975*; Record Group Number: *389*

127 Coast Artillery Journal, Nov Dec 1942

128 San Bernardino County Sun (San Bernardino, CA Wed, Jul 9, 1941.Downloaded from Newspapers.com on Jan 10, 2020.

129 San Bernardino County Sun (San Bernardino, CA) Friday Aug 22, 1941. Downloaded from Newspapers.com on May 12, 2020.

130 San Bernardino County Sun (San Bernardino, CA) Friday, June 20, 1941. Downloaded from Newspapers.com on January 10, 2020

131 Kewanne began manufacturing boilers in 1868 and was in business for 133 years until production ceased in 2002.
132 San Bernardino County Sun (San Bernardino, CA) Sun Jan 30, 1944. Downloaded from Newspapers.com on January 14 2020.
133 https://history.amedd.army.mil/booksdocs/wwii/thetechnicalservices/thetechnicalserviceshospitalizationevacuation/DEFAULT.htm
134 https://www.med-dept.com/articles/ww2-hospital-trains/
135 Telephone Directory (1946)
136 The hospital train unit is listed in the 1944 telephone directory.
137 "A" Tents had dimensions of 15'-10" x 15'-10" model M1934 254 sq. Ft. First intoduced in 1934, and "D" Tents Small Wall Tent had dimensions of 8'-10" x 9'-2" 80 sq. Ft.
138 Camp Haan Tracer. November 16, 1943. Vol. 4, No. 7
139 Coast Defense Journal (2009). Coast Artillery Organizational History, 1917-1950. Vol. 23, Issue 2.
140 War Department. (1941) 78th Coast Artillery Yearbook.
141 SB Sun June 13, 1941
142 San Bernardino County Sun (San Bernardino, CA) Wed, Jan 22, 1941. Downloaded from Newspapers.com on January 10, 2020.
143 San Bernardino County Sun (San Bernardino, CA. Thursday, July 10, 1941. Downloaded from Newspapers.com on January 10, 2020.
144 Berhow, Mark. (2015) American Seacoast Defense: A Reference Guide. 3rd ed. CDSG Press.
145 Established as Woman's Army Auxiliary Corps on 15 May 1942, PL 77-554 and was converted to active duty Woman's Army Corps on July 3, 1943.
146 Camp Haan Tracer (Camp Haan, CA) Tuesday, November 9, 1943.
147 San Bernardino County Sun (San Bernardino, CA. Thurs Feb 10, 1944. Downloaded from Newspapers.com on January 14, 2020.
148 Information excerpted from Trainees' Guidebook, Antiaircraft Replacement Training Center, Camp Callan, CA. Arts and Crafts Press, San Diego. 1940.
149 Information excerpted from Trainees' Guidebook, Antiaircraft Replacement Training Center, Camp Callan, CA. Arts and Crafts Press, San Diego. 1940.
150 Foster, L. (2018). U.S. Army Life 1941—1945: In the Letters of Theodore Pattengill Foster.
151 LA Times (Los Angeles, CA) Thursday October 21, 1943. Downloaded from Newspapers .com on January 13, 2020.
152 Press-Enterprise, Sunday, June 4, 1989. Tom Patterson. "Camp Haan had significant role in World War II
153 The Press-Enterprise (Riverside, CA) October 9, 1993. Downloaded from Newsbank.com on May 17, 2020.
154 Coast Artillery Journal, Aug-Sep 1941
155 San Bernardino County Sun (San Bernardino, CA. Sun Oct 23, 1943. Downloaded from Newspapers.com on January 13, 2020.
156 San Pedro News (San Pedro, CA) Wednesday, September 29, 1943. Downloaded from Newspapers.com on January 14, 2020.

[157] *Invading America*, 1943, written by Clifford Cole, is an eyewitness account of the British Battery's US tour illustrated with 200 period photographs. It is published by Loaghtan Books. For further details, please visit www.loaghtanbooks.com.

[158] Excerpt from a quote of Major Cole, found in the Journal of the Riverside Historical Society, No. 17, February 2013 article titled The British Invade Riverside, 1943 by Sara Goodwins.

[159] A general combat engineer is often called a *pioneer* or *sapper*, terms derived respectively from the French and British armies. In some armies, *pioneer* and *sapper* indicate specific military ranks and levels of combat engineers, who work under fire in all seasons and may be allocated to different corps.

160 Maj. Russell Price, AAJ

[161] Camp Haan Tracer. Tuesday, November 3, 1943. Vol.4, no. 6

162 Monrovia Daily News Post (Monrovia, CA) Thursday, February 11, 1943. Downloaded from Newspapers.com on January 14, 2020.

163 Long Beach Independent (Long Beach, CA) Sun January 24, 1943. Downloaded from Newspapers.com on January 13, 2020

164 Risch, E; Kieffer, C (1995) The Quartermaster Corps: Organization, Supply, and Services Vol. II. Center for Military History, CMH Pub 10-13-1. Washington, D.C.

165 San Bernardino County Sun (San Bernardino, CA) Wed April 2, 1941. Downloaded from Newspapers.com on January 10, 2020.

166 San Bernardino County Sun (San Bernardino, CA) Saturday, July 12, 1941. Downloaded from Newspapers.com on Jan 10, 2020.

167 San Bernardino County Sun (San Bernardino, CA. Sun July 27, 1941. Downloaded from Newspapers.com on January 10, 2020.

[168] Source – Letter from Col. William A. Ryan to Sharon Anthony, April 18, 1988.

169 in honor of Major General George LeRoy Irwin, commander of the 57th Field Artillery Brigade during World War I, and it was subsumed into the Desert Training Center as one of its cantonment areas and some of its ranges. Two years later, Camp Irwin was deactivated and placed on surplus status.

170 Sharon Anthony Papers (1988), letter from William A. Ryan.

171 Letter to Sharon Anthony from Col. (ret) William A. Ryan about life at Camp Haan

172 Source: Combat Reports - for "Tired Training." By Lt. James Riley amd John Thornton, published in the Coast Artillery Journal

173 San Bernardino County Sun (San Bernardino, CA) Monday April 7, 1941. Downloaded from Newspapers.com on January 9, 2020

174 San Bernardino County Sun (San Bernardino, CA) Friday, March 28, 1941. Downloaded from Newspapers.com on January 10, 2020

175 Desert Sun (Palm Springs, CA), July 25, 1941. Downloaded January 10, 2020 from Newspapers.com

176 LA Times (Los Angeles, CA) Sunday, September 28, 1941. Downloaded from Newspapers.com on January 9, 2020.

CAMP HAAN
THE HISTORY OF RIVERSIDE'S WORLD WAR II ANTI-AIRCRAFT TRAINING CENTER

177 Oakland Tribune (Oakland, CA) Wednesday, June 23, 1943. Downloaded from Newspapers.com on January 13, 2020.
[178] Camp Haan v. Fresno State football program. October 4, 1941.
179 The Press-Enterprise (Riverside, CA) May 5, 1995. Downloaded from Newsbank.com on 16 May 2020.
180 The Press-Enterprise (Riverside, CA) May 5, 1995. Downloaded from Newsbank.com on 16 May 2020.
181 SB Sun Feb 21, 1941
[182] Gallagher, Robert. World War II Story. Chapter 3 – Camp Haan, California. Retrieved from https://gallagherstory.com/ww2/chapter3.html.
183 https://www.nationalww2museum.org/war/articles/hollywood-hospitality-hollywood-canteen
184 Camp Haan Tracer, May 4, 1943
185 https://www.nationalww2museum.org/war/articles/hollywood-hospitality-hollywood-canteen
[186] Jezek, George Ross; Wanamaker, Marc (October 1, 2002). Hollywood: Past and Present. San Diego, Calif.: George Ross Jezek Photography & Publishing. pp. 92–93. ISBN 978-0970103611.
[187] Gallagher, Robert. World War II Story. Chapter 3 – Camp Haan, California. Retrieved from https://gallagherstory.com/ww2/chapter4.html.
188 San Bernardino County Sun (San Bernardino, CA) Wed Mar 19, 1941. Downloaded fron Newspapers.com on January 10, 2020.
189 A permanent location for the show in San Bernardino was selected in 1923 in the area south of Mill Street between Arrowhead Avenue and "E" street.
190 San Bernardino County Sun (San Bernardino, CA) Thurs, Oct 9, 1941. Downloaded from Newspapers.com on January 10, 2020.
191 Coast Artillery Journal, Volume 86 No. 1 United States Coast Artillery Association, 1943, Pg. 91
192 San Bernardino County Sun (San Bernardino, CA) Tuesday December 5, 1944. Downloaded from Newspapers.com on January 14, 2020.
193 San Bernardino County Sun (San Bernardino, CA) Wed Jul 15, 1945. Downloaded from Newspapers.com on Jan 10, 2020.
194 San Bernardino County Sun (San Bernardino, CA) Friday August 22, 1941. Downloaded from Newspapers.com on January 10, 2020.
195 LA Times (Los Angeles, CA) Wednesday, December 19, 2945. Dowloaded from Newspapers.com on January 10, 2020.
196 Santa Cruz Sentinel (Santa Cruz, CA) Wednesday July 18 1945. Downloaded from Newspapers.com on January 10, 2020.
197 Santa Ana Register (Santa Ana, CA) Wednesday November 11, 1942. Downloaded from Newspapers.com on January 13, 2020.
198 National Cemetery Administration. U.S. Veterans' Gravesites, ca.1775-2006 [database on-line]. Provo, UT, USA: Ancestry.com Operations Inc, 2006.
199 https://www.findagrave.com/memorial/74472355

Post Register; Publication Date: 22/ Oct/ 2009; Publication Place: Idaho Falls, Idaho, USA; URL:

[273] United States Air Force. Biography Lieutenant General Archie Old Jr. Retrieved from: http://www.477fg.afrc.af.mil/bios/bio_print.asp?bioID=6650&page=1. Downloaded on February 3, 2021.
[274] Boyne, W. (1997) Beyond the Wild Blue: A History of the United States Air Force. St. Martin's Griffin, New York.
275 https://www.pe.com/2016/04/03/riverside-housing-project-could-close-general-old-golf-course/
[276] Department of Veteran Affairs (2018). Proposed Riverside National Cemetery Expansion. Retrieved from: https://www.cem.va.gov/CEM/docs/EA/Riverside_NEPA_EA_AppendixA.pdf. Downloaded on February 3, 2021.
[277] Inland Empire.us (2019). Riverside National Cemetery to Expand. Retrieved from https://inlandempire.us/riverside-national-cemetery-to-expand/. Downloaded on February 3, 2021.
[278] Ibid
[279] March Joint Powers Authority (2010). Vision 2030: March JPA General Plan.
280 Wasch, D.; Bush, P.; Landreth, K; Glass, J. (nd) World War II and the U.S. Army Mobilization Program: A History of 700 and 800 Series Cantonment Construction. Legacy Resource Management Program, Department of Defense.
281 Wasch, D.; Bush, P.; Landreth, K; Glass, J. (nd) World War II and the U.S. Army Mobilization Program: A History of 700 and 800 Series Cantonment Construction. Legacy Resource Management Program, Department of Defense.
282 Wasch, D.; Bush, P.; Landreth, K; Glass, J. (nd) World War II and the U.S. Army Mobilization Program: A History of 700 and 800 Series Cantonment Construction. Legacy Resource Management Program, Department of Defense.
[283] Smith JA, Doidge M, Hanoa R, Frueh BC. A Historical Examination of Military Records of US Army Suicide, 1819 to 2017. JAMA Netw Open. 2019 Dec 2;2(12):e1917448. doi: 10.1001/jamanetworkopen.2019.17448. PMID: 31834395; PMCID: PMC6991201.

CAMP HAAN
THE HISTORY OF RIVERSIDE'S WORLD WAR II ANTI-AIRCRAFT TRAINING CENTER

251 U.S Army Corps of Engineers (1994) Defense Environmental Restoration Program. Archives Search Report Findings: March Air Force Base and Associated Sites. U.S Army Corps of Engineers, St. Louis District.
252 Form IF 990 WAA. Dated July 20, 1948. National Archives at Riverside.
253 Fire Protection and Security Report: Camp Haan. March 17, 1947.
254 Report of Protection and Maintenance Field Survey. (January 15, 1948) from J. Larson, engineer. National Archives at Riverside
255 Telegram dated August 20, 1947 from Robert P. Alford, Dep. Regional Director for the Office of Real Property Disposal, WAA. (National Archives Riverside.pdf)
256 The Press-Enterprise (Riverside, CA) September 26, 1994. Downloaded from Newsbank.com on May 16, 2020.
257 San Bernardino County Sun (San Bernardino CA) Monday Feb 9 1948. Downloaded on January 11, 2020.
258 (Santa Cruz, Sentinel Sun, 10/17/1948)

Verified by telegram 11-10-48 by Don Biggs, director of disposals
259 Office of Real Property Periodic Inspection Report, dated September 17, 1948 from V.I. Graham, Chief of Property Management Division. Report prepared by A. Esner.
260 http://www.themetrains.com/rbbb-circus-trains-roster-1947-1956-the-wwii-hospital-cars.htm
261 LA Times (Los Angeles, CA) Tuesday January 10, 1950. Downloaded from Newspapers.com on January 11, 2020.
262 LA Times (Los Angeles, CA) Thursday, December 14, 1950. Downloaded from Newspapers.com on January 11, 2020.
263 March Joint Powers General Plan. Http://marchjpa.com/documents/docs_forms/draft_general_plan.pdf. Accessed December 3, 2019.
[264] Verified by William Woerz III on April 9, 2022.
[265] U.S. Army Corps of Engineers (1994). Archives Search Report Findings: March Air Force Base and Associated Sites. Defense Environmental Restoration Program for Formally Used Defense Sites.
266 http://www.rvcfire.org/stationsAndFunctions/AdminSppt/Training/Pages/BCTCHistory.aspx
267 Air University Review, November-December 1974. CMSgt Donald S. eshore
268 The Riverside National Cemetery Story by Marlowe J. Churchill
269 Redlands Daily Facts (redlands, CA) Friday July 9 1977. Downloaded from Newspapers.com on January 12, 2020.
270 https://www.cem.va.gov/cem/docs/factsheets/history.pdf

National cemeteries were first developed during the Civil War.
271 National Cemeteries Act of 1973 (PL 93-43)
272 Redlands Daily Facts (redlands, CA) Friday June 18 1976. Downloaded from Newspapers.com on December 4, 2019

CAMP HAAN
THE HISTORY OF RIVERSIDE'S WORLD WAR II ANTI-AIRCRAFT TRAINING CENTER

235 San Pedro News (San Fedro, CA) Mon February 11, 1946. Downloaded from Newspapers.com on February 22, 2020.
236 San Pedro News (San Pedro, CA) Thursday June 28, 1945. Downloaded from Newspapers.com on December 4, 2019.
237 Smith, C. (1989) United States Army in World War II: The Medical Department: Hospitalization and Evacuation, Zone of Interior. Center of Military History: Washington D.C.
238 San Pedro News (San Fedro, CA) Mon February 11, 1946. Downloaded from Newspapers.com on February 22, 2020.
239 LA Times (Los Angeles, CA) Saturday September 22, 1945. Downloaded from Newspapers.com on January 10, 2020.
240 LA Times (Los Angeles, CA) Wednesday September 19, 1945. Downloaded from Newspapers.com on January 10, 2020.
241 Center of Military History. (1993) Logistics in World War II: Final Report of the Army Service Forces. United States Army.
242 Letter from the Adjutant General's Office, Washington, D.C. Dated September 6, 1946. Signed by BG B.M. Fitch
243 San Bernardino County Sun Tues July 1946. Downloaded from Newspapers.com on January 10, 2020.
[244] If a car was to be iced, it frequently began its day at the ice house getting iced up. Six men working as a team could ice a car in 90 seconds. 300-pound blocks of ice would be moved along skids and men with sharp pronged forks called bidents knew how to hit the blocks to break them into chucks with great rapidity. Once cool and loaded with the initial ice, the car was ready to go to the shipper. After the car was loaded by the shipper it was returned to the icing platform for topping up. In the case of produce, it would be pre-cooled. Keith Jordan reports, "The purpose of precooling was to take the latent field heat out of the citrus. Typically, the cars were precooled before shipping. I'm sure some cars were precooled when empty, but probably for spotting at packing houses which had precooling rooms, thus putting cool fruit in a cool car. Warm fruit in a cool car would only bring up the ambient temperature. Precooled loads used less ice enroute." In better equipped areas, a system of flexible ducts were connected to the reefer hatches and cold air was blown through the car, like modern air conditioning. This process took about 4 hours. http://sfrhms.org/files/Sandifer/Clinics/SFRD/3.htm. Retrieved on November 24, 2020.
[245] San Bernardino County Sun (San Bernardino, California). Thursday, April 4, 1946. Pg. 11. Downloaded from Newspapers.com on November 24, 2020.
[246] San Bernardino County Sun (San Bernardino, California). Wednesday, April 10, 1946. Pg. 11. Downloaded from Newspapers.com on November 24, 2020.
247 Defense Environmental Restoation Program Report, February 11, 1994.
248 Report of disposition board January 29, 1947
249 Report of Disposition Board: Camp Haan. January 29, 1947
250 Office or Real Property Disposal, Periodic Inspection Report September 1948

218 U.S. Army Corps of Engineers, Office of Chief Engineers Real Estate Division3103 Audit, May 23, 1950
219 War Department (1943). Report of Survey of Electrical Distribution System. U.S. Engineer Office, San Bernardino, California. Report dated August 13, 1943. Prepared by C.N. Parker
220 Kirkpatrick, K. 2012. Prisoner of War Camps Across America. GenTracer, Salt Lake City.
221 Seelye, D., Frank, D. (2019) The complete Book of World War II USA POW & Internment Camp Chits. The Coin & Currency Institute, Vermont
222 Center of Military History. (1993) Logistics in World War II: Final Report of the Army Service Forces. United States Army.
223 "Brief History of World War II Advertising Campaign War Loans. Retrieved from Duke University Libraries on May 7, 2020.
https://web.archive.org/web/20111029213801/https://library.duke.edu/digital collections/adaccess/guide/wwii/bonds-loans/#victory
224 Chino Champion (Chino, CA) Friday, Nov. 2 1945. Downloaded January 10, 2020 from Nespapers.com.
225 Kirkpatrick, K. 2012. Prisoner of War Camps Across America. GenTracer, Salt Lake City.
226 The Press-Enterprose (Riverside, CA) May 6, 1995. Dowloaded from Newsbank.com on May 16, 2020
227 Wallis, E. (2018) World War II in California's Inland Empire.

https://scalar.usc.edu/works/world-war-ii-in-californias-inland-empire/camp-haancamp-haan-quartermaster-depotcamp-haan-prisoner-of-war-camp
228 Ventura County Star-Free Press (ventura, CA) Thursday Mar 4, 1948. Downloaded from Newspapers.com on May 12, 2020.
229 San Bernardino County Sun (San Bernardino, CA) Tues April 16 1946. Downloaded from Newspapers.com on Feb 22, 2020.
230 San Bernardino County Sun (San Bernardino, CA) Wed Jan 29 1947. Downloaded from Newspapers.com on January 13, 2020.

Detroit Free Press (Detroit, MI) Wed Jan 15 1947. Downloaded from Newspapers.com on May 12, 2020.
231 Pomona Progress Bulletin (Pomona, CA) Thursday, February 28, 1946. Downloaded from Newspapers.com on February 22, 2020.
232 LA Times (Los Angeles, CA) Sunday, September 10, 1944. Downloaded from Newspapers.com on February 22, 2020.
233 Kirkpatrick, K. 2012. Prisoner of War Camps Across America. GenTracer, Salt Lake City.

National Archives RG 389, Entry 458, Boxes 1444-1446, RG 467B, Boxes 1544-1551, RG 467C, Boxes 1553, Microfilm 66-538
234 Center of Military History. (1993) Logistics in World War II: Final Report of the Army Service Forces. United States Army.

CAMP HAAN
THE HISTORY OF RIVERSIDE'S WORLD WAR II ANTI-AIRCRAFT TRAINING CENTER

http://www.legacy.com/PostRegister/Obituaries.asp?Page=LifeStory&PersonID=134789958
200 Ancestry.com. U.S., Find A Grave Index, 1600s-Current [database on-line]. Provo, UT, USA: Ancestry.com Operations, Inc., 2012.
201 Hanford Sentinel (Hanford, CA) Wednesday May 27, 1942. Downloaded from Newspapers.com on January 13, 2020.
202 National Archives and Records Administration. Electronic Army Serial Number Merged File, 1938-1946 [Archival Database]; ARC: 1263923. World War II Army Enlistment Records; Records of the National Archives and Records Administration, Record Group 64; National Archives at College Park. College Park, Maryland, U.S.A.
203 Hanford Morning Journal (Hanford, CA) June 9, 1943. Retrieved January 14, 2020 from Newspapers.com
204 LA Times (Los Angeles, CA) Wed, June 9 1943. Downloaded from Nespapers.com on December 10, 2019.
205 Hospital Admission Card Files, ca. 1970 - ca. 1970. NAI: 570973. Records of the Office of the Surgeon General (Army), 1775 - 1994. Record Group 12. The National Archives at College Park, MD. USA.
206 National Archives and Records Administration. Electronic Army Serial Number Merged File, 1938-1946 [Archival Database]; ARC: 1263923. World War II Army Enlistment Records; Records of the National Archives and Records Administration, Record Group 64; National Archives at College Park. College Park, Maryland, U.S.A.
207 Ancestry.com. U.S., Find A Grave Index, 1600s-Current [database on-line]. Provo, UT, USA: Ancestry.com Operations, Inc., 2012.

https://www.findagrave.com/memorial/32988421
208 Press Democrat (Santa Rosa, CA) Tuesday Jul 27 1943. Downloaded from Newspapers.com on Jan 14, 2020.
209 San Bernardino County Sun (San Bernardino, CA) Friday, November 22, 1946. Downloaded from Newspapers.com on December 4, 2019.
210 Santa Rosa Republican (Santa Rosa, CA) Tuesday March 7, 1944. Downloaded from Newspapers.com on January 14, 2020.
211 https://ae.ucr.edu/sites/g/files/rcwecm2356/files/2019-04/north_district_historic-final_cch_w_dprs_3-15-2017.pdf
[212] Personal interview – Steve Lech via Facebook 8/16/2021.
213 The Press-Enterprise (Riverside, CA) October 1, 2015. Downloaded from Newsbank.com on MAy 16, 2020
[214] The three branches opened in July 1944 included: Eastern Branch – Green Haven, New York, Southern Branch – North Camp Hood, Texas, and the Northwest Branch – Fort Missoula, Montana.
215 San Pedro News (San Pedro, CA) Saturday, May 26, 1945. Downloaded from Newspaper.com on January 10, 2020.
216 LA Times (Los Angeles, CA) Sunday June 24, 1945. Downloaded from Newspapers.com on January 10, 2020.
[217] Youngs, R. (1983). A History of U.S. Army Corrections.

CAMP HAAN
THE HISTORY OF RIVERSIDE'S WORLD WAR II ANTI-AIRCRAFT TRAINING CENTER

177 Oakland Tribune (Oakland, CA) Wednesday, June 23, 1943. Downloaded from Newspapers.com on January 13, 2020.
[178] Camp Haan v. Fresno State football program. October 4, 1941.
179 The Press-Enterprise (Riverside, CA) May 5, 1995. Downloaded from Newsbank.com on 16 May 2020.
180 The Press-Enterprise (Riverside, CA) May 5, 1995. Downloaded from Newsbank.com on 16 May 2020.
181 SB Sun Feb 21, 1941
[182] Gallagher, Robert. World War II Story. Chapter 3 – Camp Haan, California. Retrieved from https://gallagherstory.com/ww2/chapter3.html.
183 https://www.nationalww2museum.org/war/articles/hollywood-hospitality-hollywood-canteen
184 Camp Haan Tracer, May 4, 1943
185 https://www.nationalww2museum.org/war/articles/hollywood-hospitality-hollywood-canteen
[186] Jezek, George Ross; Wanamaker, Marc (October 1, 2002). Hollywood: Past and Present. San Diego, Calif.: George Ross Jezek Photography & Publishing. pp. 92–93. ISBN 978-0970103611.
[187] Gallagher, Robert. World War II Story. Chapter 3 – Camp Haan, California. Retrieved from https://gallagherstory.com/ww2/chapter4.html.
188 San Bernardino County Sun (San Bernardino, CA) Wed Mar 19, 1941. Downloaded fron Newspapers.com on January 10, 2020.
189 A permanent location for the show in San Bernardino was selected in 1923 in the area south of Mill Street between Arrowhead Avenue and "E" street.
190 San Bernardino County Sun (San Bernardino, CA) Thurs, Oct 9, 1941. Downloaded from Newspapers.com on January 10, 2020.
191 Coast Artillery Journal, Volume 86 No. 1 United States Coast Artillery Association, 1943, Pg. 91
192 San Bernardino County Sun (San Bernardino, CA) Tuesday December 5, 1944. Downloaded from Newspapers.com on January 14, 2020.
193 San Bernardino County Sun (San Bernardino, CA) Wed Jul 15, 1945. Downloaded from Newspapers.com on Jan 10, 2020.
194 San Bernardino County Sun (San Bernardino, CA) Friday August 22, 1941. Downloaded from Newspapers.com on January 10, 2020.
195 LA Times (Los Angeles, CA) Wednesday, December 19, 2945. Dowloaded from Newspapers.com on January 10, 2020.
196 Santa Cruz Sentinel (Santa Cruz, CA) Wednesday July 18 1945. Downloaded from Newspapers.com on January 10, 2020.
197 Santa Ana Register (Santa Ana, CA) Wednesday November 11, 1942. Downloaded from Newspapers.com on January 13, 2020.
198 National Cemetery Administration. U.S. Veterans' Gravesites, ca.1775-2006 [database on-line]. Provo, UT, USA: Ancestry.com Operations Inc, 2006.
199 https://www.findagrave.com/memorial/74472355

Post Register; Publication Date: 22/ Oct/ 2009; Publication Place: Idaho Falls, Idaho, USA; URL:

www.ingramcontent.com/pod-product-compliance
Lightning Source LLC
Chambersburg PA
CBHW071328080526
44587CB00017B/2765